Grave Matters

Eight studies of First Millennium AD burials in Crimea, England and southern Scandinavia

Papers from a session held at the European Association of Archaeologists Fourth Annual Meeting in Göteborg 1998

Edited by

Martin Rundkvist

BAR International Series 781
1999

Published in 2016 by
BAR Publishing, Oxford

BAR International Series 781

Grave Matters

ISBN 978 1 84171 001 3

BAR Publishing is the trading name of British Archaeological Reports (Oxford) Ltd.
British Archaeological Reports was first incorporated in 1974 to publish the BAR
Series, International and British. In 1992 Hadrian Books Ltd became part of the BAR
group. This volume was originally published by Archaeopress in conjunction with
British Archaeological Reports (Oxford) Ltd / Hadrian Books Ltd, the Series principal
publisher, in 1999. This present volume is published by BAR Publishing, 2016.

Printed in England

BAR
PUBLISHING

BAR titles are available from:

BAR Publishing
122 Banbury Rd, Oxford, OX2 7BP, UK
EMAIL info@barpublishing.com
PHONE +44 (0)1865 310431
FAX +44 (0)1865 316916
www.barpublishing.com

Ask for me to-morrow, and you shall find me a grave man.

W. Shakespeare. The Tragedy of Romeo and Juliet, III:1.

Table of contents

List of Illustrations

Introduction

This collection of papers is based upon those read and discussed on 25 September 1998 in Gothenburg, Sweden, at a session during the Fourth Annual Meeting of the European Association of Archaeologists. The session's title was *Provincial Roman and Germanic burials in the First Millennium AD*. It was organised and chaired by the editor of the present volume. All of the authors participated at the session except for Fredrik Svanberg, who was unable to attend as planned. The manuscripts were completed and submitted to the editor from September 1998 to January 1999.

The authors had been asked to concentrate on their lines of inquiry, analytical methodology and interpretations of results more than on the presentation of burial data. The session was intended to answer the question "How are scholars of the Roman-Germanic field currently *using* burial data?".

The eight papers of this volume treat three different fields of study and have been ordered accordingly. Thus, first we have two papers on Late Scythian cemeteries in Crimea from the first three centuries AD, both written at the State Historical Museum in Moscow. Mid-First Millennium AD Anglo-Saxon England is treated in three papers, all written at British universities. Finally, southern Scandinavia in the middle to the second half of the First Millennium AD is the topic of three papers, all written at universities and museums in Sweden and Norway.

As it turns out, there are two main dimensions of society studied in these papers: ethnicity and social status; both of them as expressed and perpetuated through material culture, and more specifically through mortuary customs. These two modes of categorisation may be seen as complementary opposites: ethnicity defines the social group outwards in relation to Others, while social status defines the roles of the group's members among themselves.

The two main perspectives of this collection of fin-de-siècle burial studies are currently the focus of much research. Inquiry along those lines has been with us since the beginnings of archaeology and will most likely continue for as long as archaeology is practised in any recognisable way. Questions of personal identity are at the heart of all humanities research, as indeed the most basic expression of the humanistic question may be "What does it mean to be human?".

The papers of this volume each contribute to an answer, and also serve as a collection of methodological examples. Three different research traditions are brought together and contrasted in a way made possible only at a major international conference. Analytical scale levels and approaches vary, but the authors all take the burial place as their point of departure. It is hoped that this book will serve as inspiration for further research on graves within and beyond the three main fields of study treated here.

The editor wishes to thank warmly the EAA 1998 conference secretariat for organising a superb conference, the contributors for submitting their papers so promptly, David Davison of Archaeopress for accepting the volume for publication, Howard Williams for perceptive comments and bibliographical assistance, and Stefan Kayat for suggesting the motto.

Martin Rundkvist
2 March 1999
Stockholm, Sweden

The Roman Period necropolis of Zavetnoe in southwest Crimea. Burial structures and mortuary ritual.

Kirill Firsov

Department of Archaeology, State Historical Museum, Moscow

Introduction

The complex of Roman Period archaeological sites near the village of Zavetnoe consists of an urban site, two rural sites, flat-ground burials and fortifications on one of the peaks of the second chain of the Crimean Mountains. Zavetnoe is situated on the left shore of the Al'ma River, at the middle of its length, near Bakhchysaray in southwest Crimea (fig. 1:1-2).

The necropolis of Zavetnoe, which belonged to the urban site of Al'ma-Kermen (where a Roman military camp existed in the 2nd to early 3rd century AD), was positioned at the crossroads of very important routes – from Neapolis Scythica to Chersonesus and to the urban site of Ust'-Al'ma (Vysotskaya 1972, 1994:139), that is, in the zone of especially intensive contacts between the indigenous Late Scythian population and Sarmatians and the inhabitants of the Greek centres such as Chersonesus. Therefore it occupies a special place among the burial sites of Taurica.

The necropolis, where 294 burials of the 1st century BC to the 3rd century AD have been discovered (fig. 2), was excavated by the expedition of the Bakhchysaray Historico-Archaeological Museum and the State Historical Museum in 1954-1981 under the supervision of N.A. Bogdanova.

Burial structures

Burial structures of several types have been documented within the necropolis. The majority of burials are in *simple trenches* of rectangular shape (51%) with earthen or stone fill (fig. 3:1-3, 4:2, 8:1, 9:2).

Trenches with *earthen fill* (30.6%) were usually dug to a depth of less than 1.2 m, had a width of 0.5-0.7 m, and had a length of 1.7-2.2 m (fig. 3:1-3, 8:1). Graves of this type were constructed throughout the burial site's period of use, but most of them date from the 1st and 2nd centuries AD judging from the grave goods. Typical for them is a strict

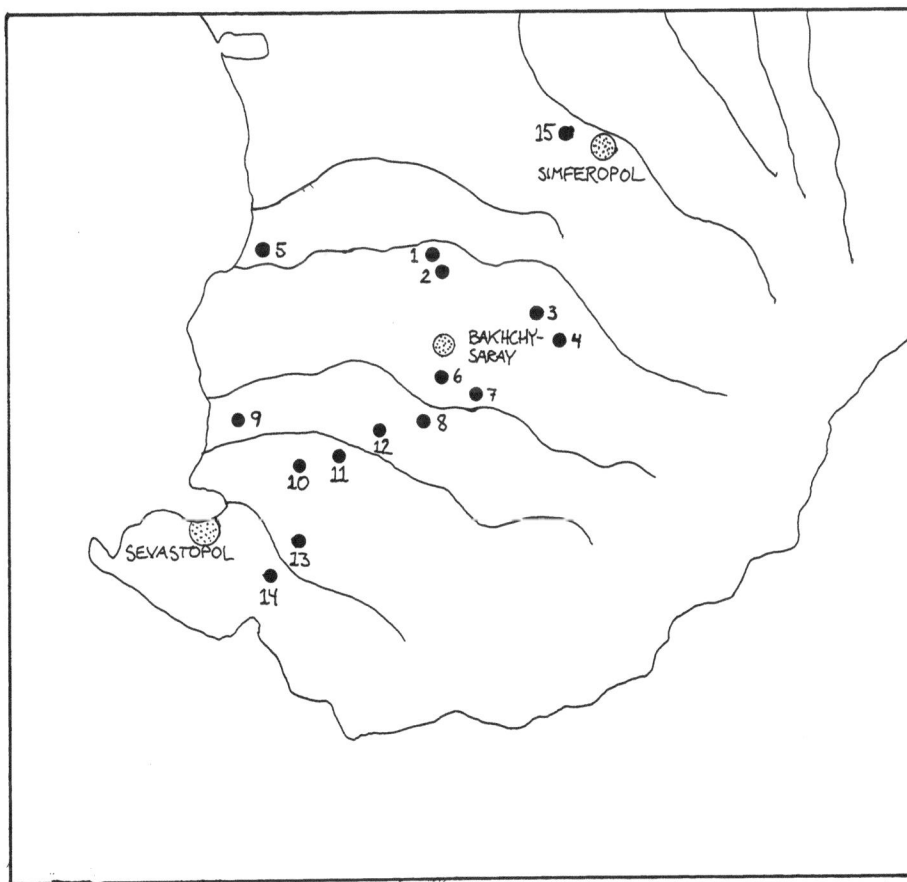

Fig. 1: Southern Crimea. Necropolises of the first centuries AD. 1-2: Zavetnoe. 3: Skalistoe II. 4: Skalistoe III. 5: Ust'-Al'ma. 6: Tankovoe. 7: Surenskii povorot. 8: Turgenevka. 9: Belbek IV. 10: Belbek I. 11: Belbek III. 12: Belbek II. 13: Sovkhoz 10. 14: Chernorechenskii. 15: Neapolis Scythica.

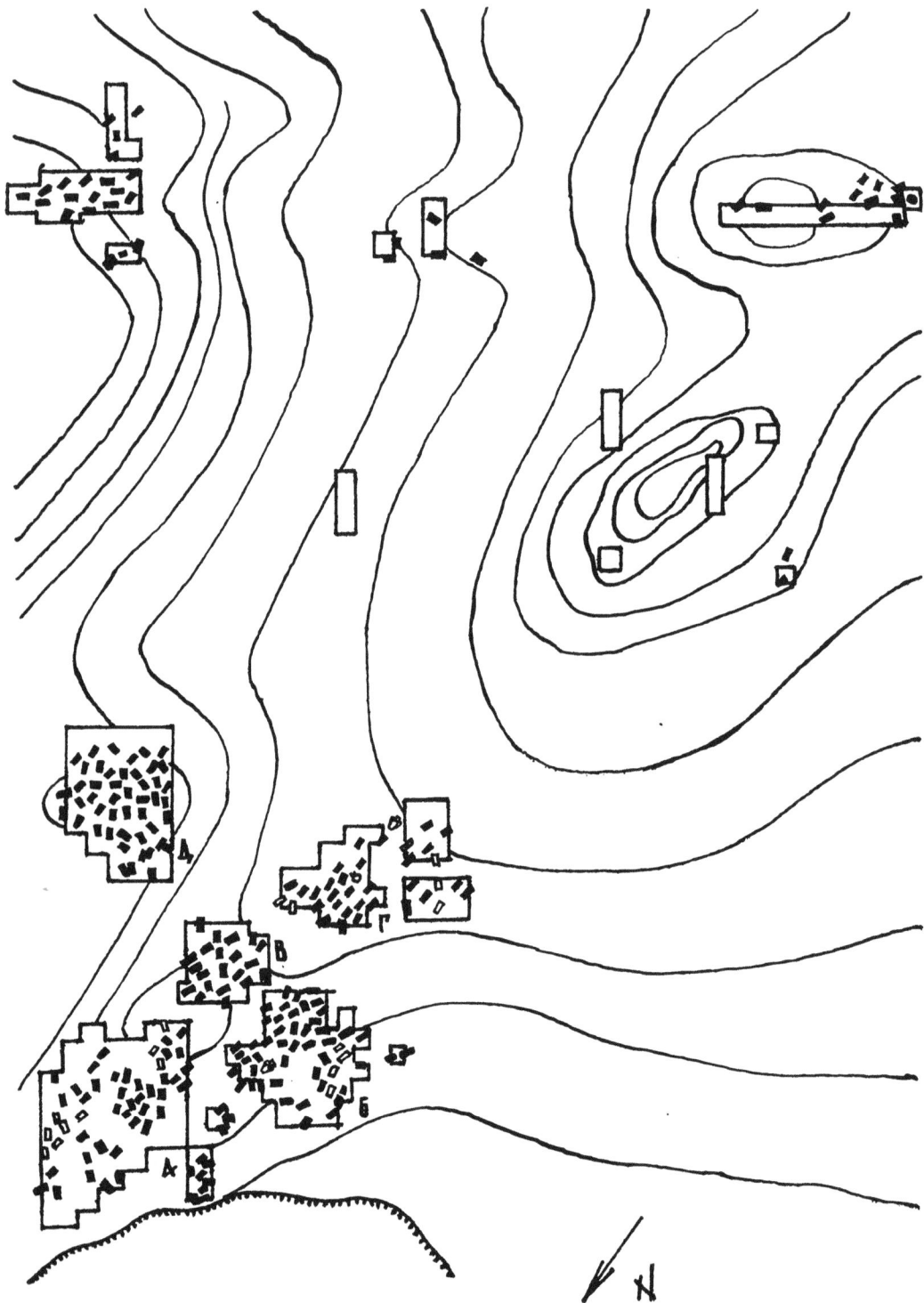

Fig. 2: *General plan of the Zavetnoe necropolis.*

southwest orientation, with small deviations. The position of the body is remarkable for its considerable diversity. Burials of this type from the 1st and 2nd centuries were commonly accompanied by abundant grave goods.

Trenches with *stone fill* (20.4%) had a depth of 0.6-1.1 m, a width of 0.9-1.9 m, and a length of 2.2-3.0 m (fig. 4:2, 9:2). The quarrystone that fills the trench, along with loam, often extends beyond its edges, forming a rectangular pavement. The burial rite is strongly formalised, with a strict southwest orientation. Generally the body is extended on its back with straightened extremities. Graves with stone covering are usually linked to Scythian burial traditions, since such burial structures were typical for the Scythians of Crimea from as early as the 5th to the 3rd centuries BC (Troitskaya 1954:7; Vysotskaya 1972:88; Yakovenko 1974:34; Ol'khovskiy 1979:12, 1991:25).

As for the burials in a *trench with shoulders* (or stairs), covered with timber lids or stone slabs, a lesser number of them has been discovered (7.4%; fig. 3:4, 4:4, 5:1). *Shouldered trenches covered with timber* had a depth >1.5 m, a length of 1.5-2.7 m, and a width of 0.9-1.4 m (fig. 3:4, 4:4). The shoulders were located at a depth of 0.5-0.6 m from the top of the trench. Similar graves with timbered covers were built by the Sarmatians of the Volga region and the Ural Mountains in the 4th to the 2nd centuries BC (Smirnov 1975:159). They appear at Crimean burial sites with the first wave of the Sarmatian invasion (Bogdanova 1982:32). These burials can be dated to the 1st century AD.

Shouldered trenches covered with stone slabs are dated to the 2nd and the beginning of the 3rd century AD (fig. 5:1). These burial trenches were made wider than the aforementioned ones, thanks to the stability of the stone slabs. They were covered with two or three well-dressed slabs, on which was a quarrystone pavement. The depth of the trenches was 0.6-0.8 m. Typical for the later graves are large stone floorings up to 3.5 x 3.0 m and deep trenches up to 2 m. The orientation, in most cases, is southwest; the position of the bodies variable. Burials in trenches covered with stone slabs are widespread in Bosporus, Chersonese and some burial sites of southwest Crimea (Skalistoe III, fig. 1:4; Shelov 1961:94, Zubar 1982:13, Korpusova 1983:17-18). The choice of material for the grave coverings was probably determined by availability – great amounts of stone and a deficiency of wood (Bogdanova 1989:21).

Stone cists – with reinforced sides and covered with stone slabs – comprised 11.5% of all graves at the necropolis (fig. 5:2-4, 6:1-3, 4:3). They were constructed in two stages: first a rectangular trench 2.2-2.5 m long and 0.7-1.2 m wide was dug and then three to four well-dressed slabs were placed against each of the long sides of the trench. Over them were laid two to four slabs and a cover of quarrystone. Burials of this type appear in the 2nd and 3rd centuries AD. Similar structures which, as a rule, have end-slabs, are known in the cemeteries of Bosporan cities as early as the middle of the 1st millennium BC onward (Bogdanova 1989:22). The appearance of cist graves at the cemeteries of southwest Crimea is probably due to the Greek influence (Vysotskaya 1972:90). However, the cist graves of the Zavetnoe necropolis lack end-slabs, which is perhaps an important factor for establishing their origin. They probably hark back to the shouldered trenches with wooden or stone covering (Bogdanova 1982:33, 1989).

25% of the burials featured *trenches with stepped-down chambers* and earthen or stone fill (fig. 6:4. 7:1-4. 8:2-4). Some indications of a Sarmatian influence can be traced in these burials. Stone-filling of the entrance trenches to stepped-down chambers is, however, not characteristic of the Sarmatian culture. This custom appears at the burial sites of Crimea in the first centuries AD, probably under the influence of Scythian rites of packing the grave with stones (Bogdanova 1982:32).

Graves with *earthen filling* of the entrance trench (12%) had a vertical entrance trench 1.6-2.2 m long, 0.5-0.7 m wide and 0.5-1.7 m deep (fig. 7:2-3). Usually in the eastern side of the trench, a chamber 2.2-2.5 m long and up to 1 m wide was dug. The entrance to the stepped-down chamber was closed with flat stone slabs, sometimes re-used. In the 2nd century AD there appeared a variant of this type – a simplified variety of the stepped-down chamber in the form of a trench divided by stone slabs (fig. 8:3-4). Such structures have analogies in the necropolis of Tanais (Shelov 1961:88). Taking into account the poor furnishings of such graves, it is possible to explain their appearance with social factors, since their construction did not require great labour expenditure. Another variant of this type is represented by the rare graves with *two* stepped-down chambers, one at either side of the trench, where relatives were probably buried (fig. 8:2).

Graves with *stone filling* of the entrance trench (13%) appeared in the late 1st to the mid-2nd century AD (fig. 6:4; 7:1, 4). Their structure was similar to the aforementioned type, but the entrance trench was packed with quarrystone. Sometimes the filling had a complicated structure, quarrystone alternating with horizontally placed flat slabs.

Earthen vaults, as a rule, are not typical of Late Scythian burial sites of southwest Taurica. Only the necropolis of Ust'-Al'ma stands out for the number of such graves (Vysotskaya 1994:51). Only one structure of this kind, from the end of the 3rd or the beginning of the 4th century AD, has been discovered at Zavetnoe (0.5%, fig. 9:3). The crypt was an oval room with a semicircular dome 2 x 1.5 m, height up to 1 m, to which led a narrow *dromos* opening, deepening at an angle, with a diameter of 0.6 m and a length of 1 m, to the round closing slab. The crypt contained four graves and the furnishings were poor.

The number of *child burials in amphorae* is also small (0.7%, fig. 9:1). In one of the graves the amphora was covered on all sides and on top with small slabs, in another rested on two handmade pots. This form of burial was in use in Greek cities of the north Black Sea coast from Hellenistic times. It also occurs at some Late Scythian urban sites (Grakov 1954:56, Shelov 1961:88, Vysotskaya 1972:38). Possibly, this constitutes a mix of the Scythian custom of burying children at urban sites and the Greek one of burying children in amphorae (Bogdanova 1982:33).

Mortuary ritual

Traces of ritual acts have been found at the necropolis. A type of structure that can be linked to funeral feasting is the sacrificial pit with burnt animal bones, fragments of moulded pottery, ashes and charcoal. Sometimes the grave fills contained remnants of funeral banquets, and in the graves themselves were found flint, ochre and chalk. In grave 266 the remains of the skeletons of three horses were found *in situ*, mixed with ash and coal. The fills of four graves contained 3-5 stone pavements with traces of fire, alternating with layers of earth (fig. 9:2, c.f. Bogdanova 1990:53-58). In some cases rich burials were marked on the surface with cross-shaped masonry. The coverings of some graves featured re-used slabs from anthropomorphic sculptures (Bogdanova 1965:233-237) and wine presses.

The cemetery featured burials in felts, typical of earlier graves, and in dug-out tree-trunks, most frequently in cist burials (fig. 4:3). The custom of trunk burial is known from Sarmatian burials from the 4th and 3rd centuries BC (Moshkova 1963:22). An interesting rite was traced in the burial 187: the head of the deceased was covered with snail shells (fig. 3:1). Such details of the burial rite as chalk, ochre, dye, coal and flint, present at Zavetnoe, are widely known in Scythian and Sarmatian graves and are undoubtedly connected with the purifying powers of fire (Smirnov 1964:96, 1975:162; Vyazmitina 1972:120).

Southwest orientation of the bodies is typical for the 1st and early 2nd century AD (90%), while 5% of the burials are oriented to the west and 2.5% to the south and to the east. In the late 2nd and the 3rd centuries southwest orientation is still predominant (72%), while west and south orientations are less frequent (18% and 10% respectively).

Grave goods and chronology

As a rule, the burials are richly furnished, but there also occur poor and unfurnished graves. The grave goods are quite varied: red slip pottery, glass and metal vessels (fig. 10:1-5, 11:1-8, 14:1-3), weapons (fig. 15:12), jewellery (fig. 12:1-6, 8-10, 15; 14:6-7), dress accessories (fig. 13:7-12), horse harness, coins, tools (fig. 15:1-2, 4) and cult objects (fig. 12:7, 11-14; 14:4, 5, 9) made of different materials have been found. In some cases a certain regularity can be observed in the positioning of the objects in graves.

Although the inventory of the necropolis shows considerable variety, rather few Roman imports have been found, unlike, for instance, the case of the Belbek IV necropolis (fig. 1:9, Guschina 1974:32-61, Guschina & Zhuravlev 1996:23, Zhuravlev in the present volume). This is, in view of the presence of a Roman camp in the vicinity, hard to explain. Possibly, the reason is the remote situation of the necropolis in relation to Chersonesus. Here, on the other hand, a number of the richest burials of the area containing gold objects have been discovered. At other necropolises only a few objects of this kind have

been found, and they are not of any remarkable diversity. At the necropolis of Ust'-Al'ma rich burials were found exclusively in earthen vaults, whereas at Zavetnoe they were discovered in simple trench graves. Also, the almost total absence of earthen vaults cannot be easily interpreted.

The rich grave furnishings at Zavetnoe make it possible to date most of the burials. The use-period of the necropolis encompasses the period from the 1st century BC to the 3rd century AD. 52% of the graves belong to the period from the 1st century to the early 2nd century AD. This group includes the four earliest burials of the site, which may go back to the late 1st century BC on the verge of the new era. Interestingly, the richest burials of the site, including gold objects, date to the 1st century AD; that is to the time when the Roman military outpost had not yet been established. 18.6% of the burials date from the late 1st to the early 3rd century AD, while 4.2% date from the mid-2nd to the 3rd century AD. Planigraphically speaking, contemporary burials are located in compact groups. Quite frequently they have similar furnishings between which typological analogies can be established. However, no such grouping can be discerned for the different types of grave structure; most of them are distributed randomly.

The Zavetnoe necropolis reflects the final floruit of the Scythian tribes, complicated by Classical as well as considerable Sarmatian influence. They illustrate Sarmatian penetration into the local Late Scythian environment. As for the distinguishing characteristics of this necropolis, possibly due to its relative closeness to steppe areas, they consist of a high degree of Sarmatisation, which can be traced in the burial rites and grave goods, the presence of Late Scythian and Graeco-Roman elements notwithstanding (Dashevskaya 1991, Firsov 1998:128).

References

Bogdanova, N.A. 1965. Skifskie i sarmatskie stely Zavetninskogo mogilnika. *Sovyetskaya Arkheologia* 3, pp 233-237. Institute of Archaeology, Russian Academy of Sciences. Moscow.

Bogdanova, N.A. 1982. Pogrebal'nyi obryad sel'skogo naseleniya pozdneskifskogo gosudarstva v Krymu. Talis, D.L. (ed.). *Arkheologicheskiye issledovaniya na yuge Vostochnoy Evropy.* Trudy GIM (Papers of the State Historical Museum) vol. 54, pp 31-39. Moscow.

Bogdanova, N.A. 1989. Mogil'nik pervykh vekov nashei ery u s. Zavetnoe. Abramova, M.P. (ed.). *Arkheo-logicheskiye issledovaniya na yuge Vostochnoy Evropy.* Trudy GIM (Papers of the State Historical Museum) vol. 70, pp 17-70. Moscow.

Bogdanova, N.A. 1990. Rol' ognya v pogrebal'nom rituale mogilnika pervykh vekov nashey ery u s. Zavetnoe. Studzitskaya, S.V. (ed.). *Problemy arkheologii Evrazii (po materialam GIM).* Trudy GIM (Papers of the State Historical Museum) vol. 74, pp 53-58. Moscow.

Dashevskaya, O.D. 1991. *Pozdnie skify v Krymu.* Svod Arkheologicheskikh Istochnikov A1-7. Moscow.

Firsov, K. 1998. Scythian, Sarmatian and Graeco-Roman elements in the burial rite of the population of South-Western Crimea of the Roman period: archaeological sites of the Zavethoye village. *Abstracts Book. EAA 4th*

Annual Meeting. Göteborg. Sweden. September 23-27 1998. Department of Archaeology, University of Gothenburg.

Grakov, B.N. 1954. *Kamenskoe gorodishche na Dnepre.* Materialy i issledovaniya po arkheologii SSSR 36. Institute of Archaeology, Russian Academy of Sciences. Moscow.

Guschina, I.I. 1974. Naselenie sarmatskogo vremeni v doline reki Belbek v Krymu (po materialam mogilnikov). Talis, D.L. (ed.). *Arkheologicheskie issledovaniya na yuge Vostochnoi Evropy.* Trudy GIM (Papers of the State Historical Museum), pp 32-64. Moscow.

Guschina, I.I. & Zhuravlev, D.V. 1996. Rimskiy import iz mogilnika Belbek IV. Zhuravlev, D.V. & Firsov, K.B. (eds.). *Tezisy dokladov Otchetnoy sessii GIM po itogam polevykh arkheologicheskikh issledovaniy i novykh postupleniy v 1991-1995 g,* pp 45-50. Moscow.

Korpusova, V.N. 1983. *Nekropol' Zolotoe. K etno-kul'turnoi istorii evropeiskogo Bospora.* Kiev.

Moshkova, M.G. 1963. *Pamyatniki prokhorovskoi kultury.* Svod Arkheologicheskikh Istochnikov D1-10. Moscow.

Ol'khovskiy, V.S. 1979. *Pogrebal'nye obryady naseleniya stepnoi Skifii (VII–III vv. do n.e.).* Avtoreferat diss... kand. ist. nauk. Moscow.

Ol'khovskiy, V.S. 1991. *Pogrebal'no-pominal'naya obryadnost' naseleniya stepnoy Skifii (VII-III vv. do n.e.).* Moscow.

Shelov, D.B. 1961. *Nekropol' Tanaisa.* Materialy i issledovaniya po arkheologii SSSR 98. Institute of Archaeology, Russian Academy of Sciences. Moscow.

Smirnov, K.F. 1964. *Savromaty. Rannyaya istoriya i kul'tura sarmatov.* Moscow.

Smirnov, K.F. 1975. *Sarmaty na Ileke.* Moscow.

Troitskaya, T.N. 1954. *Skifskie pogrebeniya v kurganax Kryma.* Avtoreferat diss... kand. ist. nauk. Simferopol'.

Vysotskaya, T.N. 1972. *Pozdnie skify v Yugo-Zapadnom Krymu.* Kiev.

Vysotskaya, T.N. 1994. *Ust'-Al'minskoye gorodische i nekropol'.* Kiev.

Vyazmitina, M.I. 1972. *Zolotobalkovskiy mogil'nik.* Kiev.

Yakovenko, E.V. 1974. *Skify skhidnogo Krimy v V–III st. do n.e.* Kiev.

Zubar, V.M. 1982. *Nekropol' Khersonesa Tavricheskogo I–IV vv. n.e.* Kiev.

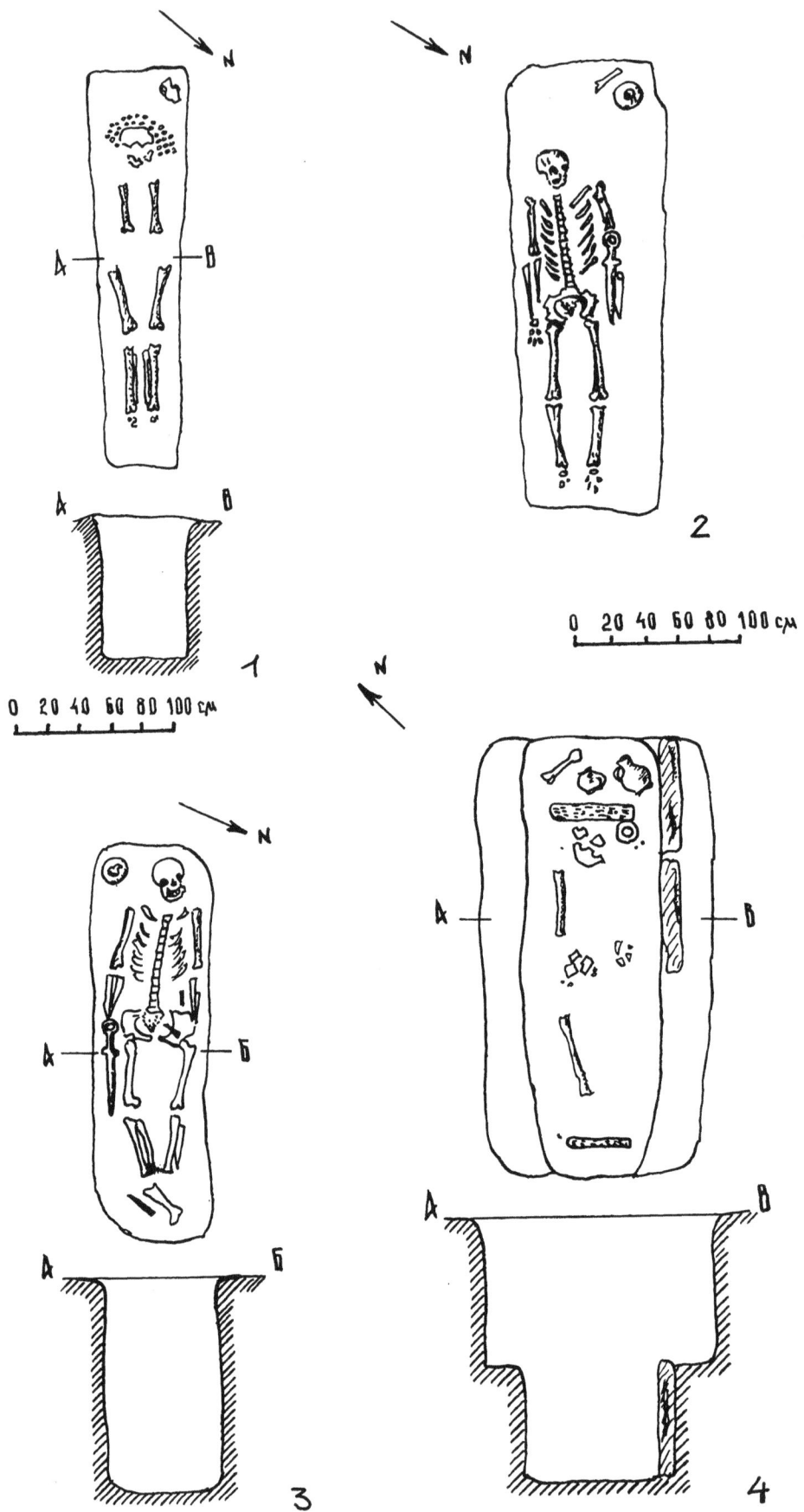

Fig. 3: *Burial structures at the Zavetnoe necropolis. 1: grave 187. 2: 250. 3: 227. 4: 186.*

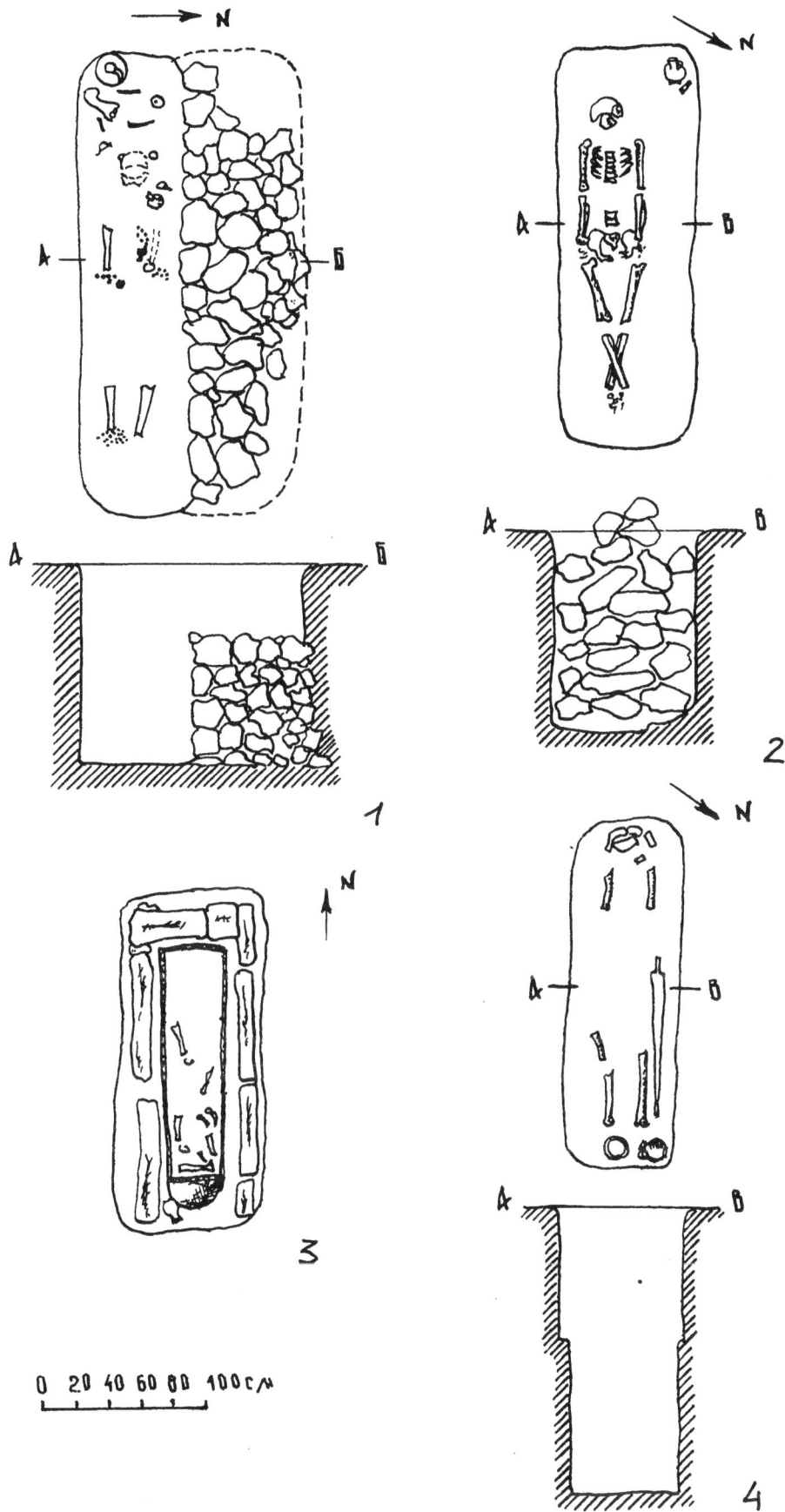

Fig. 4: *Burial structures at the Zavetnoe necropolis.: 1: grave 217. 2: 208. 3: 103. 4: 196.*

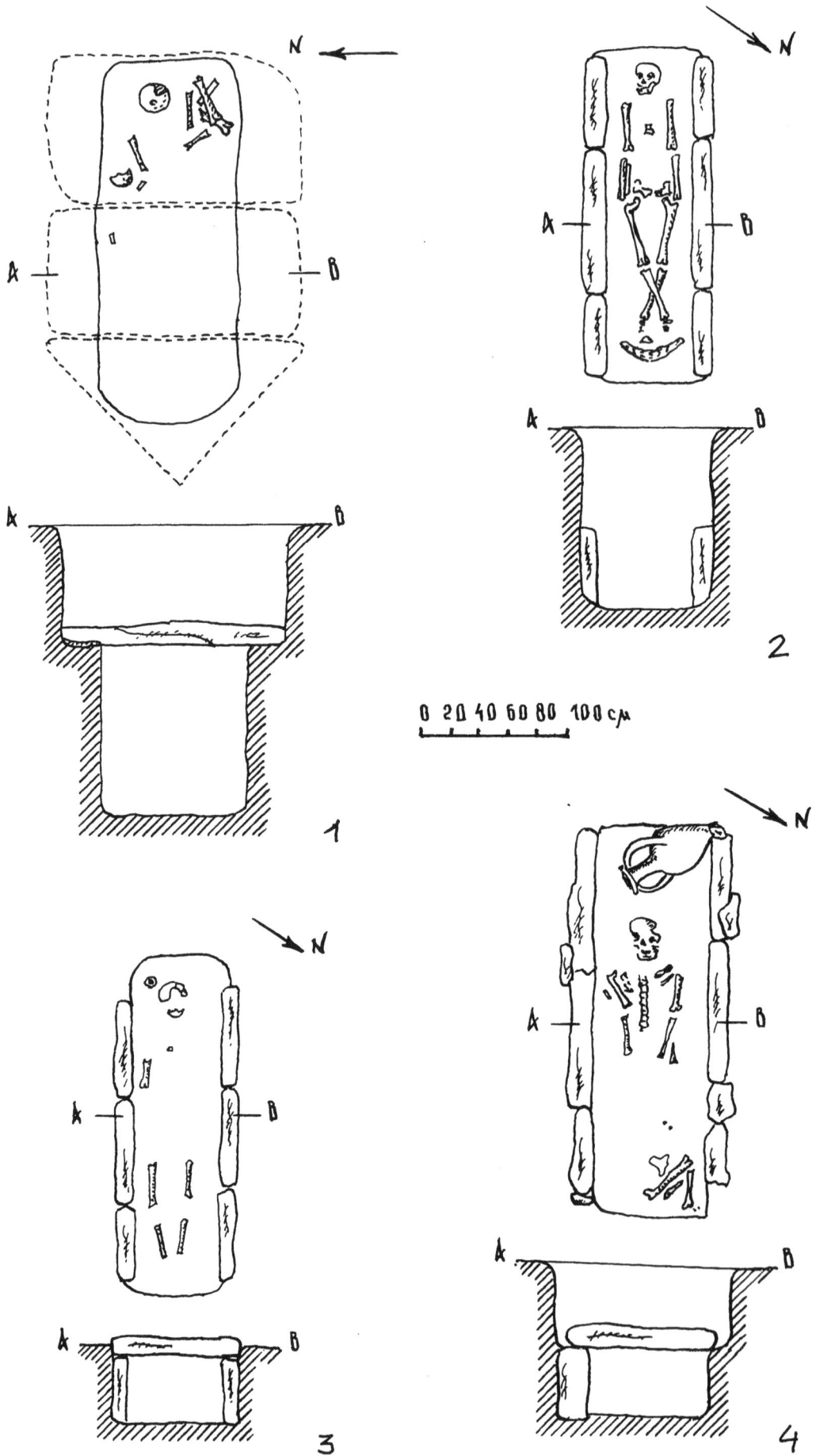

Fig. 5: *Burial structures at the Zavetnoe necropolis. 1: grave 191. 2: 203. 3: 200. 4: 267.*

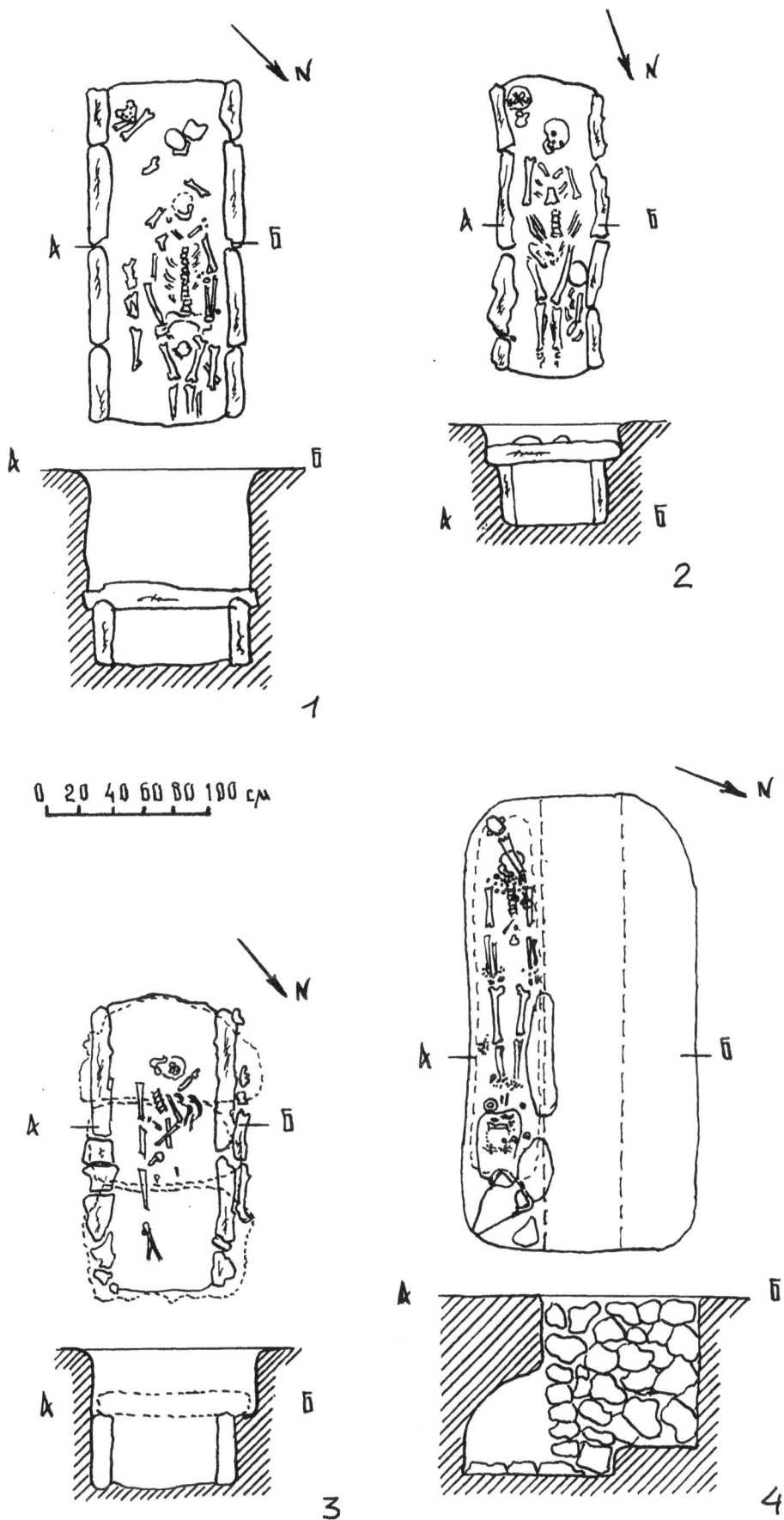

Fig. 6: *Burial structures at the Zavetnoe necropolis. 1: grave 268. 2: 270. 3: 262. 4: 216.*

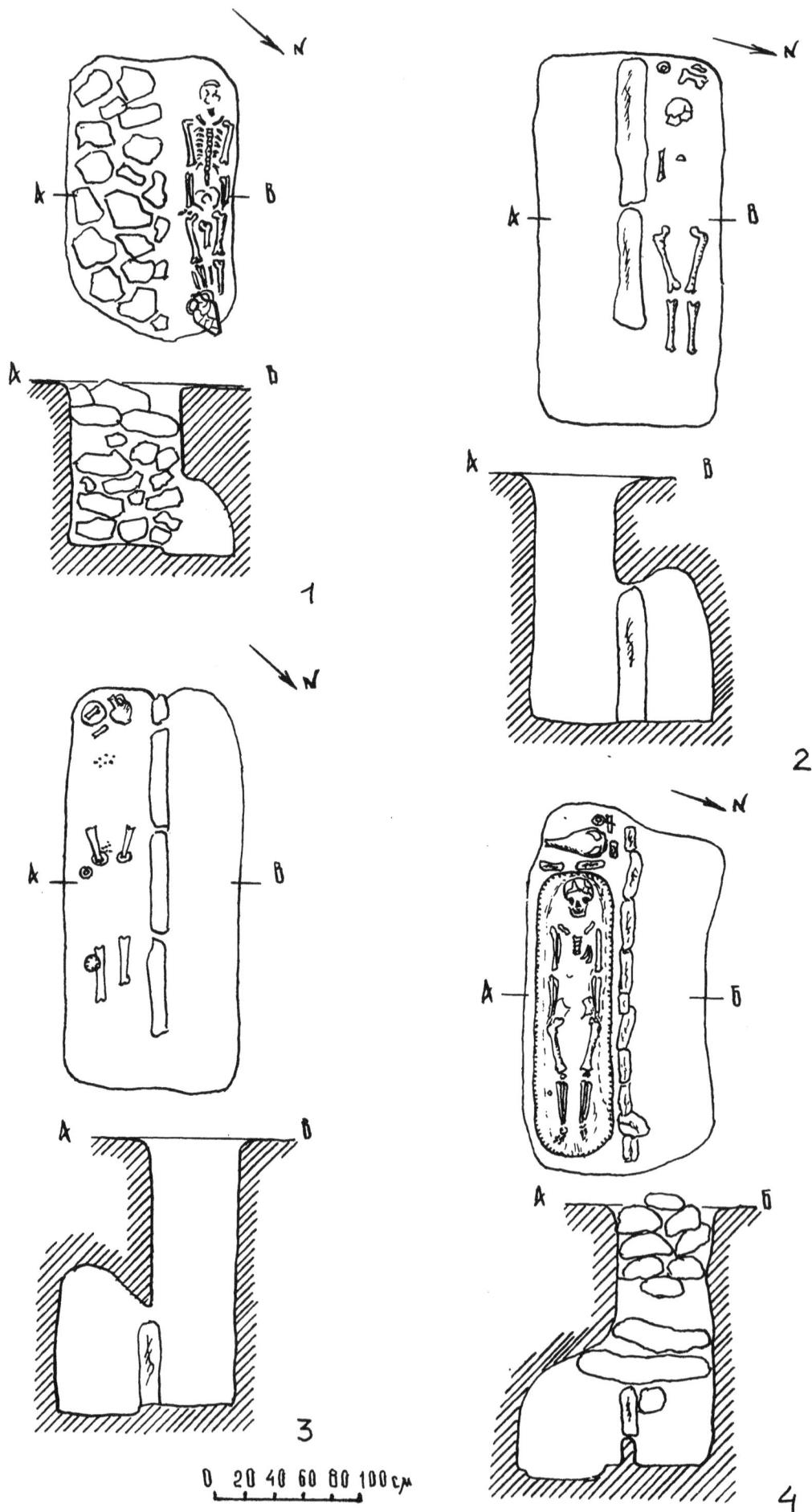

Fig. 7: Burial structures at the Zavetnoe necropolis. 1: grave 252. 2: 205. 3: 189. 4: 287.

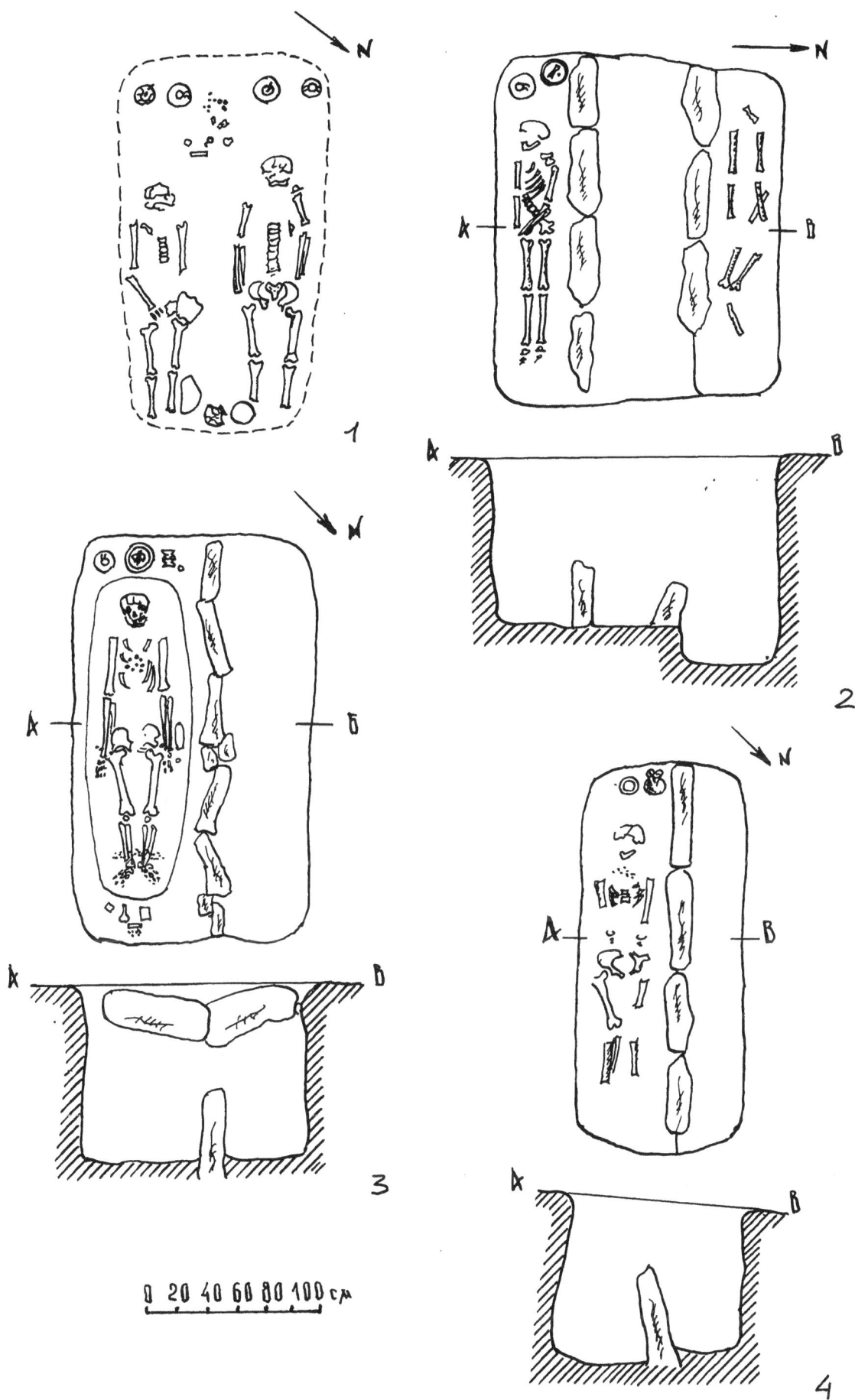

Fig. 8: Burial structures at the Zavetnoe necropolis. 1: grave 225. 2: 202. 3: 294. 4: 207.

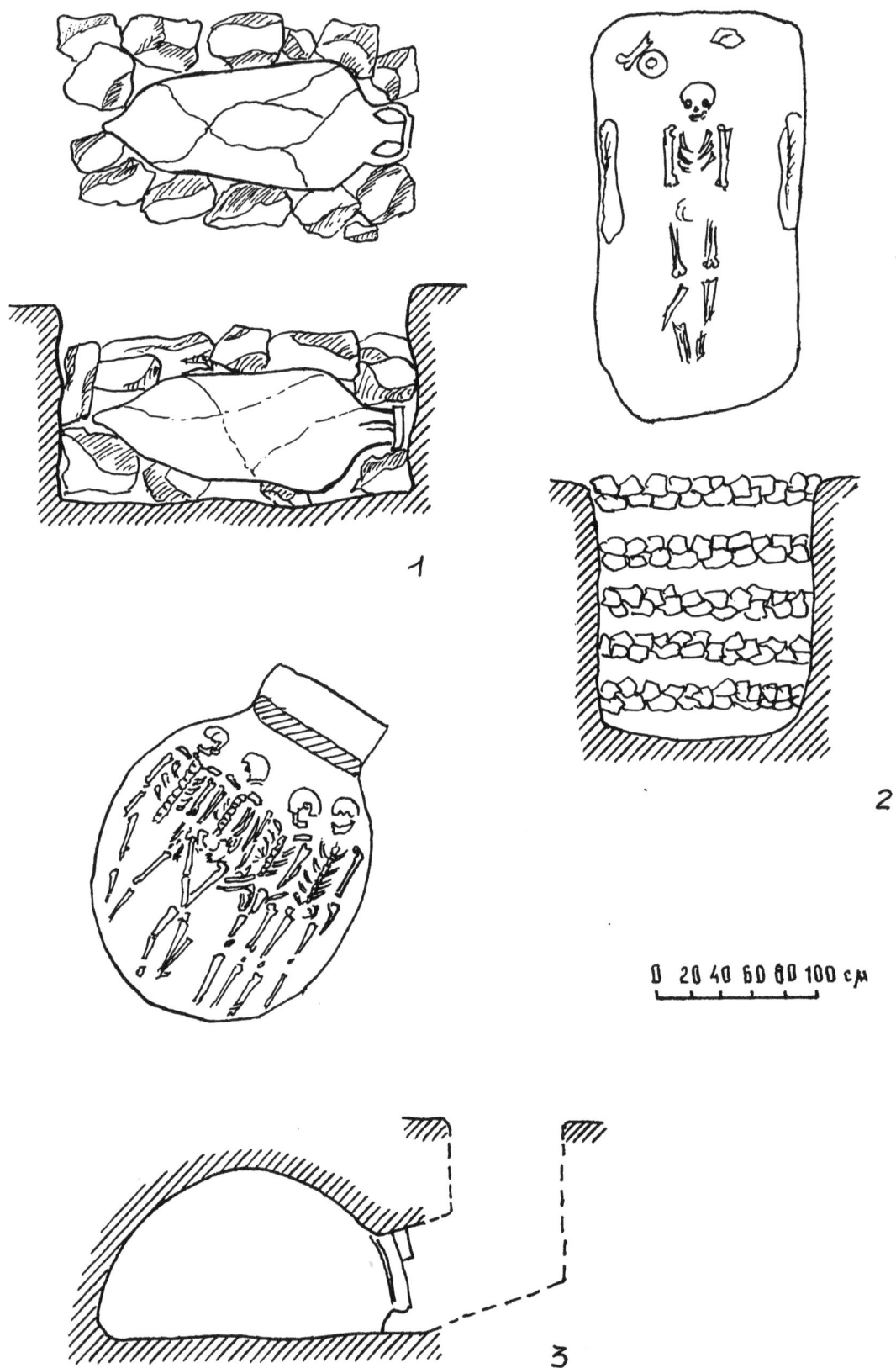

Fig. 9: Burial structures at the Zavetnoe necropolis. 1: grave 201. 2: 153. 3: 92.

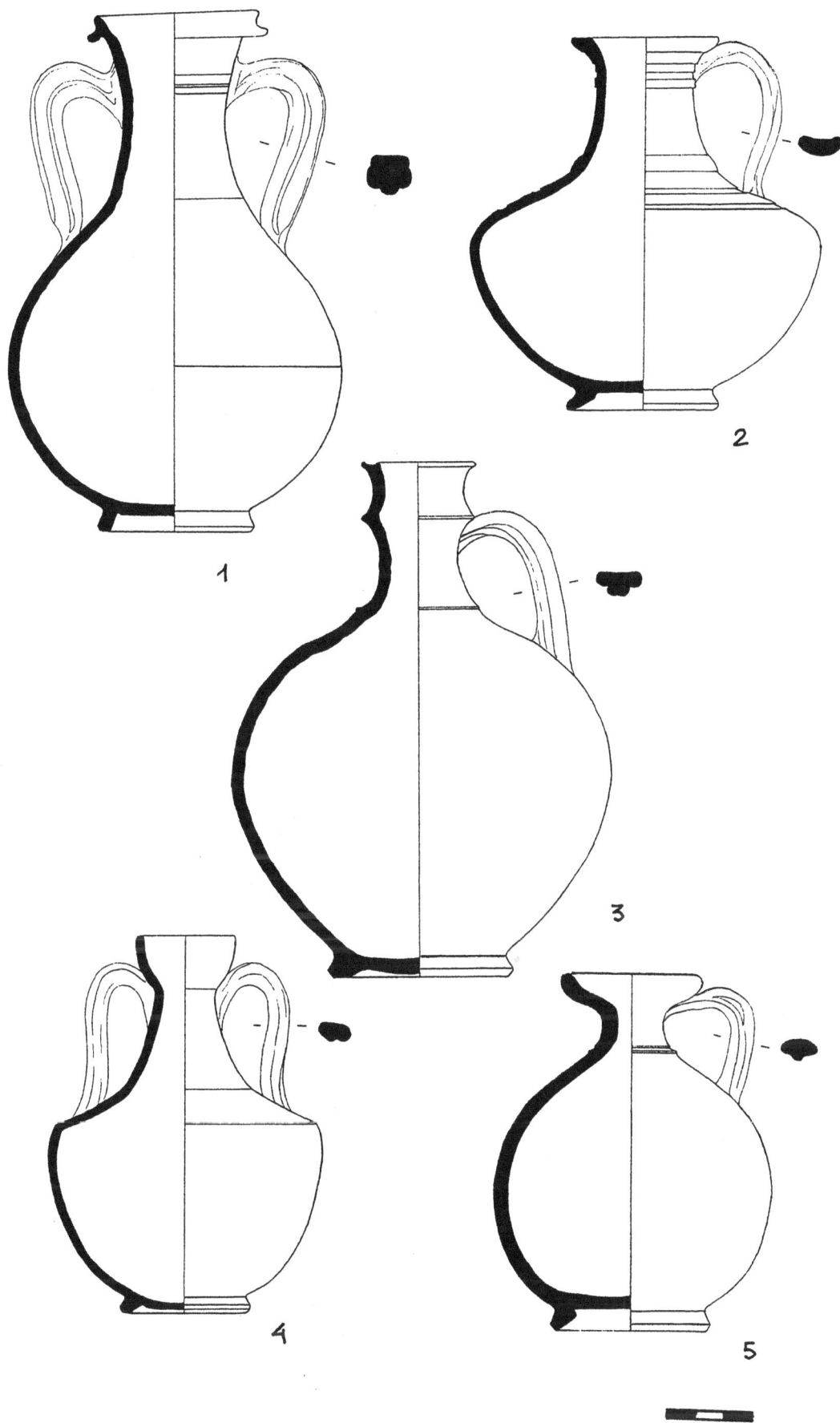

Fig. 10: *Pottery from the Zavetnoe necropolis. 1: grave 292. 2: 294. 3: 200. 4: 288. 5: 192.*

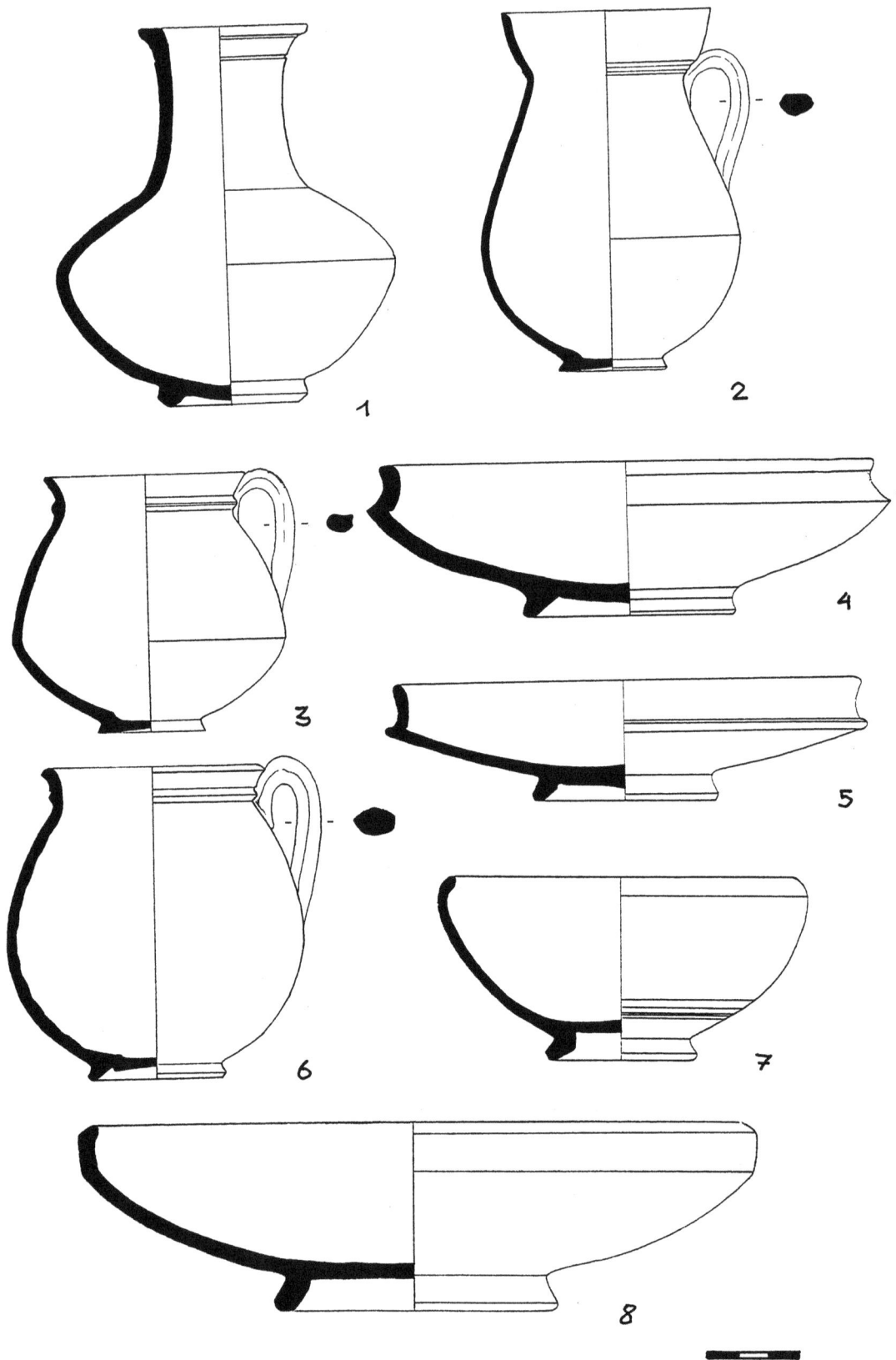

Fig. 11*: Pottery from the Zavetnoe necropolis. 1: grave 283. 2: 281. 3: 284. 4: 282. 5: 285. 6: 282. 7: 292. 8: 294.*

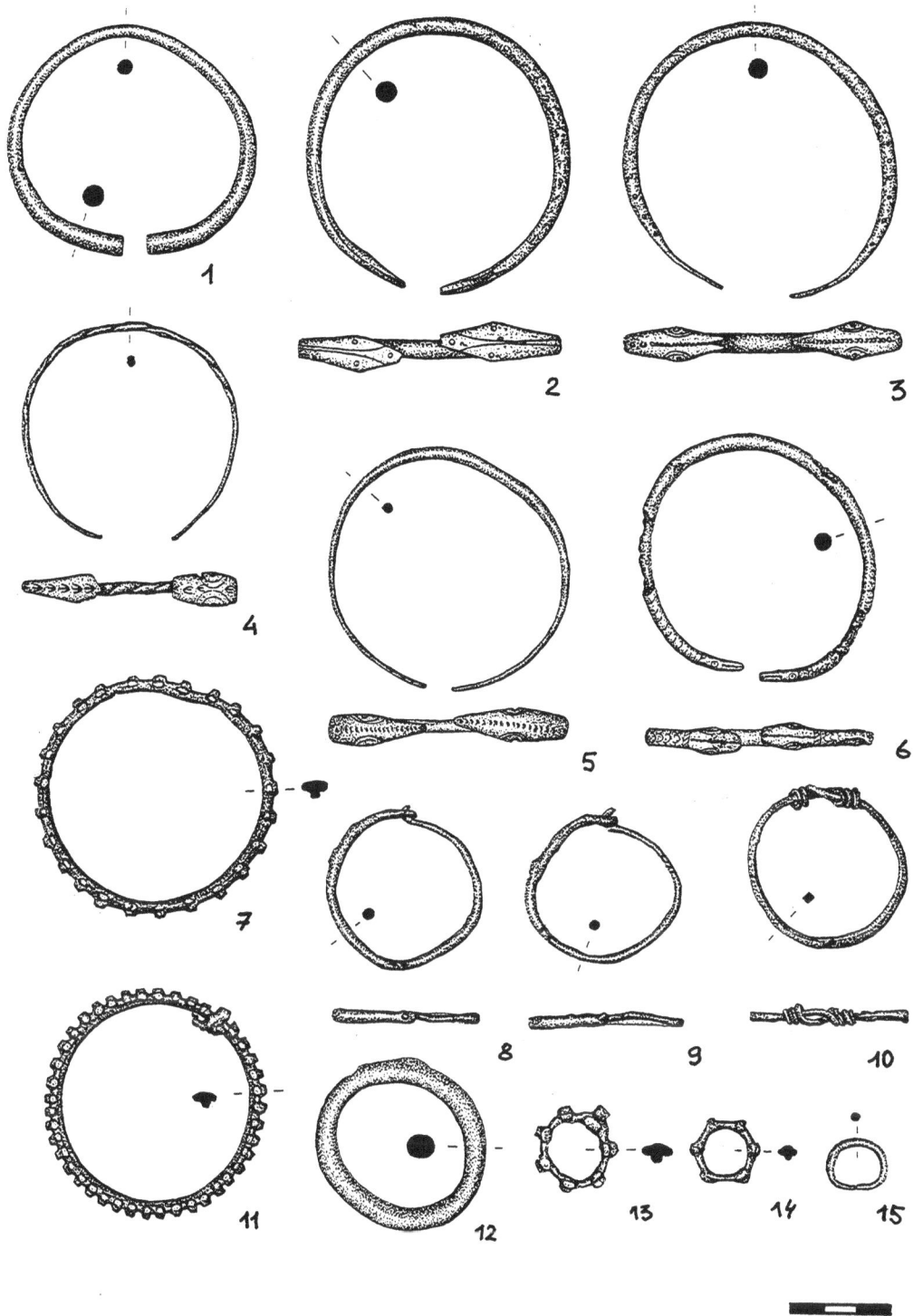

Fig. 12: *Bracelets and finger-rings from the Zavetnoe necropolis. 1: grave 184. 2: 189. 3: 184. 4: 189. 5: 282. 6: 140. 7: 189. 8-9: 182. 10: 184. 11-12: 294. 13: 284. 14: 182. 15: 263. 1-14: bronze. 15: silver.*

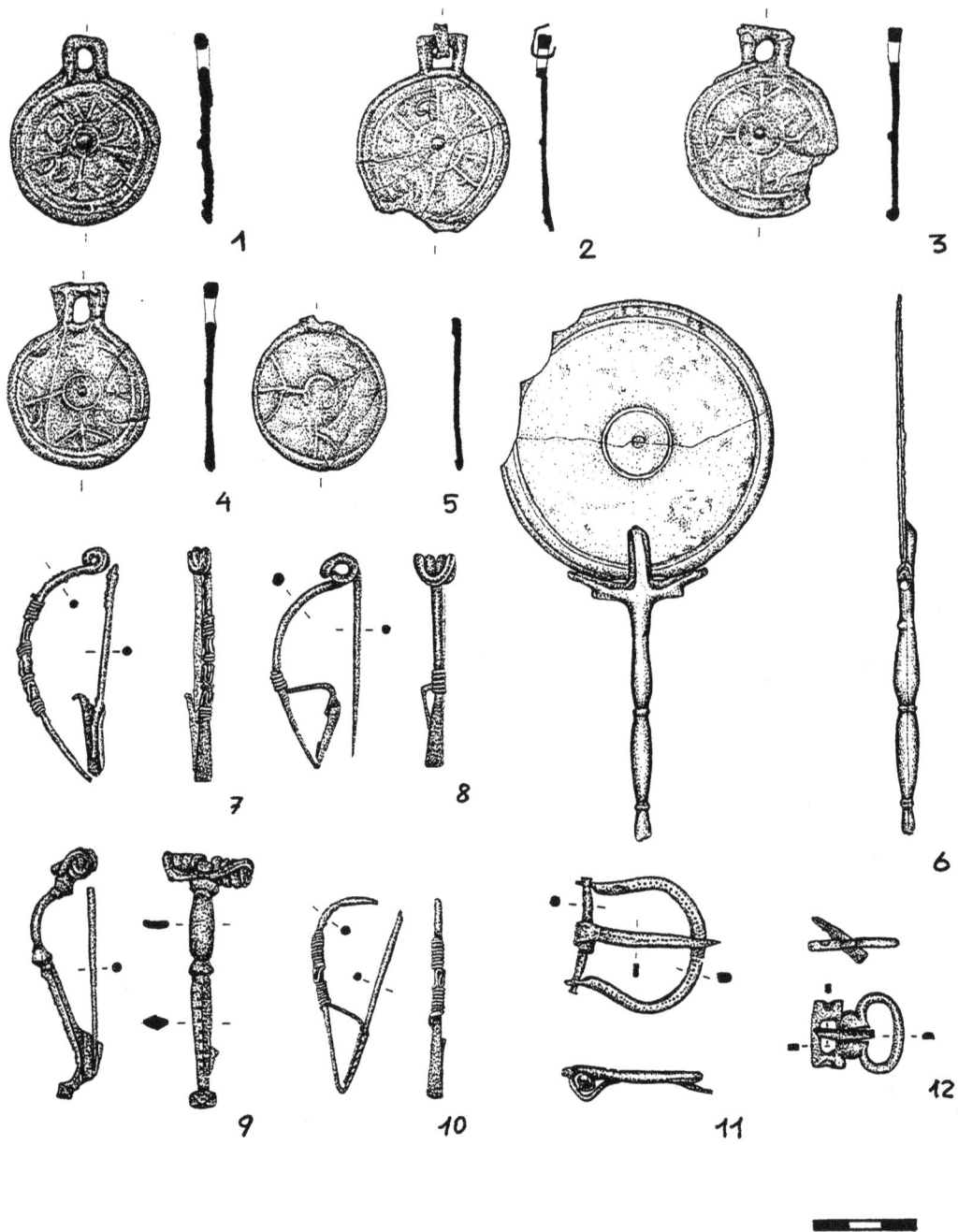

Fig. 13: *Mirrors, fibulae and belt buckles from the Zavetnoe necropolis. 1: grave 214. 2: 286. 3: 193. 4: 294. 5: 284. 6: 93. 7: 284. 8: 102. 9: 225. 10-11: 182. 12: 284. All bronze, 2 with a leather strap fragment.*

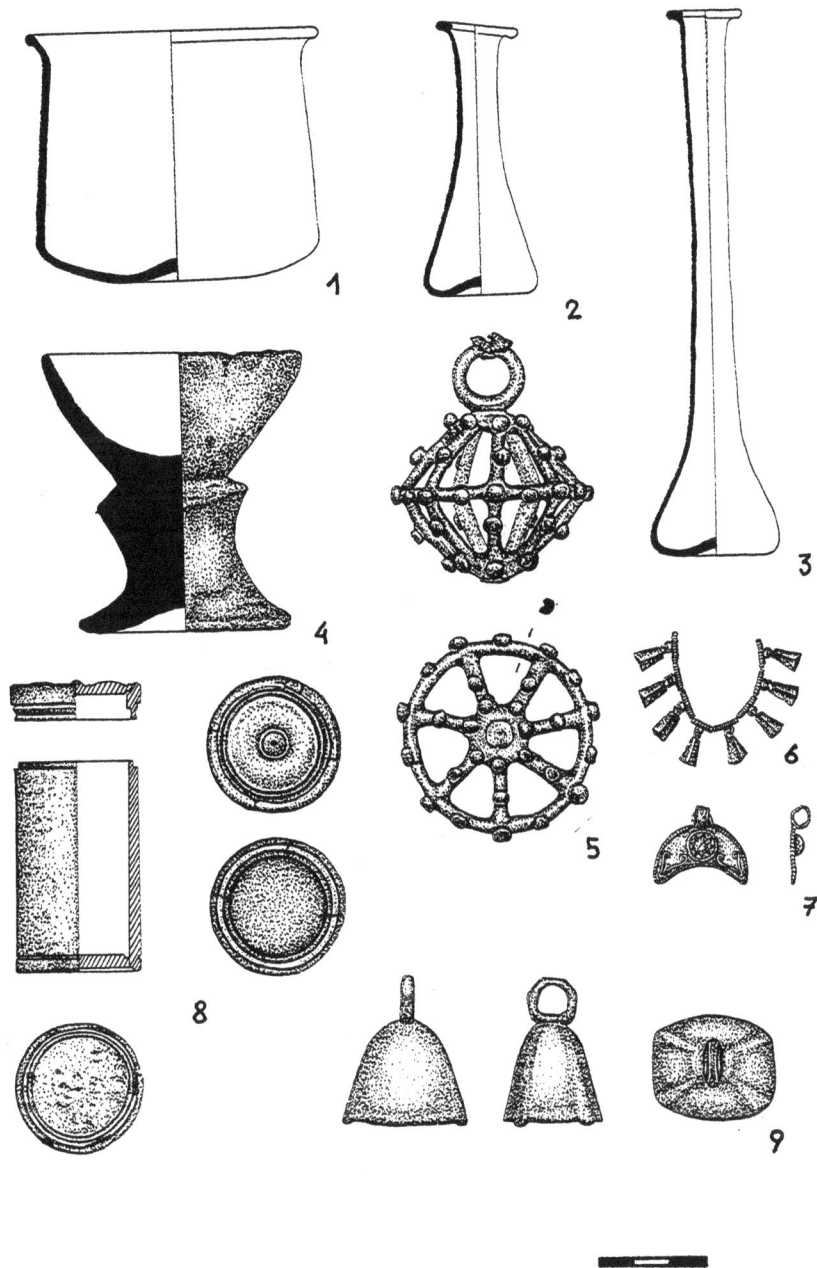

Fig. 14: *Miscellaneous artefacts from the Zavetnoe necropolis. 1: grave 284. 2-5: 294. 6-7: 286. 8: 140. 9: 294. 1: drinking glass. 2-3: balsamaria. 4: incense cup. 5, 7: pendants. 6: necklace. 8: pyxis. 9: bell. 1, 3: glass. 4: pottery. 5-9: bronze. 6-7: gold. 8: bone.*

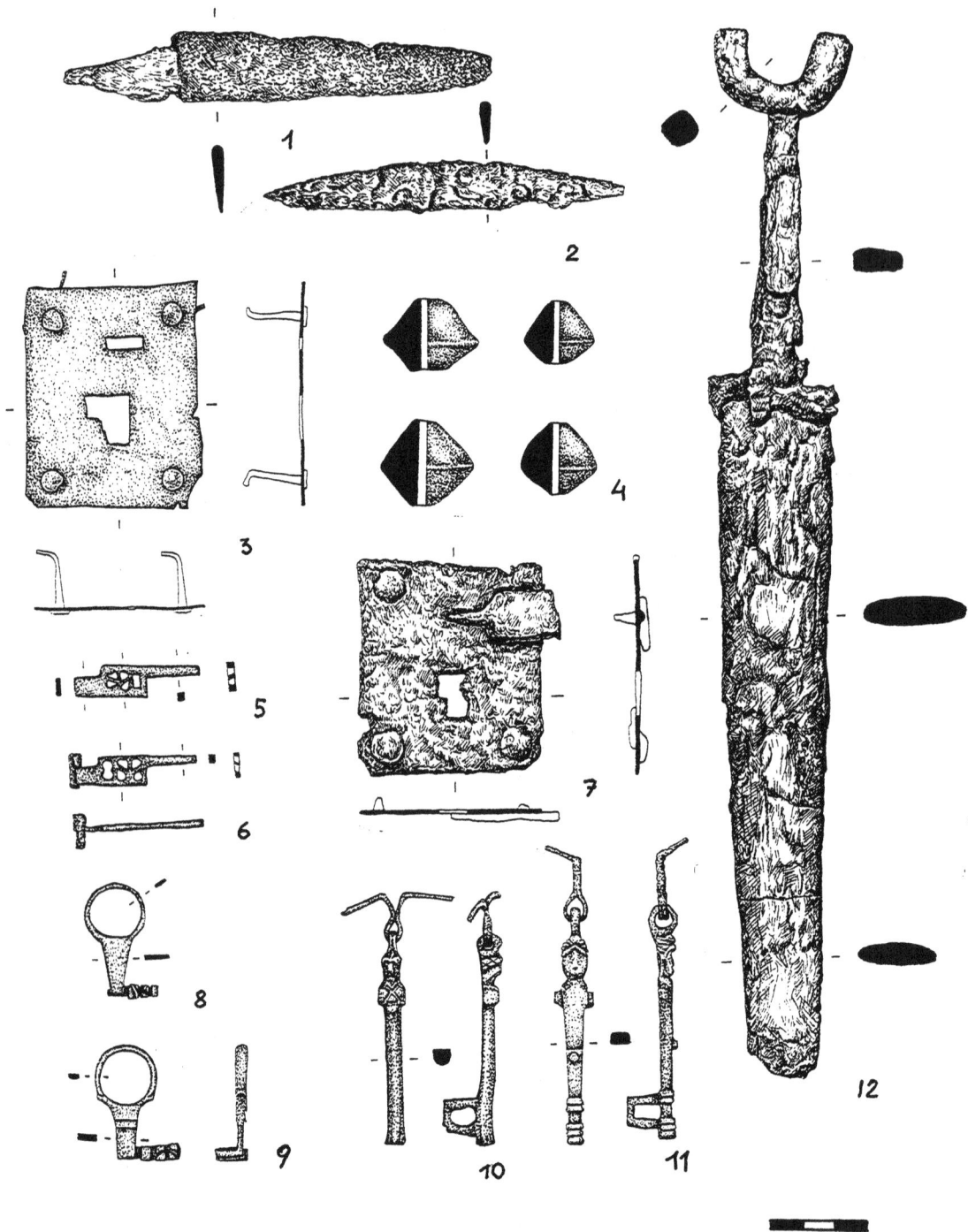

Fig. 15: *Miscellaneous artefacts from the Zavetnoe necropolis. 1: grave 284. 2: 293. 3: 286. 4: 263. 5: 286. 6-7: 294. 8: 217. 9: 286. 10: 217. 11: 286. 12: 102. 1-2: knives. 3, 5-7, 10-11: casket fittings. 4: spindle whorls. 8-9: keys. 12: short sword. 1-3, 7, 12: iron. 4: pottery. 8-11: bronze.*

The Late Scythian burial rite in the Belbek Valley of southwest Crimea in the Roman Period

Denis Zhuravlev
Department of Archaeology, State Historical Museum, Moscow

Introduction

At the turn of the 3rd and 2nd centuries BC, Crimea (now the territory of Ukraine) became the centre of the Late Scythian state. The final floruit of the Late Scythian culture, accompanied both by Graeco-Roman influence and by Sarmatian penetration into the area, as well as the subsequent dissolution of the state under the attacks of Goths and then Huns, can be clearly seen in the archaeological record of the Belbek river valley.

The burial customs of the Late Scythian population of the Belbek Valley vividly illustrate the complex ethnic composition of the region in the Roman Period (1st to mid-3rd centuries AD) at the necropolises of Belbek I-IV, the Mamay-Oba barrow and the barrow near the Bratskoye cemetery – c.f. map in Firsov, fig. 1, the present volume. There is a preliminary publication of the burial rite of the region (Guschina 1997), and also two articles about the burial rite of southwest Crimea in general (Bogdanova 1982, Puzdrovskiy 1994).

Burial structures

Two main types of burial structures were predominant in southwest Crimea in this period: tombs with stepped-down chambers and simple trenches. They are south-oriented with some deviations (36%). Orientation towards the north (28%) is typical of later burials.

Simple trenches (fig. 16) are of rectangular shape, with rounded corners, sometimes slightly narrower toward the feet (length up to 2 m, width up to 0.9 m, depth up to 1.6 m). Trenches with earth or stone filling account for 30-40% of burial structures. Remarkably, burials with stone filling are situated close to each other. Bogdanova supposes that the rite of filling the burial trench with stone goes back to Scythian burial traditions (Bogdanova 1982:31). One variety of trench has shoulders and is oriented from north to south with small deviations. A step up to 0.4 m wide is located at a depth of 1 m from the edge of the trench. The shoulders served as support when covering the graves with stone slabs.

The advance of Sarmatian tribes into Crimea in the second half of the 1st century AD caused an increase in the number of burials with stepped-down chambers (fig. 17), such that they account for 40-50% of the burial structures from the 2nd and 3rd century. The prevalent orientation is from the northwest to the southeast. The narrow rectangular entrance trench (length up to 2.2 m, width up to 0.6 m) has a stepped-down chamber 0.45 to 0.75 m wide on one of its long sides, mostly the west one. The floor of the chamber is usually 0.15 to 0.2 m, sometimes 0.35 m lower than the bottom level of the entrance trench. The chamber is closed with vertically positioned stone slabs which under the pressure of the earth become strongly inclined. The stepped-down chamber burials are distributed rather evenly over the Belbek IV cemetery, but in some parts of it they are predominant. At the same time (after the mid-2nd century) their numbers increased in the necropolis of ancient Chersonesus, a fact attributed by many scholars to the increased Sarmatian presence in the region (e.g. Zubar 1977:71, for another opinion see Dashevskaya 1984). Some stepped-down chambers were secondarily dug into Bronze Age barrows, e.g. at Mamay-Oba and Bratskoye (Zubar & Savelya 1989:74-83).

Proceeding from the predominance of the stepped-down chamber burials at the Belbek IV necropolis as well as at the sites of Skalistoe II and III, Vysotskaya supposes a stronger influence of Sarmatian traditions in the "rural, provincial" necropolises, in comparison with necropolises of large urban sites (Vysotskaya 1983:19). According to Dashevskaya, stepped-down chamber graves are a criterion not primarily of ethnic, but rather of social differentiation, since stepped-down chamber burials are "usually poor" (Dashevskaya 1984:57). It must be noted that even if this thesis is true for the Belyaus cemetery, the analysis of Belbek IV shows a different picture. Some quite rich burials in stepped-down chamber burials can be pointed out.

To Raevskiy's mind, it was precisely the individual character of burials that was typical for the Sarmatian burial rite, a fact which he linked to the weakening of family ties in Late Scythian society (Raevskiy 1971:64). Dashevskaya explains the appearance of individual burials in stepped-down chamber graves with the "solitary family status of the persons buried and the meagre conditions resulting therefrom" (Dashevskaya 1984:59). According to Puzdrovskiy, the proliferation of the stepped-down chamber graves was connected not only with the influx of a new population, but also with a new form of social organisation which resulted in an increasing number of individual burials (Puzdrovskiy 1994:117).

Single burials are prevalent and only rarely does one find two stepped-down chambers or two or more bodies to one trench. One of these exceptions is grave 223 in the Belbek IV necropolis (fig. 18), where the skeleton of the buried man was shifted and a deceased woman was placed beside it. Bogdanova suggests that in such cases the shared burial could be imposed by considerations not only of parenthood, but also of social status. She states that such burials are invariably poorly furnished (Bogdanova 1982:32). Contrary to this statement, grave 223 at Belbek IV is one of the richest at the site. A man and a woman were buried here within a small timespan. The furnishings – fragments of a suit of chain mail armour, an iron sword,

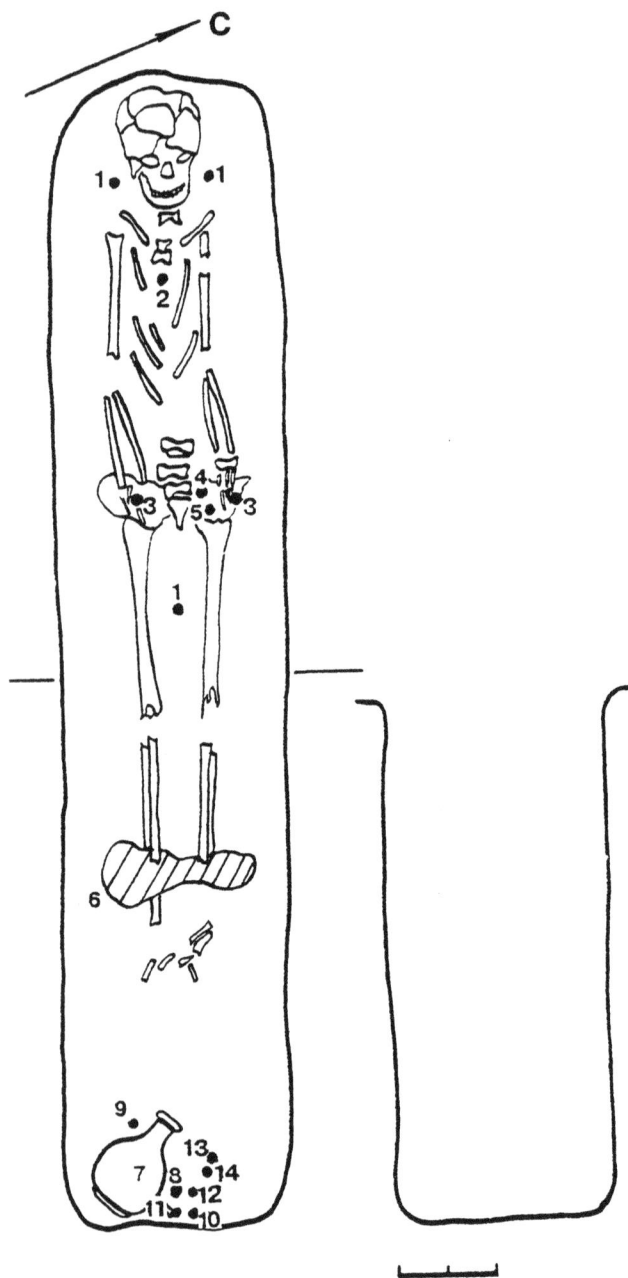

Fig. 16. Belbek IV, grave 295 (Guschina 1997).

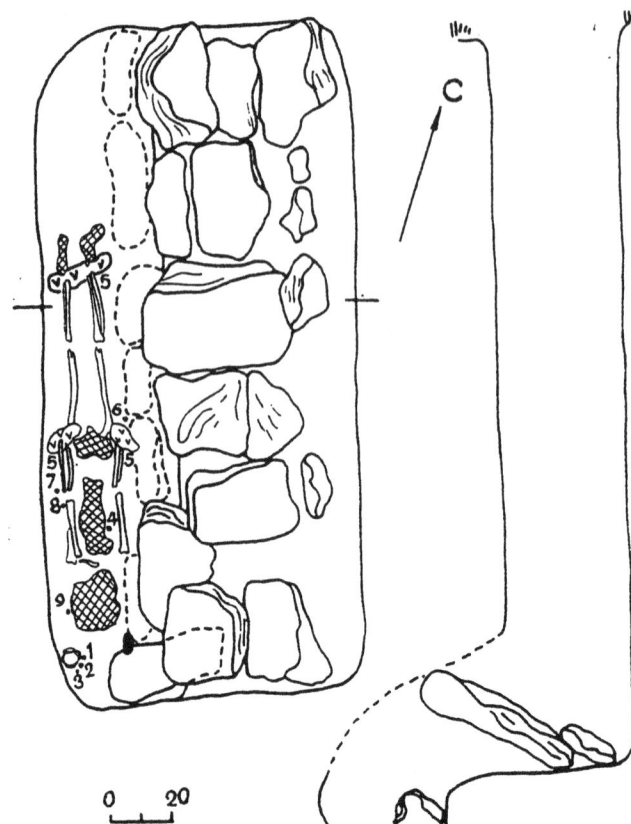

Fig. 17. Belbek IV, grave 314 (Guschina 1997).

pelvis or the legs crossed at the shins. The position of one or both hands on the waist as well as crossed legs is by some scholars identified as a Sarmatian tradition. On the other hand, the opinion has been voiced that this particular trait cannot be regarded as an ethnic indicator either of the Sarmatians or of the Meotians, who followed this custom much earlier (Moshkova 1983:31 ff). This rite can probably be linked to religious ideas according to which the feet of the deceased had to be tied together before burial (Bogdanova 1982:36). It should also be noted in passing that such traits as the positioning of the hands on the waist or on the thighs, legs crossed at the shins and bodies lying on their side were typical for the Crimean Scythians in the 4th and 3rd centuries BC as well (Ol'khovskiy 1991:139). In some cases the face of the deceased is turned eastwards.

In some graves wooden flooring has been traced in the burial trench (fig. 19). In some cases, grave goods were placed on this floor. Traces of fire have been observed on the wooden planking. Here, we are probably dealing with the rite of purification with fire, widespread among a number of ancient peoples including the Sarmatians. Together with finds of flints and censers in the graves this lets us state that the cult of fire played a quite important role in the religion of the population of the Belbek Valley (Bogdanova 1990:53-58).

A very interesting and unusual rite has been observed in grave 221 at Belbek IV (fig. 20-21). On the bottom of a rectangular burial trench oriented from the northwest to the southeast stood vertically placed rectangular stone slabs:

remnants of horse harness, enamelled fibulae, silver and gold jewellery, a bronze statuette of Eros – testify to the high social status of those buried, possibly a married couple.

An interesting rite was observed in one of the burials: a woman was initially buried in the stepped-down chamber grave, and then the poorly furnished burial of a man was placed in the entrance trench. Both burials date to the second half of the 2nd century AD.

Most bodies are extended on their backs, the arms stretched along the sides, although some corpses are slightly contorted, with the arms sometimes placed on the

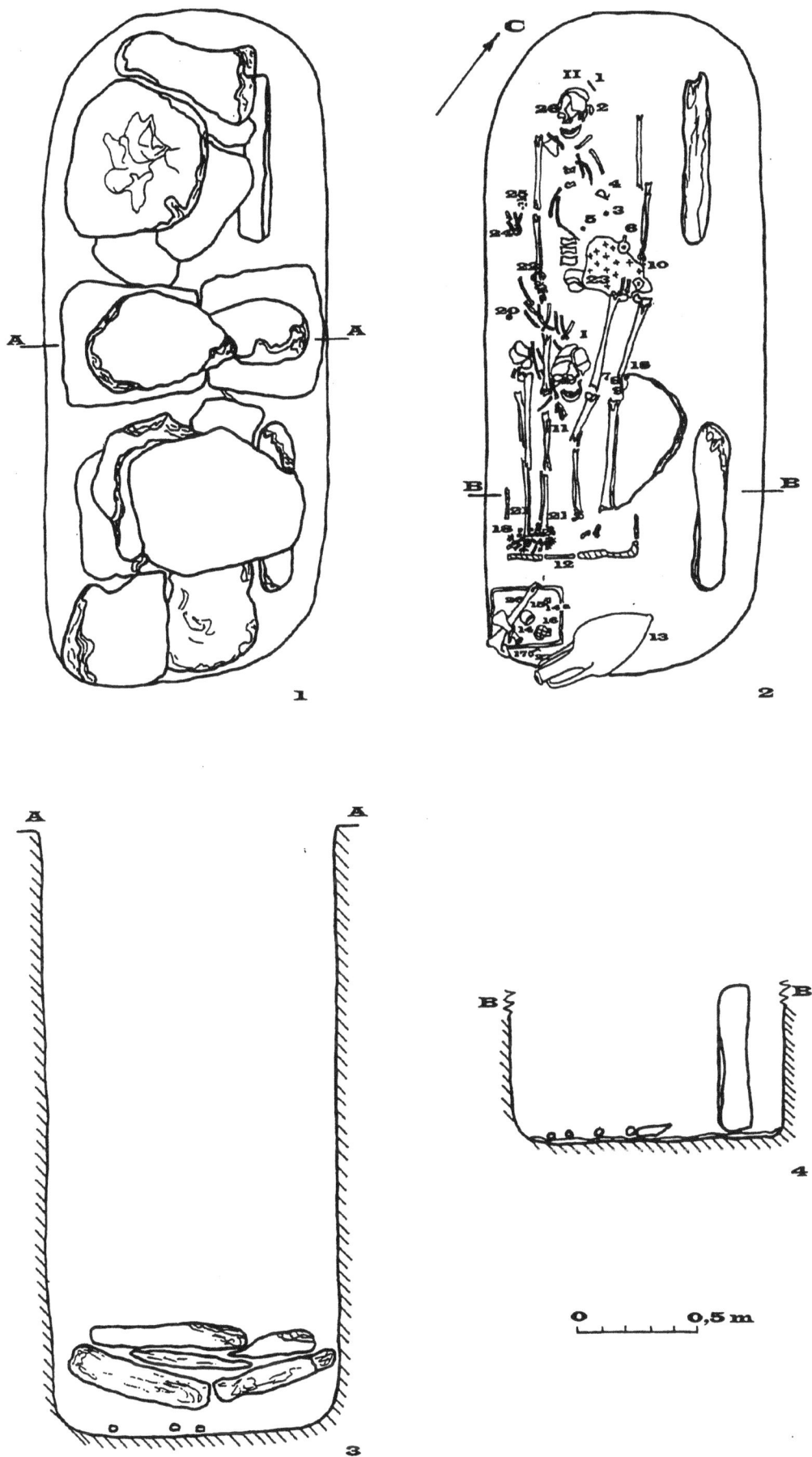

Fig. 18. *Belbek IV, grave 223*.

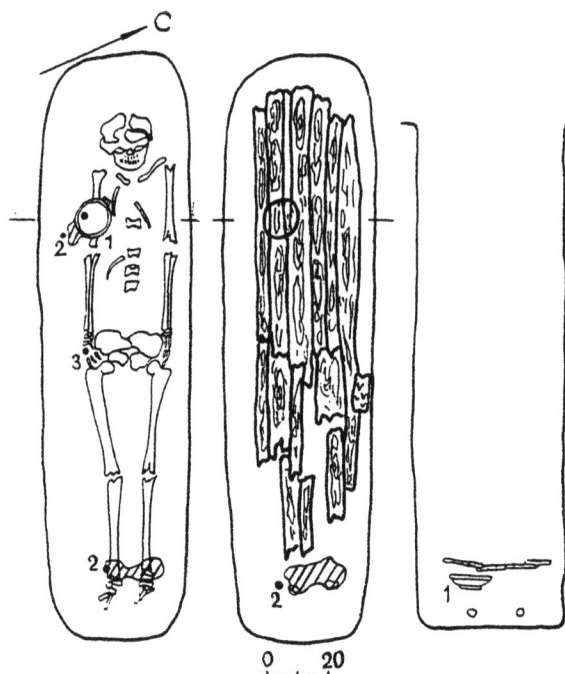

Fig. 19. Belbek IV, grave 290 (Guschina 1997).

the pit (between the two vertical slabs). In the opposite part of the grave behind the vertical slab nothing was found except traces of the continuing wooden flooring. It can be assumed that in the part of the burial where the artefacts were found there was a child burial on the floor – as a rule, bones are not preserved in such cases. However, the lack of system in the placement of the grave goods seemingly contradicts this supposition (Guschina 1997:33-34). The purpose of the other part of the trench remains enigmatic – as does, admittedly, the whole rite of this burial.

The Belbek Valley has yielded no collective burials in earthen vaults, which are widespread in other parts of southwest Crimea (Puzdrovskiy 1994:118-119). Cenotaphs are extremely rare which a number of scholars regard as an example of the influence of Greek culture. Grave superstructures are not common, although earthen mounds did exist in antiquity, since regular rows of graves can be traced practically everywhere and later graves do not disturb earlier ones. All the graves of the same period are situated in the neighbouring area of the necropolises. Unlike the case of the Zavetnoe cemetery (Bogdanova 1965), only one anthropomorphic stele was found in the necropolis of Belbek IV.

one at the northwest end of the trench and the other in a parallel position at the centre of the grave, dividing it into two parts. Another stone slab stood in the southeast part of the grave along its east side. In the northwest part of the grave shapeless blocks of stone were placed horizontally over these slabs. On the bottom of the burial trench were found traces of wooden flooring of burnt and charred poles of round profile, up to 30 cm in diameter, which lay along the pit and in some places also across it. The grave goods were found in situ on the flooring in the northwest part of

In the second half of the 2nd century AD stone cists appear (fig. 22), most of which are accompanied by a rich inventory. The cist graves are made of vertically placed flat slabs (usually four at each side) which form a sort of stone box without end-slabs. This type of burial structure occurs quite rarely in southwest Crimea. It must be noted that the majority of the cist graves in the burial sites of southwest Crimea were robbed already in antiquity (Bogdanova 1982:34), which can probably be taken as testimony to the opulence of the grave goods and / or of a special social status of those buried in such graves. The cist graves are one of the last types of burial structures of the

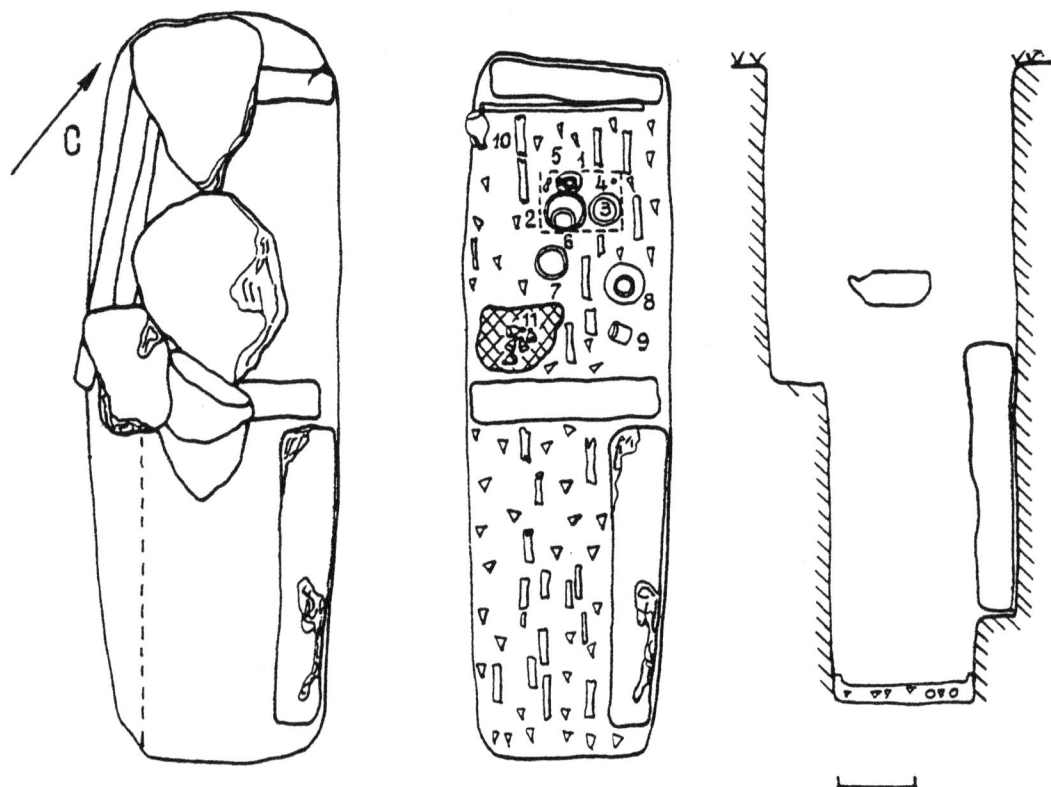

Fig. 20. Belbek IV, grave 221.

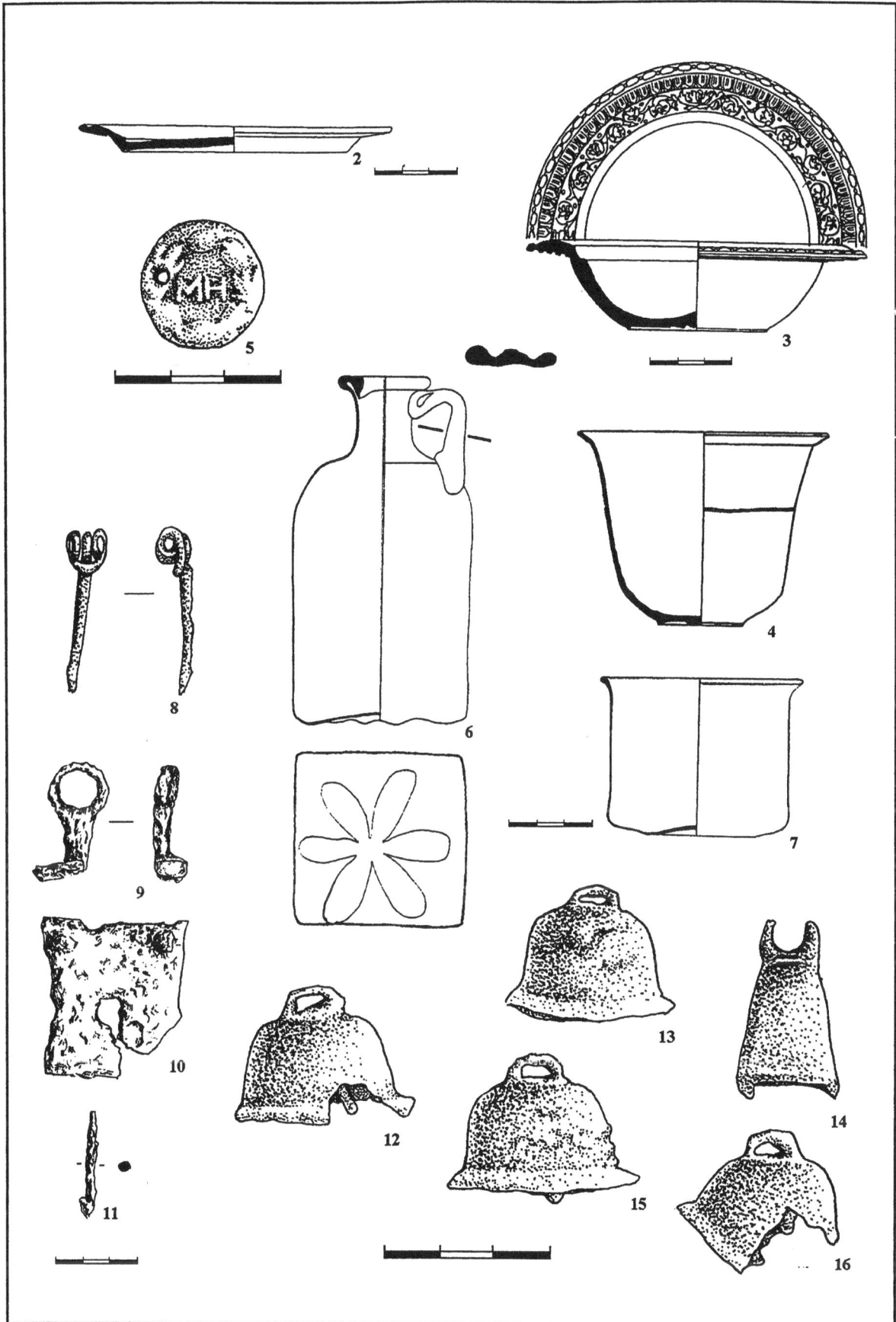

Fig. 21. Belbek IV, grave 221. Grave goods. Incorrect find numbers; 1 should be subtracted from each number, making the coin no 4 etc.

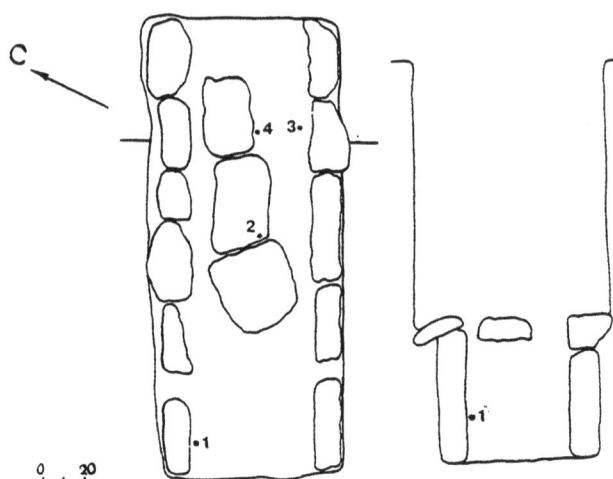

Fig. 22. Belbek IV, grave 284.

Crimean Scythians, appearing in the 2nd and 3rd centuries AD. The Belbek I necropolis yielded 17 stone cists out of 22 graves (Guschina 1974:32). According to Vysotskaya, this grave type was adopted by the population of southwest Crimea from the Greeks (Vysotskaya 1972:90). Bogdanova, on the other hand, was of the opinion that the cist graves were a development of the local grave trenches with shoulders (Bogdanova 1982:33).

Puzdrovskiy supposes that the aforementioned type of burial structure is a result of the convergence of the graves with shoulders and of those with a stone ceiling. He does not rule out that their appearance may have been influenced by the traditions of the Chernyakhov culture – if the cremations in stone cists found at Belbek I should be taken into account, although they are of a considerably later date (Puzdrovskiy 1994:116-117). In the second half of the 3rd century cremation burials appear at Belbek I, Skalistoye III etc, which some scholars link to the influence of provincial Roman customs (Vysotskaya 1972:99). It should be noted, however, that cremation was typical not only of the Romans, but of the Sarmatians and the Chernyakhov culture as well (Puzdrovskiy 1994:124).

Mortuary ritual

Traces of funeral banquets have been recorded in the form of potsherds in grave trenches and several ritual areas have been found at the cemeteries.

In a number of burials various traces of fire were found: pieces of charcoal, ash strewing or partial cremation. This custom was widespread in Late Scythian society (Vysotskaya 1994:65). Besides that, partial cremation is known to have been employed by the Scythians of the Lower Dnepr region and by the Sauromatians (Vyazmitina 1972:110, Smirnov 1964:225). Very probably Late Scythians lit a brief fire on the chest of the deceased (Yatsenko 1998:68-69). A purifying fire was probably also lit in the grave, sometimes before the burial (as evidenced by a layer of ashes beneath the skeleton), while sometimes the deceased was covered with embers and branches from the fire. Remains of charred wooden boards have been found in some burials. They may pertain both to the burnt

ceiling of the burial trench and to the coffin boards (Vysotskaya 1994:65).

Red paint found in the burials was used as body ornament and for ritual purposes, probably as an symbolic evocation of fire. Bessonova, analysing the finds of red paint in Scythian burials, suggests that it could also "be associated with fertility and signify the transitional state of the organism between life and death, a hope for the continuation of life; rebirth, that is, the resurrection of the dead" (Bessonova 1990:31). It cannot be ruled out that the dye may have been kept or prepared in the seashells found in several burials, a common feature also of graves of Sauromatian priestesses (Smirnov 1964: 254 - 255). Admittedly, there is another point of view, according to which the red paint was used as body ornament only (Ilynskaya 1968:150, Zuev 1996:59).

A quite rare phenomenon is the presence of pieces of chalk or chalk strewing in the graves. This rite is known from many burial sites of southwest Crimea and is usually linked to the Sarmatian influence (Dashevskaya 1991: 26, Vysotskaya 1994:66). Pieces of flint have also been found in some burials. Such finds are quite frequent also in contemporary graves in the region north of the Black Sea (Vysotskaya 1994:68, Shilov 1959:430, Rikman 1975: 320). The finds of smooth pebbles are surely also connected with elements of the burial rite. In some graves traces of decayed fabric have been observed, possibly from spread-out textiles or felt in which the deceased were wrapped. A similar rite has been traced in many burial sites of the Late Scythian culture.

Grave goods

The location of the grave goods in the burials is typical for Late Scythian culture. The pottery was placed at the head of the deceased, or, less frequently, at the hands or feet. Other items (brooches, fibulae, bead necklaces, pendants), as a rule, were placed where they belonged in life. Sometimes the vessels (up to five in one burial) were placed one into another, upside down or covering each other. In a number of burials the jug or cup was covered with a flat stone or a fragment of an amphora side (c.f. Vysotskaya 1994, fig. 27).

The burials were practically always accompanied by funeral food (beef, mutton or goat meat, sometimes poultry) in a plate or bowl, often together with an iron knife. Grape pips were found in one of the graves.

Among the inventory, besides items typical for Late Scythians, there is an enormous number of imported Classical objects: coins, amphorae, terra sigillata, bronze and glass vessels and so on (Guschina & Zhuravlev 1996:45-50, 1999). Greek graffiti are also fairly numerous. The placement of clay lamps in graves can be interpreted as a Graeco-Roman influence (Chrzanovski & Zhuravlev 1998:86-87).

Pendants, amulets, mirrors, seashells etc can be classified as ritual objects. These objects are usually found in female or child burials, less frequently in the male ones

Fig. 23. Bronze mirrors with tamgas, Sarmatian clan emblems.

(Bogdanova 1980:79-88). Many of the Classical bronze objects found have been re-used, in particular as amulets.

A field of great interest is the analysis of *tamgas* – clan emblems – on the mirrors from Belbek IV (fig. 23). The conclusion has been reached that the buried women were connected to two large clans, from which the locals could take their wives. For one of the clans a northward orientation of burials was typical, and, for the other, southward; with corresponding chronological differences (Yatsenko & Zhuravlev, in print). The custom of breaking a mirror at burial was common among the inhabitants of the valley.

Bead-trimmed edges occur frequently on various parts of the female dress (Yatsenko 1987:166-176, Vysotskaya 1994:63-65). A difference can be observed in the use of such ornaments between burials oriented northwards and southwards. The bead-trim on the hems of the skirts is known in three varieties. The first, a line of beads across the middle of the tibiae, is most widespread among female Sarmatian burials. At Belbek IV this type is noted only in female graves with a northward orientation. The border was sometimes formed by two or more rows of beads. The trim of low skirt-hems at the ankle level was found in burials of both orientations, and those oriented southwards also had two or more rows of beads. A very short skirt (bead-trim above the knees) has been found in one grave oriented southwards. Bead-trimming across the chest is rare, gold ornaments are usually prevalent; they are known from burials of both orientations. The sleeves carried bead-trimming in two burials oriented northwards. In one of these cases the sleeves were rather short (above the wrists) and wide (15 cm). In the other one the left sleeve had four rows of beads of blue faience and jet along the edge. A belt (?) trimmed with of a row of beads across the upper edge of the pelvis has been found in several female burials, all of them oriented northwards.

Male dress (shirt and cloak) as well as the female one was fixed with fibulae. Among the Sarmatians of the 2nd-1st centuries BC cloaks were most frequently fixed with a fibula on the left shoulder by women, and on the right one by men. At Belbek IV this rule was not observed. A fibula could fix a woman's cloak both on the left and on the right shoulder.

Beside metal bracelets, bead bracelets are also common in female burials. A great diversity of variants and placement is typical for burials with a northward orientation. In complexes of both types the most common way to wear bead bracelets was at the wrists without metal ones.

Unfortunately, the extremely bad state of preservation of bones at the Belbek sites precluded the use of anthropological definitions. Only in some burials could preliminary observations be made, e.g. deformed skulls was traced in four of the male graves (Belbek I (1), II (2), IV (1); a trait regarded as an indicator of the Sarmatian culture.

Chronology

The grave finds from the Belbek valley necropolises allow us to distinguish three chronological groups of burials. The first is dated to the mid-1st to early 2nd century AD. The second group comprises burials from the early 2nd century AD to the third quarter of the same century. The third one dates to the last quarter of the 2nd to the first half of the 3rd century AD.

In the earliest group of burials female and child graves are prevalent, whereas in the second group the male graves dominate. The earliest burials have been discovered at the very top of the hill; later the burial site expanded to the south and to the east. This is also a feature of other Late Scythian burial sites.

Virtually all the burials belong to the rank-and-file population – very few rich burials have been found, although there is a considerable variation in grave goods. However, this is testimony to chronological differences rather than to social stratification. Generally, the burials of group 1 are much richer than the burials of group 2, and only a few relatively rich burials fall into group 3. At the same time, numerous contemporary rich vault burials have been documented at the Ust'-Al'ma necropolis, which beside the usual grave goods contain many gold objects and are undoubtedly the graves of top-level aristocrats (Puzdrovskiy, Zaitsev & Loboda 1997:98-100).

The Classical influence

The close proximity of Classical Chersonesus and the co-existence of different ethnic groups resulted in the formation in the region of a Late Scythian culture in fact very similar to the provincial Roman one.

Sarmatian traits of the burial rite and artefact-types usually linked to Sarmatian presence or influence appear in the mid-1st and early 2nd centuries AD at the burial sites of central and southwest Crimea, and somewhat later at the Chersonesus necropolis as well. In the necropolises of Neapolis and Zavetnoe there appear wooden coffins, and the custom of crossing the legs of the deceased spreads. Mirror-pendants and fragments thereof adorned with Sarmatian *tamgas* become common. Sarmatian weapons and moulded censers appear. According to Raevskiy (1971:140-141), this period represents the middle stage of the Sarmatians' penetration into Crimea. He dates the first stage to the 2nd and 1st centuries BC. The late Sarmatian culture made a strong impact on the population of Crimea. In central Crimea near Neapolis, the capital of the Late Scythian kingdom, a number of richly furnished burials appear at this time, interpreted by many authors as Sarmatian, e.g. grave 4 of the Nogaichinskiy barrow (Simonenko 1993:70-74) and finds from the village of Konstantinovka (Orlov & Skoriy 1989). In southwest Crimea Sarmatian burials were inserted into Bronze Age barrows. Zubar & Savelya suppose that the Late Scythians and Sarmatians inhabited the same urban sites and buried their dead in the same cemeteries (Zubar & Savelya 1989:82).

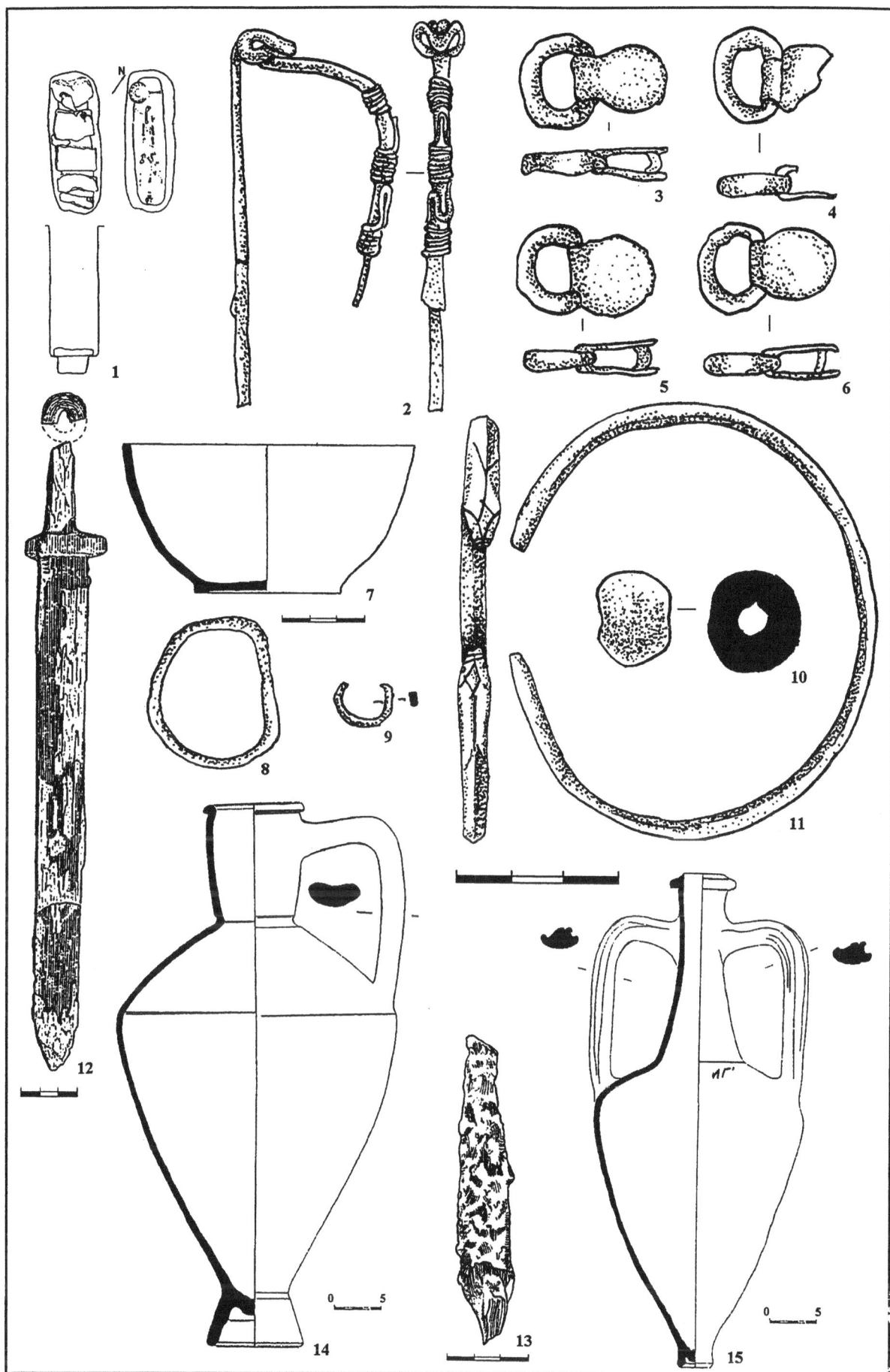

Fig. 24. Belbek IV, grave 215. Plan and grave goods.

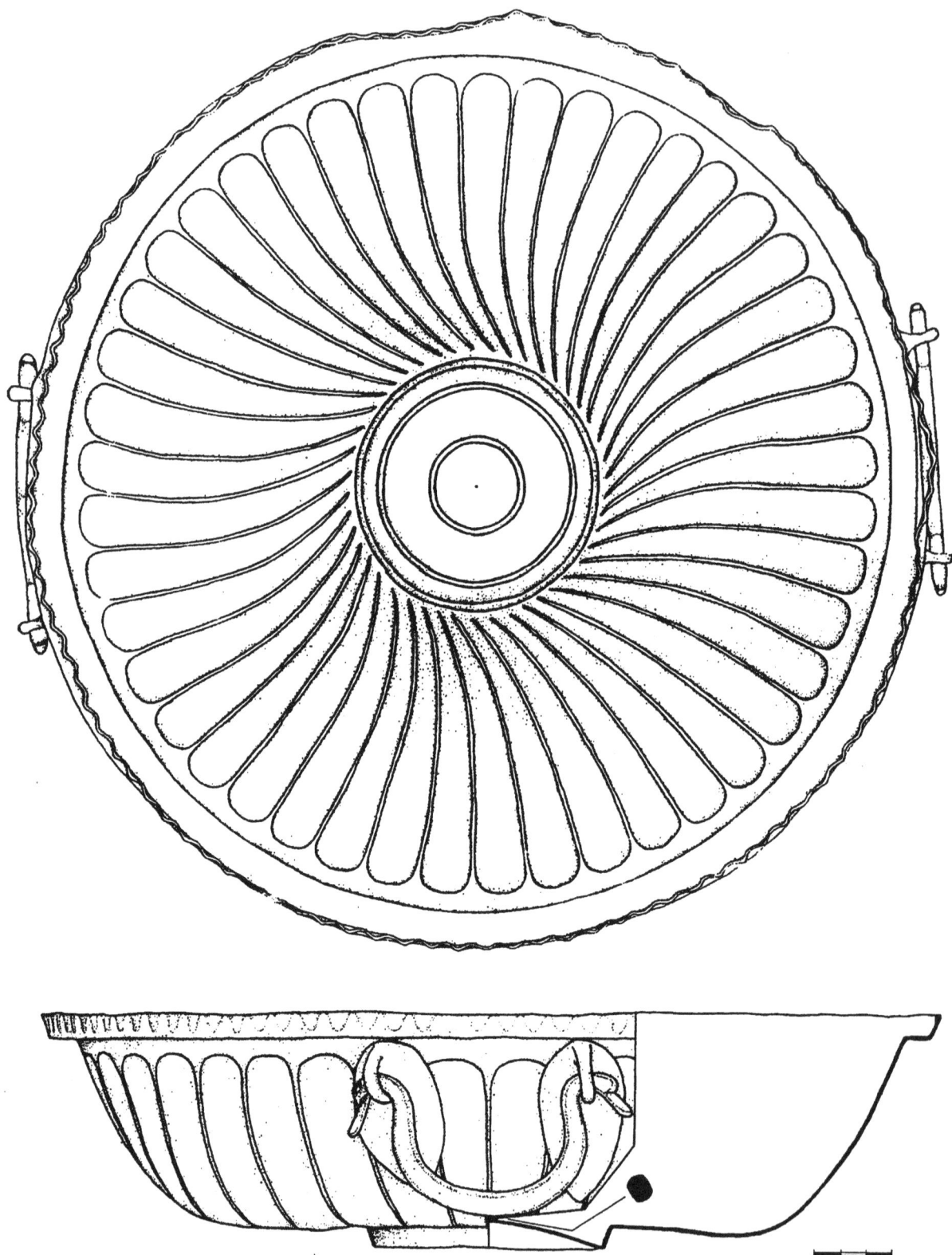

Fig. 25. *Belbek IV, grave 215. Bronze vessel.*

The close proximity of these barbarians to Chersonesus became a threat to the city's security. Historical sources indicate a barbarian onslaught on Chersonesus in the early 60s of the 1st century AD (IOSPE I.2:369), which was fought off by Roman troops (CIL XIV:3608). Incidentally, it is at this time that stepped-down chamber graves appear in Late Scythian necropolises. In my opinion, the rise of imports in the third quarter of the 1st century and a large number of the Greek graffiti on terra sigillata vessels from the burials may be closely linked to a military expedition to Chersonesus led by the legate of the province of Moesia, Titus Plautius Silvanus, between AD 63 and 66 (Zubar 1988:19-27). Also relevant in this connection are the Roman military detachments stationed in the Chersonesus area and the fact that right at this time peaceful relations were for a short period established between the Chersonesites and the indigenous population of Taurica, so that Chersonesus became an intermediary trade centre.

The Belbek Valley at that time apparently remained in the hands of barbarian tribes. As indicated by Sorochan, in the 1st century AD a process had just begun whereby close economic connections between Chersonesus and southwest Crimea were strengthened (Sorochan 1981:27). The dependence of Chersonesus on grain from southwest Crimea is obvious (Sorochan 1994:69), and this may explain the large number of objects of Graeco-Roman types in the burials, as well as the scarcity of weapons.

In the first half of the 2nd century the military and political situation of Chersonesus was again aggravated through increased barbarian activity. A similar picture may be observed in the Bodrak river valley at the Ozernoe I-III cemeteries (Kadeev & Sorochan 1989:85). At several burial sites in this region a common trend of the burial rite can be traced: in the mid-2nd century grave orientation changes from southward to northward. Bogdanova linked the change in orientation to the two waves of the Sarmatian penetration into Crimea (Bogdanova 1982:35).

The next stage of the Sarmatian penetration into southwest Crimea came after the victory of the Bosporan King Sauromates II over the Scythians (CBN no. 1237) and the settlement of the conquered territories of Taurica in the late 2nd to early 3rd centuries. The weaponry (fig. 24:12) and horse graves (at Belbek I, II, IV) found at the burial sites are dated to this period. As an example we might point out a horse grave from Belbek IV. The horse lay, its legs tucked in, in an oval-shaped pit oriented from the north to the south. The burial was accompanied by an iron bit with cheek rings and a saddle-girth buckle, and was linked to a warrior burial nearby.

A contemporaneous increase in Bosporan imports has been established at several burial sites of southwest Crimea, in the form of pottery, including red slip ware with zoomorphic handles, a clay rattle with the image of Eros, isolated coins struck at Bosporus etc. Military colonists from Sarmatian tribes penetrated the territory of Taurica in the late 2nd century, and the area came into the Bosporan sphere of interest.

In the late 2nd to the first half of the 3rd century AD another peak in Graeco-Roman imports can be observed, probably due to the granting of *eleutheria* (an at least nominal freedom) to Chersonesus and the stationing of Roman garrisons in Taurica. Individual features of the so called "Late Scythian culture" gradually almost disappeared under the impact of the levelling effect of provincial Roman culture (Malyukevich 1992:54).

A system of Roman roads, water-supplies, military outposts, fortifications etc was created at this time in southwest Crimea, which, according to certain scholars, resembles the features of a classical *limes*. Numerous finds of Roman objects from the area are widely known, among them the tombstones of legionaries. Near Balaklava remains not only of Roman fortifications, but also of a temple were found in 1996 (Zubar, Savelya & Sarnovskiy 1997). Admittedly, far from all scholars agree with the hypothesis of the presence of a *limes* in Taurica (for complete references see Zubar 1994:65-78).

The convenient geographic location at the mouth of the Belbek River could very well have led to the stationing here of a small Roman detachment. Several burials at the site stand out not only through their unusual furnishings with a large number of imported Graeco-Roman items, but also through the burial rite, which is markedly different from that of adjacent graves, with the use of slabs or wooden constructions. The burials richest in imported items could arguably belong to people somehow connected to a Roman garrison. Certainly, the people buried at Belbek were not Roman legionaries, but the graves may very well belong to soldiers of auxiliary troops; such as, for instance, the man buried in grave 215 of Belbek IV; or to people connected to the garrison in other ways. This hypothesis gains weight as the material culture of the inhabitants of the Belbek Valley was in many aspects similar to the provincial Roman one. On the other hand, due to their proximity to the Roman soldiers, the local people had access to more imported goods than their more remote neighbours.

Apparently, the burial site was used by the population of a large Late Scythian settlement in which, or near which, Roman detachments could be stationed – just as at the urban sites of Al'ma-Kermen or Ust'-Al'ma.

The end of the Scythian culture

Probably no later than the mid-3rd century, many Late Scythian urban sites of southwest Crimea were devastated. Numerous closed complexes with traces of destruction are dated to that time at different urban sites, e.g. at the settlements of Neapolis, Ust'-Al'ma and Al'ma-Kermen (Raevskiy 1970:105, Vysotskaya 1994:145 ff). A similar situation has been observed for the burial sites: the majority of them ceased to be used already by the mid-3rd century. Coin hoards in Scythia are also dated to the late second quarter of the same century (Dashevskaya 1991:22). Possibly this devastation can be linked to the invasion of the Gothic tribal union, which resulted in the destruction of many cities on the northern coast of the Pontus (Pioro 1990:25). According to Raevskiy, Alans may also have taken part in this invasion: they were "drawn into Crimea by the Goths and participated together with them in the destruction of the Late Scythian capital" (Raevskiy 1971:151). This is indirectly supported by the find of a Sarmato-Alan burial of the 3rd century at the Ust'-Al'ma settlement (fig 26). A man lacking his right hand, equipped with a sword – probably an invader maimed in war – was found in a grave untypical for the region (Vysotskaya 1994:145, fig. 42).

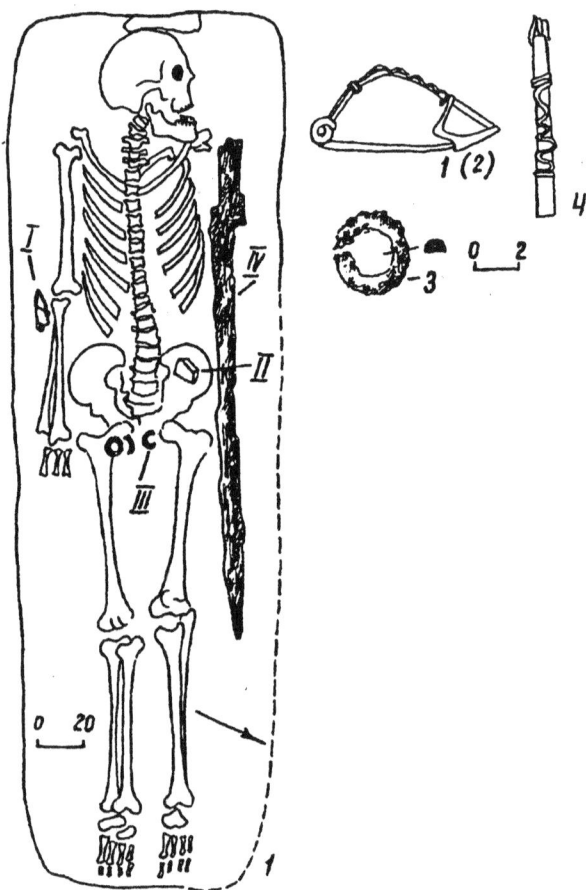

Fig. 26. Ust'-Al'ma settlement, Sarmato-Alan burial (Vysotskaya 1994).

At the same time – i.e. the mid-3rd century or a bit later – the burial site of Belbek IV also ceased to be used, and the population of the valley apparently resettled up the river Belbek, where habitation continued in the 4th-5th centuries and later.

Acknowledgements

I would like to thank Dr. Irina Guschina (State Historical Museum, Moscow) for her help and for the opportunity to work with as yet unpublished materials. A general publication of the Belbek IV necropolis is forthcoming (Guschina & Zhuravlev in print).

References

Bessonova, S.S. 1990. Skifskie pogrebalnye kompleksy kak istochnik dlya rekonstruktsii ideologicheskikh predstavleniy. Zubar, V.M. (ed.). *Obryady i verovaniya drevnego naseleniya Ukrainy*, pp 17-40. Kiev.

Bogdanova, N.A. 1965. Skifskie i sarmatskie stely Zavetninskogo mogilnika. *Sovyetskaya Arkheologia* 3, pp 233-237. Institute of Archaeology, Russian Academy of Sciences. Moscow.

Bogdanova, N.A. 1980. Semantika i naznachenie nekotorykh amuletov iz mogilnikov pervykh vekov n.e. Yugo-Zapadnogo Kryma. Popova, T.B. & al. (eds.). *Istoriya i kultura Evrazii po arkheologicheskim dannym*. Trudy GIM (Papers of the State Historical Museum) vol. 51, pp 79-88. Moscow.

Bogdanova, N.A. 1982. Pogrebal'nyi obryad sel'skogo naseleniya pozdneskifskogo gosudarstva v Krymu. Talis, D.L. (ed.). *Arkheologicheskiye issledovaniya na yuge Vostochnoy Evropy*. Trudy GIM (Papers of the State Historical Museum) vol. 54, pp 31-39. Moscow.

Bogdanova, N.A. 1990. Rol' ognya v pogrebal'nom rituale mogilnika pervykh vekov nashey ery u s. Zavetnoe. Studzitskaya, S.V. (ed.). *Problemy arkheologii Evrazii (po materialam GIM)*. Trudy GIM (Papers of the State Historical Museum) vol. 74, pp 53-58. Moscow.

CBN. *Korpus Bosporskikh nadpisey* (Corpus of Bosporan inscriptions). Moscow-Leningrad 1965.

Chrzanovski, L. & Zhuravlev, D. 1998. *Lamps from Chersonesos in the State Historical Museum, Moscow*. L'ERMA di Bretschneider. Studia Archaeologica 94. Rome.

Dashevskaya, O.D. 1984. O podboynykh mogilakh u pozdnikh skifov. Melyukova, A.I. & al. (eds.). *Drevnosti Evrazii v skifo-sarmatskoe vremya*, pp 53-60. Moscow.

Dashevskaya, O.D. 1991. *Pozdnie skify v Krymu*. Svod Arkheologicheskikh Istochnikov A1-7. Moscow.

Guschina, I.I. 1974. Naselenie sarmatskogo vremeni v doline reki Belbek v Krymu (po materialam mogilnikov). Talis, D.L. (ed.). *Arkheologicheskie issledovaniya na yuge Vostochnoi Evropy*. Trudy GIM (Papers of the State Historical Museum), pp 32-64. Moscow.

Guschina, I.I. 1997. O pogrebalnom obryade naseleniya Belbekskoi doliny (Po materialam mogilnika Belbek IV v yugo-zapadnom Krimu. Belotserkovskaya, I.V. (ed.). *Arkheologicheskiy sbornik. Pogrebalniy obryad*. Trudy GIM (Papers of the State Historical Museum) vol. 93, pp 29-37. Moscow.

Guschina, I.I. & Zhuravlev, D.V. 1996. Rimskiy import iz mogilnika Belbek IV. Zhuravlev, D.V. & Firsov, K.B. (eds.). *Tezisy dokladov Otchetnoy sessii GIM po itogam polevykh arkheologicheskikh issledovaniy i novykh postupleniy v 1991-1995 g*, pp 45-50. Moscow.

Guschina, I.I. & Zhuravlev, D.V. 1999. Pogrebeniya s bronzovoi posudoi iz mogilnika Belbek IV v Yugo-Zapadnom Krymu. *Rossiyskaya Arkheologiya* 2. Institute of Archaeology, Russian Academy of Sciences. Moscow.

Guschina, I.I. & Zhuravlev, D.V. In print. *Belbek IV – a Late Scythian necropolis of Roman time in the South-Western Crimea*. Steppenvölker Eurasiens. Bd.IV. Moscow -Berlin.

Il'inskaya, V.A. 1968. *Skify dneprovskogo lesostepnogo levoberezh'ya*. Kiev.

IOSPE. *Inscriptiones antiqua orae septentrionalis Ponti Euxini graecae et latinae*.

Kadeev, V.I. & Sorochan, S.B. 1989. *Ekonomicheskie svyazi antichnykh gorodov Severnogo Prichernomor'ya v I v.do n.e.- V v.n.e. (na materialakh Khersonesa).* Kharkov.

Malyukevich, A.E. 1992. Phenomen pozdneskifskoy kul'tury. Vanchugov, V.P. (ed.). *Severo-Zapadnoye Prichernomor'ye. Ritmy kulturogeneza. Tezisy dokladov seminara,* pp 52-54. Odessa.

Moshkova, M.G. 1983. K voprosy o katakombnykh pogrebal'nykh sooruzheniyakh kak spetsificheskom etnicheskom opredelitele. Skripkin, A.S. (ed.). *Istoriya i kul'tura sarmatov,* pp 18-34. Saratov.

Ol'khovskiy, V.S. 1991. *Pogrebal'no-pominal'naya obryadnost' naseleniya stepnoy Skifii (VII-III vv. do n. e.).* Moscow.

Orlov, K.S. & Skoryi, S.A. 1989. Kompleks z bronzovim posudom rims'kogo chasu iz pohovann'ya v Tsentral'nom Krimu. *Arkheologiya* 2, pp 63-73. Kiev.

Puzdrovskiy, A.E. 1994. O pogrebalnykh sooruzheniyah Yugo-Zapadnogo i Tsentralnogo Kryma v pervye veka n.e. Mogarichev, Yu.M. (ed.). *Problemy istorii i arkheologii Krima,* pp 114-126. Simpheropol.

Puzdrovskiy, A.E.; Zaitsev, Yu.P. & Loboda, I.I. 1997. Pogrebeniya sarmatskoy znati I v. n.e. na Ust'-Alminskom necropole (po materialam raskopok 1996 g.). *Chersones v antichnom mire. Istorico-arkheologicheskiy aspect. Tezisy dokladov.* Sevastopol.

Raevskiy, D.S. 1970. Kompleks krasnolakovoy keramiki iz Neapolya. Verzhbitskiy, V.G. (ed.). *Ezhegodnik GIM za 1965-1966 gg,* pp 91-105. Moscow.

Raevskiy, D.S. 1971. Skify i sarmaty v Neapole (po materialam necropolya). Liberov, P.D. & Gulyaev, V.I. (eds.). *Problemy skifskoy arkheologii.* Materialy i issledovaniya po arkheologii SSSR 177, pp 143-151. Institute of Archaeology, Academy of Sciences of the USSR. Moscow.

Rikman, E.A. 1975. *Etnicheskaya istoriya naseleniya Pridnestrov'ya i prilegayuschego Podunav'ya v pervye veka n.e.* Moscow.

Shilov, V.P. 1959. *Kalinovskiy kurgannyi mogil'nik.* Materialy i issledovaniya po arkheologii SSSR 60. Institute of Archaeology, Academy of Sciences of the USSR. Moscow.

Simonenko, A.V. 1993. *Sarmaty Tavrii.* Kiev.

Smirnov, K.F. 1964. *Savromaty. Rannyaya istoriya i kul'tura sarmatov.* Moscow.

Sorochan, S.B. 1981. Ekonomicheskie svyazi Khersonesa so skifo-sarmatskim naseleniem Kryma v I v. do n.e. - V v. n.e.. *Antichnye gosudarstva i varvarskiy mir.* Ordzhonikidze.

Sorochan, S.B. 1994. Mify i realii khersonesskogo hlebnogo eksporta. Kadeev, V.I. (ed.). *Drevnosti,* pp 66-72. Kharkov.

Vysotskaya, T.N. 1972. *Pozdnie skify v Yugo-Zapadnom Krymu.* Kiev.

Vysotskaya, T.N. 1983. *Svoeobrazie kultury pozdnikh skifov v Krimu, in Naselenie i kultura Krima v pervye veka nashey ery.* Kiev.

Vysotskaya, T.N. 1994. *Ust'-Al'minskoye gorodische i nekropol'.* Kiev.

Vyazmitina, M.I. 1972. *Zolotobalkovskiy mogil'nik.* Kiev.

Yatsenko, S.A. 1987. K reconstruktsii zhenskoy plechevoi odezhdy Sarmatii. *Sovyetskaya Arkheologia* 3, pp 166-176. Institute of Archaeology, Russian Academy of Sciences. Moscow.

Yatsenko, S.A. 1998. Sarmatskie pogrebal'nye ritualy i osetinskaya etnografiya. *Rossiyskaya Arkheologiya* 3, pp 67-73. Institute of Archaeology, Russian Academy of Sciences. Moscow.

Yatsenko, S.A. & Zhuravlev, D.V. In print. *Bronze mirrors from the Belbek IV necropolis.*

Zubar, V.M. 1977. Pidbiyni mogili Khersonesskogo nekropolya. *Arkheologiya* 24, pp 68-73 Kiev.

Zubar, V.M. 1994. *Khersones Tavricheskiy i Rimskaya imperiya. Ocherki voenno-politicheskoy istorii.* Kiev.

Zubar, V.M. & Savelya, O.Ya. 1989. Noviy sarmatskiy mogilnik vtoroi poloviny 1- nachala 2 vv. n.e. v Yugo-Zapadnom Krimy. *Arkheologiya* 2, pp 74-83. Kiev.

Zubar, V.M.; Savelya, O.Ya. & Sarnovskiy, T. 1997. Novi latinski nadpisi z rimskogo hramu v okolitsyah Khersonesa Tavriiskogo. *Arkheologiya* 4, pp 67-88. Kiev.

Zuev, V.Yu. 1996. Nauchniy mif o "savromatskih zhritsakh". Alekseev, A.Yu. & al. (eds.). *Zhrechestvo i shamanizm v skifskuyu epokhu,* pp 54-68. Saint Petersburg.

The Early Anglo-Saxon burial rite: moving towards a contextual understanding

Sam J. Lucy, Department of Archaeology, University of Durham

Introduction

The term "Anglo-Saxon" encompasses a number of different meanings (Reynolds 1985:395). Calling a burial "Anglo-Saxon" can be taken to mean (a) that the deceased was interred during the Anglo-Saxon period (c. 450 AD to 700 AD in the case of furnished burials in eastern England), (b) that the burial was accompanied by artefacts which have stylistic parallels in north-west Europe between the fifth and seventh centuries, or (c) that the burial is thought to represent an immigrant, or the descendant of an immigrant from northern continental Europe during this period. "Anglo-Saxon" is thus at the same time a chronological term, a way of characterising artefact styles, and the name given to the inhabitants of eastern England in the fifth to seventh centuries AD on the assumption that they migrated from the continent.

These multiple meanings are often equated – a burial containing artefacts identified as "Anglo-Saxon" is frequently taken to be the burial of a person of Germanic ancestry and, in addition, that person is assumed to have been an "Anglo-Saxon" (more properly "Old English") speaker, although this cannot be proven through the use of archaeology. Within this limited terminology, therefore, resides a mass of assumptions about how funerary evidence from the fifth to seventh centuries should be interpreted, and about the very nature of ethnic identities, and their relationships with origins and language.

This paper intends to question the idea that such identities can be unproblematically and simplistically "read off" from the archaeological evidence. Instead, a different way of looking at burials will be proposed – that they are the result of many individual decisions of the mourners, who often have quite localised and continually changing ideas about how individuals should be buried. It will be suggested that these ideas about burial are, to a certain extent, archaeologically recoverable; that, due to the geographical and temporal perspective which archaeology can offer, some of these ideas can start to be reconstructed, but only when the evidence is examined in sufficient detail and with a critical eye.

Equating artefacts and identities

When artefacts began to be recognised as early Anglo-Saxon in the late eighteenth and early nineteenth centuries, there was already in existence a generally accepted historical framework, derived from Bede's *Ecclesiastical History* and the *De Excidio* of Gildas, which outlined the fifth and sixth century movements of Germanic tribes such as Angles, Saxons and Jutes (e.g. Turner 1799-1805). During the course of the later nineteenth century this narrative was expanded and embellished by historians, such as the "Oxford School" of Freeman, Stubbs and Green (Freeman 1869, 1872, 1881, 1888; Stubbs 1870, 1880, 1906; Green 1874, 1881, 1883). These historians are generally held to have been instrumental in the creation of "Anglo-Saxonism", a version of the past which claimed superiority for the Germanic peoples, especially the Anglo-Saxons, and saw "Anglo-Saxon" characteristics as contributing greatly to the success of the "English nation" in the Victorian period (Curtis 1968:11-12, Lucy 1998:10). Green (1881), for example, "presented the advance of the Anglo-Saxons, hewing their way through the dank forests, as the forward march of progress, civilisation and English colonialism" (Sims-Williams 1983:3).

In conjunction with this historical work, archaeology was helping to confirm the nature and progress of the Germanic movements. The first identification of parallels between the material culture of Britain and north-west Germany in the fifth and sixth centuries was made by J.M. Kemble (1856), with his observation of the similarities between pottery in Hanover Museum and English vessels published by Akerman in 1855. He thought that by comparisons of such urns "we are brought ... many steps nearer to our forefathers on the banks of the Elbe and its tributary rivers, and we can henceforth use indifferently the discoveries of Englishmen and North Germans for the elucidation of our national treasures" (Kemble 1863:230). From the middle of the nineteenth century, therefore, it was assumed that the movements of these early peoples, as described in the early historical sources, could be mapped through plotting distributions of early Germanic material culture, such as "pagan" pottery and the distinctive brooch types.

Thus, by the later nineteenth century, if an artefact found in eastern England could be paralleled by one in northern Germany (where Bede stated the Saxons came from), then that artefact was termed "Saxon". A burial in a cemetery which exhibited Anglian, Saxon or Jutish material came, in time, to be called "Anglo-Saxon". There was little doubt among most archaeologists that these remains indicated the burials of immigrants from these continental areas or their direct descendants (e.g. Wright 1855, Bateman 1861:xiii, Rolleston 1870). Even material found in these cemeteries which was unparalleled on the continent, such as annular brooches, came to be termed Anglo-Saxon because of its associations with the general assemblage. There was thus a widely held view in the later nineteenth century that the vast majority of the later fifth and sixth century population of eastern England were of Germanic ancestry. For example, Rolleston (1870:118) stated "we know, from finding cremation urns of the Anglo-Saxon type all over England nearly, that the whole of the country was overrun by a heathen population". In addition, the historians' emphasis on the Anglo-Saxon ancestry of the English, and the hostility expressed towards "Celtic" characteristics (Curtis 1968:64-5, 89) meant that any mixing of the Celtic and Anglo-Saxon "races" in the past was discounted.

From the early decades of the twentieth century, however, this view began to be challenged, possibly due to an increasing aversion to a Germanic myth of origin for the English people (Zachrisson 1927, Lucy 1998:14-15). Some archaeologists in the late 1930s became especially interested in the fate of the British population in the face of Germanic invasions (perhaps unsurprising, given the contemporary political climate), and invested effort into trying to identify artefacts which could indicate their continued existence. E.T. Leeds, for example, identified some classes of artefact, such as the penannular brooch, as belonging to a native substratum in Anglo-Saxon culture (Leeds 1936:3). T.D. Kendrick thought that the fine gold and garnet jewellery found in Kent and other areas, now dated to the later sixth and seventh century, actually belonged to what he termed "Arthurian Britain", seeing it as "a natural resurgence of barbaric tendencies set free by the withdrawal of the Romans", which could only have been produced by the native peoples (Kendrick 1938:59-60).

From the 1950s other developments in archaeology reinforced this view that the native population of Britain could not have been entirely wiped out by migrations from the continent. The refinement of aerial photography (Crawford 1953, St Joseph 1966) led to the realisation that Iron Age and Roman Britain were far more densely settled than had previously been thought, with estimates for the Roman population of perhaps four or five million people (Taylor 1983:106). Environmental research (for example, pollen analysis) demonstrated a substantial element of continuity in land management during the fifth and sixth centuries (Bell 1989:275-7). Probable continuity of field boundaries also challenged assumptions of mass population replacement in the fifth and sixth centuries (Bell 1989:280). Other work, such as that by Crabtree (1989) on animal bone assemblages, suggests further evidence for striking similarities in everyday activities such as animal husbandry and butchery practices between the late Roman and early Anglo-Saxon periods.

The accumulation of such evidence resulted in a growing acceptance of considerable native survival, which was marked from the late 1970s by a renewed search for objects or traits which could be equated with the British element in Anglo-Saxon society, such as the crouched burials found in East Yorkshire (Faull 1979:85, Higham 1992:184 – see Lucy forthcoming for a critical review of these interpretations). This view has been given a slightly different twist in, among others, the work of Higham (1992), who has proposed a model for the Roman-Saxon transition whereby an elite invasion and take-over from the continent brought the impetus for societal, linguistic and material culture change in the fifth and sixth centuries, with these elite influences then filtering down through the

rest of the (native) population. There is thus still current a widespread agreement that the material culture change of the fifth and sixth centuries was due ultimately to some form of population movement, whether that be mass migration (for those who favour low levels of native survival) or an elite invasion (for those who see such survival as considerable). Such interpretations are, however, open to debate, for they rest on a specific understanding of what material culture represents, on particular readings of the historical sources, and, it will be argued, on a misconception of what ethnicity is, and how ethnic groups would have been constituted in the past.

Challenging the equation

Although native survival has become an acceptable idea in many quarters, there still remains the implicit assumption – the same as can be seen in the work of Leeds and Kendrick – that a material object or trait can be directly indicative of the ethnic origins or identity of the person buried. However, this methodology, with its automatic equation of grave goods (or burial practices) and ethnicity, had first been challenged as early as the 1950s. Lethbridge, in 1956, stated: "Because a large number of ornaments are found in a series of graves and it can be shown that the origin of the style of ornaments lies in some continental district or other, is it any proof that the people in those graves were descended from those in the land in which that style of ornament was formerly common? Of course it is not" (1956:113). He maintained that "no one could prove that the wearers of these ornaments were Saxons, or Angles, or Romano-Britons or a mixture of them all. The wearers became Anglo-Saxons in name only ... Because we speak of a collection of objects as Anglo-Saxon, we must not assume that they indicate the presence of a pure-blooded Teutonic stock in the district in which they were found. They indicate no more than the presence in that district of people with a taste for barbaric ornaments of Teutonic type" (ibid:114). This radical perspective was, however, dismissed with disdain by his contemporaries: "Lethbridge writes in characteristic vein" (Hunter Blair 1956), and it is only in recent years that archaeologists have been looking at the equation made between material culture and ethnicity in a similarly critical light.

The impetus for this critique has arisen in several different quarters: the growing awareness among archaeologists of the political and historical contexts in which many of the assumptions and frameworks on which they rely arose; a similarly contextual approach to the interpretation of material culture; reconsideration by anthropologists and sociologists of the nature of ethnicity and the constitution of ethnic groups; and increasingly critical re-analysis of the historical sources on which many of these ideas about the nature of such groups were ultimately based.

A growing body of work on the history of later nineteenth century archaeology has demonstrated how links between material culture and "racial" origins arose. In the context of the time, "race" was thought to be fundamental. Although Darwinism had shown that humans could not have multiple origins, they were still conceptualised as being of different ancestral stocks, from which personal characteristics had been inherited (Jones 1997:43). There was thus an interest in tracing back the history and the culture of such "national" groups as far as possible (Olsen & Kobylínski 1991:9). Inevitably, this was to have a major impact on the way that archaeologists viewed their material.

In the 1860s and 1870s, the "direct ethno-historical method" being developed by Vocel and Montelius attempted to trace particular named groups of people back into prehistory on the basis of find associations and horizons (Malina & Vasícek 1990:63, Jones 1997:15). During the same period, classifications were being developed for material culture, language and physical anthropology. In 1895, Kossinna propounded the idea that archaeology was capable of isolating cultural areas ("Kulturprovinzen" or "Kulturkreise"), which could be identified with specific ethnic or national units and traced back into prehistory (Malina & Vasícek 1990:62). The combination of this method with the three kinds of classification led to the development of a paradigm which expressed a direct relationship between language, material culture and a people (Olsen & Kobylínski 1991:9). Kossinna (1911:3 cited in Veit 1994:37) thus came to believe that "[s]harply defined archaeological culture areas correspond unquestionably with the areas of particular peoples or tribes", and it was assumed that cultural continuity indicated ethnic continuity (Jones 1997:16).

Kossinna thus defined and systematically applied the concept of an archaeological culture in combination with the newly-developed direct ethno-historical method (Jones 1997:16). Despite the racist interpretations which both Kossinna and later archaeologists made on the basis of this method, it became almost a fundamental paradigm in archaeology, due to its seeming resonance with the contemporary political situation:

"Kossinna had a powerful set of ingredients with which to produce his picture of the European past and the method on which it was based: a belief, derived from the present, of nation-states as historical actors, whose predecessors were the 'peoples' whose character and movements were described by classical authors at the dawn of recorded history; and an explanation of variations in social and economic patterns in terms of the innate capacities of the 'peoples' producing them, ranked on a widely agreed scale of evolutionary superiority".
(Shennan 1994:8)

In prehistoric archaeology, as well as Anglo-Saxon archaeology, therefore, there arose an idea of human history as being peopled by groups with clearly identifiable "cultures" and static boundaries. Change within an area could only be accounted for by events such as contacts, migrations and conquests (Jones 1996:65, 1997:12). Even after the damnation of Kossinna following

World War II, culture areas were still seen as expressions of ethnic groups or peoples, and equated with the tribes first documented historically in a given area (Veit 1994:39-40). Thus Kossinna's model of migrations was partly provided by the movements of post-Roman "barbarians" as described by the early chroniclers (Anthony 1990b:896). However, historians' interpretations of these early sources have been shown to be strongly affected by their own notions (and the dominant frameworks) of how the past was constituted (Shennan 1991:29-30, Geary 1983, Pohl 1997). In turn, those Early Medieval sources, depicting migrations and other population movements, can be seen to be drawing heavily on a tradition of biblical allegory and symbolism (Harrison forthcoming). From the foundations of the idea of archaeological cultures right up to the present, the debate has rested on a circular argument: historians have accepted archaeologists' interpretations of "tribes" or "peoples" in the past, and archaeologists have based their interpretations partly on those of the historians. Both camps ultimately depend on the assumption that the past was populated by bounded entities (whether they are called tribes, peoples, or ethnic groups), and that those groups named in the historical sources (Saxons, Franks, Thuringians, Goths etc) could be equated with groups recorded by archaeology and linguistics, and perhaps physical anthropology (more recently molecular biology). These groups have thus been seen as the true subjects of history, rather than as only one of a number of types of grouping which may have given meaning to peoples' actions (Pohl 1997:12).

However, this notion of ethnic groups as bounded entities with language, culture and biology in common is increasingly being challenged by a number of researchers in different fields. In recent decades, the notion of both present-day and past ethnicity as an objective identity has been strongly disputed.

Arising out of contemporary observations by anthropologists and sociologists of how human groups define themselves and others, there now seems to be general agreement that ethnicity is not an objective, biological attribute, which can be independently observed by others. Rather, it is something which is lived and created, a "self-defining system" which is emphasised in certain situations, but not others (Barth 1969; Epstein 1978; Geary 1983; Jones 1997:60). The creation of feelings of both similarity (to members of one's own group) and difference (to members of others) is important in the construction of such groups (Bentley 1987:34; Jones 1997:93). Language, artefacts and everyday practices do not coincide in the expression of neatly bounded groups, although such things can be consciously seized on in the expression of ethnic allegiance (McGuire 1982:160-1; Jenkins 1997:76-7; Jones 1997:95, 125). Thus, ethnicity and ethnic groups do not exist separately from the people involved in them − it is only when a group of individuals see themselves as forming an ethnic group (usually in opposition to others), and act in accordance with that sense of belonging, that an ethnic group can be said to exist

(Jones 1997:84). In this light, ethnic groups are continually imagined (though not imaginary) groups (Jenkins 1997:77) and are "ideational beings" (Olsen & Kobylínski 1991:12), which can have no fixed boundaries, as they are not solid, bounded categorisations. In addition, ethnicity may only be one aspect of an individual's sense of identity – they may experience an "ethnic" sense of belonging on various different levels of inclusiveness and exclusiveness (Cohen 1978:387, Bentley 1987:36, Jenkins 1997:85), as well as being subject to social norms regarding their age, gender and status.

While, on an intuitive level, it seems obvious that what we understand to be the "ethnic identity" of a person can be recognised from their appearance, when such identifications are looked into more closely (especially from the contemporary perspectives offered by anthropology and sociology), ethnicity becomes more complex, and harder to concretely identify. What seems "common-sense" at first sight, in fact rests on a series of assumptions derived from modern western historico-political contexts, where all belong to a nation, with a national language, and distinct national differences in ways of dressing and acting (all things which themselves change with time and are often not clear-cut). However, it would be a mistake to back-project the illusion of the inevitability of such contemporary differences into the identification of difference in the past. As Amory (1993:3) has argued: "Ethnic consciousness, so universal and so important in the modern world, is often assumed to have been universal and primary in the past as well, although in the hothouse culture of Late Antiquity, status and religious sect may have been more important defining traits. It is particularly difficult to shed the ancient notion that a group called by a given name maintained itself as a static and self-perpetuating biological community, a race". This is especially true, given that many of the names used for groups were either applied retrospectively, or by contemporary outsiders.

Historians too have been looking at interpretations of Early Medieval ethnicity with a critical eye. With regard to the documentary sources, Geary (1983:18) has highlighted the assumptions often used by historians when dealing with Early Medieval texts (such as that ethnicity would have been recognisable to others, would not change except over several generations, and was a source of friction in society), and has demonstrated how such assumptions have coloured their readings of the sources. In addition, the contexts of ethnic naming have been re-examined, and the conclusion drawn that such groups as the Franks (James 1988), the Burgundians (Amory 1993) and the Anglo-Saxons (Wormald 1983, Reynolds 1985, Pohl 1997) are as much historical creations as anything; that documentary records have helped to create that which they purported to describe. The role of the church and its historians has been emphasised as being a major factor in this process (Pohl 1997:19). It has been pointed out that many individuals mentioned in Early Medieval sources were not given any ethnic attribution at all, and it has been suggested that perhaps an ethnic identity was only important for certain

(elite) sections of the population, and that such identities were brought into being in connection with certain members of the elite (Amory 1994; Pohl 1997:23). Peoples did not produce kings – kings produced peoples (James 1989:47). Thus, the historical basis which provided the foundation for interpretations of both prehistoric and Early Medieval ethnicity in the past has been shown to be far more illusory than was thought to be the case.

Similarly, a small number of archaeologists have questioned the very existence of ethnic groups as fixed, bounded entities in the past (Shennan 1994:11-12, Jones 1997:109). The idea that a "people" and a language necessarily coincide has been called into doubt (Olsen & Kobylínski 1991:15-16, Robb 1993, Moore 1994, Zvelebil 1995:41, Pluciennik 1996), as have correlations between material culture distributions and population groups (Håland 1977, Zvelebil 1995:40-42). In addition, the nature of those material culture distributions is being discussed more intensively. It has been recognised that the distributions of archaeological types comprising a "culture" do not exactly coincide with each other (Clarke 1968:363, Shennan 1978:113, see also Hodder 1978:12-13), and that archaeological distributions comprise an enormous variety of cross-cutting patterns, produced by different factors (Shennan 1994:13). As Jones (1997:104) has said, "[e]thnic groups are not neatly packaged territorially bounded culture-bearing units in the present, nor are they likely to have been in the past". If archaeological "cultures" do not exist, if ethnic groups are imagined, rather than real, where does this leave Anglo-Saxon archaeologists in their attempts to interpret their material?

The implications for Anglo-Saxon archaeology

Ethnicity is a self-conscious identity; it should be something that archaeologists rigorously look for, rather than the first thing they assume. Unfortunately, it is extremely difficult for archaeologists to move away from these assumptions, for they even underpin the most basic aspects of classification such as typologies and chronologies. In Anglo-Saxon archaeology these are based on inherent assumptions about what is "Germanic" material culture (despite many now accepting late Roman provincial antecedents for several pottery and metalwork forms and decorative styles). Indeed, chronologies for such material are often held to start in AD 450/1, the traditional starting date for the "Germanic" migrations.

Interpretations given by Anglo-Saxon archaeologists for material culture change still rest largely on an implicit equation of material culture with language and genetic grouping. Explanations for material culture change are therefore usually predicated on a version of the migration/invasion hypothesis for this period. However, even if such population movements can be demonstrated (and they do need to be demonstrated, rather than assumed, given the doubts now expressed about the veracity of the historical sources), they are not necessarily the explanation for social and material change.

In fact, recent work on migration in the social sciences has stressed that it is a self-conscious, intentional social strategy, through which individuals and groups can compete for social and economic power (Anthony 1997:29). People must see a clear advantage in migrating, but they rarely migrate to unknown destinations: migration "proceeds in streams towards known targets, not in broad waves that wash heedlessly over entire landscapes" (Anthony 1997:24). Information about destinations is often provided by returning migrants (migration is rarely one-way), who may use their role as "founder" families as the dynamic for the development of status differences (Anthony 1990:900-901, 904). Above all: "Cultures don't migrate; people do. Even large-scale movements usually consist of numerous clustered episodes of chain migration" (Anthony 1997:27). Similarly, language change has been viewed as an intentional social strategy, which must be seen as having a clear advantage to the speaker (Robb 1993:748, Anthony 1997:29). Language change is therefore not an inevitable result of migration, and thus migration cannot be inferred from language change.

In recent years archaeologists have been focusing on the active role of material culture, pointing out that the objects and artefacts that people use in their day to day lives do not directly reflect social conditions, but in fact participate in reproducing, restructuring and transforming those conditions (Barrett 1990:179). Material culture is an integral part of social life, which can express, create and transform rules of meaning (Barrett 1991:3; Sørensen 1991:121). In addition, meanings of objects are given primarily by their contexts (Hodder 1987; Sørensen 1987, 1991:121), and therefore that meaning will change with its context (Barrett 1991:3). Social systems are seen as constructed out of social practices, and those social practices take place within the specific cultural and historical systems which they maintain (Barrett 1988:30, 1989:305). The things that people use are therefore the result of many separate choices, rather than inevitable aspects of their society. Migration is not the only explanation for changes in particular artefact types. In order to establish a true comparative basis for studying material culture in the fifth and sixth centuries, what we really need are detailed understandings of both everyday practices, and also overtly symbolic practices such as burial rituals, in the late Roman period around the North Sea, rather than relying on ideas about what is "Germanic" about an object, and using this to date it. Instead, distributions of, and variations within, all the different factors which go to make up material culture and how it is used in practice must be examined in detail on a local level.

We also need a new conceptual framework for analysing Anglo-Saxon cemeteries. Rather than just seeing them as containing evidence for continental ancestry, they can be used to gain a fine-grained understanding of how identities are created and maintained through the burial ritual – not an everyday practice, but a deliberately articulated one (Barrett et al 1991:7). The mourners are the active participants in burial rituals (Barrett 1990:182), and the treatment of the dead is a powerful symbolic resource (Barrett 1988:30, Thomas 1991). Burial rites are not static – there is nothing "natural" about them. Rather, they are the result of many different culturally-situated decisions. A person's identity cannot be "read off" from the way in which they were buried, but their burial can shed light on the aspects of the deceased which the mourners thought important to emphasise through the use of material culture and other aspects of the ritual (Lucy 1998:107). The advantage of the long time-scale available to archaeology is that in this way a picture can be built up of developments within an area over time, which have contributed to the reproduction of the social system or changes within it (Barrett 1988:30).

Through such a contextual analysis of burials, the archaeologist can start to observe the construction of gender and age-based identities using material culture, and how such identities changed over time (Pader 1982, Lucy 1998). For example, different assemblages of grave goods, with associated textiles, can give an in-depth picture of how people of different ages and sexes (ascertained by examination of skeletal material) were dressed for burial. In terms of the preparation and provisioning of burial costumes, this can indicate how different groups were viewed differently by the mourners. Such provisioning will not directly reflect the role of the deceased in life, but we can start to see the complex patterning of ideas about death and the dead held by the mourners. We can then start to ask what the relationship might have been between those ideas held about the dead, and those held about the living, and we can perhaps ask if material culture is helping to reinforce, and on one level even create, such ideas.

On a wider level, after accounting for the variation within communities represented by varying gender, sex, age, and perhaps status; we can look for other patterning, perhaps on a local or regional level, which might suggest deliberate reinforcement of local or regional identities by the mourners. However, we cannot assume these at the outset – they must be demonstrated, and they may well intersect with these other aspects of identity. If such patterns can be seen, they must be recognised as deliberate and symbolic, and the possibility entertained that the arena of burial was the only context in which such identities were articulated.

Conclusions

It can be argued that the historical sources, on which much of our archaeological interpretation ultimately rests, have themselves been misinterpreted due to long-standing preconceptions about the nature of the groups which appear to be given ethnic names within them. Recently, historians have shown that these Early Medieval sources refer mainly to the elite, and have demonstrated how Early Medieval sources gave a person an ethnic attribution primarily when they were involved in contexts of allegiance or conflict. They have also argued for the importance of opposition in definition, and highlighted the role of pivotal figures in creating ethnic groups around themselves, possibly making use of myths of origin for providing the legitimation for this.

Anglo-Saxon archaeologists have largely accepted the basic tenets of the traditional historical framework (even while debating its finer points) and have thus helped reconstruct an ethnic history of the fifth and sixth centuries, which makes for a satisfying origin myth, but fares poorly as an explanation for cultural change. Work in the social sciences has shown how the different aspects assumed to coincide in a "culture" in fact form a whole series of overlapping phenomena. Changes in material culture cannot necessarily be equated with changes in language or in population. In order to be able to interpret archaeological evidence, a detailed understanding of developments in local areas must first be developed, before trying to explain changes over wider areas. If large-scale patterns can be seen (such as the distribution of a particular brooch type across Eastern England), they must be recognised as being the result of many more complex patterns and practices, which seem simple when viewed from a great enough distance.

Burial evidence must be accepted for what it is, which is a palimpsest of individual decisions made by different generations of mourners. While careful contextual analysis can shed light on processes of identity construction and maintenance, they may be able to tell us little of ethnic histories. If this disturbs us, we should perhaps be asking why.

Acknowledgements

I am extremely grateful to Simon James and Geoff Harrison for their helpful criticisms and comments on a draft of this paper.

References

Akerman, J.Y. 1855. *Remains of pagan Saxondom.* London.

Amory, P. 1993. The meaning and purpose of ethnic terminology in the Burgundian laws. *Early Medieval Europe* 2(1), pp 1-28. Harlow.

Amory, P. 1994. Names, ethnic identity and community in fifth and sixth-century Burgundy. *Viator* 25, pp 1-30. Los Angeles.

Anthony, D. 1990. Migration in archaeology: the baby and the bathwater. *American Anthropologist* 92(4), pp 895-914. American Anthropological Association. Washington D.C.

Anthony, D. 1997. Prehistoric migration as social process. In Chapman, J. & Hamerow, H. (eds.). *Migrations and invasions in archaeological explanation.* British Archaeological Reports, International Series 664, pp 21-32. Oxford.

Barrett, J.C., Bradley, R. & Green, M. 1991. *Landscape, monuments and society: the prehistory of Cranbourne Chase.* Cambridge University Press.

Barrett, J. 1988. The living, the dead, and the ancestors: Neolithic and early Bronze Age mortuary practices. In Barrett, J. & Kinnes, I. (eds.). *The archaeology of context in the Neolithic and Bronze Ages,* pp 30-41. Department of Archaeology and Prehistory, University of Sheffield.

Barrett, J. 1989. Food, gender and metal: questions of social reproduction. In Sørensen, M.L.S. & Thomas, R. (eds.). *The Bronze-Age – Iron-Age transition in Europe.* British Archaeological Reports, International Series 483, pp 304-320. Oxford.

Barrett, J. 1990. The monumentality of death: the character of early Bronze Age mortuary mounds in Southern Britain. *World Archaeology* 22(2), pp 179-189. London.

Barrett, J. 1991. Towards an archaeology of ritual. In Garwood, P.; Jennings, D.; Skeates, R. & Toms, J. (eds.). *Sacred and profane: proceedings of a conference on archaeology, ritual and religion, Oxford 1989.* Oxford University Committee for Archaeology, Monograph 32, pp 1-9.

Barth, F. (ed.). 1969. *Ethnic groups and boundaries.* London.

Bateman, T. 1861. *Ten years' digging in Celtic and Saxon grave hills in the Counties of Derby, Stafford and York, from 1848 to 1858.* London.

Bell, M. 1989. Environmental archaeology as an index of continuity and change in the Medieval landscape. In Aston, M; Austin, D. & Dyer, C. (eds.). *The rural settlements of Medieval England,* pp 269-286. Oxford.

Bentley, G. 1987. Ethnicity and practice. *Comparative studies in society and history* 29, pp 24-55. Cambridge.

Clarke, D.L. 1968. *Analytical archaeology.* London.

Cohen, R. 1978. Ethnicity: problem and focus in anthropology. *Annual review of anthropology* 7, pp 379-403. Palo Alto, California.

Crabtree, P. 1989. *West Stow, Suffolk: early Anglo-Saxon animal husbandry.* East Anglian archaeology report 47. Norwich.

Crawford, O.G.S. 1953. *Archaeology in the field.* London.

Curtis, L.P. 1968. *Anglo-Saxons and Celts.* New York University Press.

Epstein, A.L. 1978. *Ethos and identity. Three studies in ethnicity.* London.

Faull, M. 1979. *British survival in Anglo-Saxon Yorkshire.* Unpublished PhD dissertation. University of Leeds.

Freeman, E.A. 1869. *Old English history for children.* London.

Freeman, E.A. 1872. *The growth of the English constitution.* London.

Freeman, E.A. 1881. *The historical geography of Europe.* London.

Freeman, E.A. 1888. *Fifty years of European history: Teutonic conquest in Gaul and Britain.* London.

Geary, P. 1983. Ethnic identity as a situational construct in the Early Middle Ages. *Mitteilungen der Anthropologischen Gesellschaft in Wien* 113, pp 15-26. Vienna.

Green, J.R. 1874. *A short history of the English people.* London.

Green, J.R. 1881. *The making of England.* London.

Green, J.R. 1883. *The conquest of England.* London.

Håland, R. 1977. Archaeological classification and ethnic groups: a case study from Sudanese Nubia. *Norwegian Archaeological Review* 10(1-2), pp 1-17. Oslo.

Harrison, G. Forthcoming. Quoit brooches and the Roman-Medieval transition. In Forcey, C.; Witcher, R.; Baker, P. & Jundi, S. (eds.). *TRAC 98 – Proceedings of the eighth annual theoretical Roman archaeology conference.*

Higham, N. 1992. *Rome, Britain and the Anglo-Saxons.* London.

Hodder, I. 1978. Simple correlations between material culture and society: a review. In Hodder, I. (ed.). *The spatial organisation of culture*, pp 3-24. London.

Hunter Blair, P. 1956. Review of D.B. Harden (ed.). Dark Age Britain. *The Cambridge Review,* June 2. Cambridge.

James, E. 1988. *The Franks.* Oxford.

James, E. 1989. The origins of barbarian kingdoms: the continental evidence. In Bassett, S. (ed.) *The origins of Anglo-Saxon kingdoms*, pp 40-52. Leicester University Press.

Jenkins, R. 1997. *Rethinking ethnicity: arguments and explorations.* London.

Jones, S. 1996. Discourses of identity in the interpretation of the past. In Graves-Brown, P. et al (eds.). *Cultural identity and archaeology: the construction of European communities*, pp 62-80. London.

Jones, S. 1997. *The archaeology of ethnicity.* London.

Kemble, J.M. 1856. On mortuary urns found at Stade-on-the-Elbe, and other parts of North Germany, now in the Museum of the Historical Society of Hanover *Archaeologia* XXVI, pp 270-283. Oxford.

Kemble, J.M. 1863. *Horae ferales; or Studies in archaeology of the Northern Nations* London.

Kendrick, T.D. 1938. *Anglo-Saxon art to AD 900.* London.

Kossinna, G. 1911. *Die Herkunft der Germanen: zur Methode der Siedlungsarchäologie* Würzburg.

Leeds, E.T. 1936. *Early Anglo-Saxon art and archaeology.* Oxford.

Lethbridge, T. 1956. The Anglo-Saxon settlement in eastern England: a reassessment. In Harden, D.B. (ed.). *Dark Age Britain – studies presented to E.T. Leeds*, pp 112-122. London.

Lucy, S. 1998. *The Early Anglo-Saxon cemeteries of East Yorkshire: an analysis and re-interpretation.* British Archaeological Reports, British Series 272. Oxford.

Lucy, S. Forthcoming. Early Medieval burials in East Yorkshire: reconsidering the evidence. In Geake, H. & Kenny, J. (eds.). *Anglo-Saxon Yorkshire 1994: conference proceedings.*

Malina, J. & Vasícek, Z. 1990. *Archaeology yesterday and today.* Cambridge University Press.

McGuire, R.H. 1982. The study of ethnicity in historical archaeology. *Journal of Anthropological Archaeology* 1, pp 159-178. Academic Press.

Moore, J.H. 1994. Putting anthropology back together again: the ethnogenetic critique of cladistic theory. *American Anthropologist* 96(4), pp 925-948. American Anthropological Association. Washington D.C.

Olsen, B. & Kobylínski, Z. 1991. Ethnicity in anthropological and archaeological research: a Norwegian-Polish perspective. *Archaeologia Polona* 29, pp 5-27. Wroclaw.

Pader, E.-J. 1982. *Symbolism, social relations and the interpretation of mortuary remains.* British Archaeological Reports, British Series 130. Oxford.

Pluciennik, M. 1996. A perilous but necessary search: archaeology and European identities. In Atkinson, J.A.; Banks, I. & O'Sullivan, J. (eds.). *Nationalism and archaeology*, pp 35-58. Glasgow.

Pohl, W. 1997. Ethnic names and identities in the British Isles: a comparative perspective. In Hines, J. (ed.). *The Anglo-Saxons from the Migration Period to the Eighth Century. An ethnographic perspective*, pp 7-40. Woodbridge.

Reynolds, S. 1985. What do we mean by Anglo-Saxon and Anglo-Saxons? *Journal of British Studies* 24(4), pp 395-414. Chicago.

Robb, J. 1993. A social prehistory of European languages. *Antiquity* 67, pp 747-760. Cambridge.

Rolleston, G. 1870. On the character and influence of the Anglo-Saxon conquest of England, as illustrated by archaeological research. *Proceedings of the Royal Institute* 6, pp 116-119. London.

Shennan, S. 1978. Archaeological "cultures": an empirical investigation. In Hodder, I. (ed.). *The spatial organisation of culture*, pp 113-139. London.

Shennan, S. 1991. Some current issues in the archaeological identification of past peoples. *Archaeologia Polona* 29, pp 29-37. Wroclaw.

Shennan, S. 1994. Introduction: archaeological approaches to cultural identity. In Shennan, S. (ed.). *Archaeological approaches to cultural identity*, pp 1-32. London.

Sims-Williams, P. 1983. The settlement of England in Bede and the Chronicle. *Anglo-Saxon England* 12, pp 1-41. Cambridge.

Sørensen, M.L.S. 1987. Material order and cultural classification: the role of bronze objects in the transition from Bronze Age to Iron Age in Scandinavia. In Hodder, I. (ed.). *The archaeology of contextual meanings*, pp 90-101. Cambridge University Press.

Sørensen, M.L.S. 1991. The construction of gender through appearance. In Walde, D. & Willows, N. (eds.). *The archaeology of gender. Proceedings of the 22nd Chacmool conference*, pp 121-129. University of Calgary Archaeological Association.

St Joseph, J.K. (ed.). 1966. *The uses of air photography: nature and man in a new perspective.* University of Cambridge Committee for Air Photography. London.

Stubbs, W. 1870. *Select charters and other illustrations of English constitutional history from the earliest times to the reign of Edward the First.* 9th ed. 1913 revised by H.W.C. Davies. London.

Stubbs, W. 1880. *The constitutional history of England* vol I. 1st ed. 1874-8. Oxford.

Stubbs, W. 1906. *Lectures on Early English history* (ed. A. Hassall). London.

Taylor, C.C. 1983. *Village and farmstead.* London.

Thomas, J. 1991. *Rethinking the Neolithic.* Cambridge University Press.

Turner, S. 1799-1805. *A history of the Anglo-Saxons.* London.

Veit, U. 1994. Ethnic concepts in German prehistory: a case study on the relationship between cultural identity and objectivity. In Shennan, S. (ed.). *Archaeological approaches to cultural identity*, pp 35-56. London.

Wormald, P. 1983. Bede, the *Bretwaldas* and the origins of the *Gens Anglorum*. In Wormald, P. (ed.). *Ideal and reality in Frankish and Anglo-Saxon society*, pp 99-129. Oxford.

Wright, T. 1855. On Anglo-Saxon antiquities, with a particular reference to the Faussett collection. *Transactions of the Historic Society of Lancashire and Cheshire* 7, pp 1-39. Liverpool.

Zachrisson, R.E. 1927. Romans, Kelts and Saxons in Ancient Britain. *Skrifter utgivna av K. Humanistiska Vetenskaps-Samfundet i Uppsala* 24(12), pp 1-94. Uppsala.

Zvelebil, M. 1995. Farmers our ancestors and the identity of Europe. In Graves-Brown, P.; Jones, S. & Gamble, C. (eds.). *Cultural identity and archaeology: the construction of European communities*, pp 145-166. London.

Zvelebil, M. 1995. At the interface of archaeology, linguistics and genetics: Indo-European dispersals and the agricultural transition in Europe. *Journal of European Archaeology* 3:1, pp 33-70. Aldershot.

Theoretical and methodological approaches to Migration Period burials

Mads Ravn, Department of Archaeology, University of Århus

> *Wealhtheow moved, mindful of courtesies,*
> *the queen of Hrothgar, glittering to greet the*
> *Geats in the hall, peerless lady; but to the*
> *land's guardian she offered first the flowing*
> *cup, bade him be blithe at the beer drinking,*
> *gracious to his people; gladly the conqueror*
> *partook of the banquet, tasted the hall-cup.*

(Beowulf vv 613-620, translation Alexander 1973).

The following is a discussion of the use of burial analyses in post-Roman archaeology in Europe. Here I will, firstly, present an outline of the history of burial analysis in the Anglo-American world, the Continent (mainly German scholarship) and in Scandinavia, with an emphasis on south Scandinavian (Danish) burial archaeology. Secondly, I will present my theoretical and methodological approach to burials in general. Thirdly, I will discuss a specific case-study. Very brief as it is, it is meant to serve as an illustration of the potential of the use of multivariate analysis. Lastly, I will outline a preliminary interpretation of the meaning of the analysed Anglo-Saxon burials. My argument here will be that we can identify symbols in material culture if we explore appropriate theories and methods which keep the context in focus.

A history of the archaeology of death

Binford was the first to explicitly express the theoretical potential of burials as a means to understanding social aspects of the past. In a classic paper, he reached the conclusion that variability of a burial is a *reflection* of social differentiation (Binford 1972). Goldstein (1981) developed this approach, claiming that the emergence of bounded cemeteries reserved for the dead indicates the presence of unilineal descent groups monopolising access to some vital resource, often land. Others followed suit, and it resulted in the 1981 volume *The Archaeology of Death*, edited by Chapman and Randsborg. This volume set the agenda for burial archaeology for the next decade within the Anglo-American archaeological tradition. In general, graves were seen as a *reflection* of past society. Hodder (1980, 1982a) and others (cf. Parker Pearson 1982: 101) challenged this approach by proposing from the viewpoint of ethnoarchaeological studies that burials at the most could be seen as an *indirect reflection* of society, because burials constitute remains of *rites de passage* and are thus distorted by ideology.

After the fiercest post-modern and mainly Marxist criticism of processualism (e.g. Shanks & Tilley 1987) had made its point, the approach towards burials, in my view, developed in two constructive directions (Härke 1997:21). The first was the *symbolic and contextual approach*, which assumed that human action is expressed in symbols, and that the patterning of symbols was expressed in the archaeological record (Hodder 1986). Material culture was seen as an analogy to language or text (Patrik 1985), in that both consisted of signs (signifiers) the meaning of which (the signified) only became clear in context. Thus, graves were seen as a symbolic language that needed decoding. A related approach draws on sociology, as advocated by Giddens' *structuration theory* (1984). I shall return to these approaches below. Here, I shall emphasise a few examples, which, to me, appear to be the most constructive in the field of burial analysis.

Pader (1982), who pursued a symbolic approach, made a substantial methodological point, although the results of her analyses of graves did not reveal a clear pattern. The rather primitive computer facilities available for her multivariate analyses, as well as her small sample, may explain the lack of results. Richards' (1987) interesting analysis of artefact form and decoration in relation to sexed skeletons in Anglo-Saxon society did reach some interesting conclusions, but here also limitations were imposed by the statistical computer packages then available. Morris' analyses of Greek grave material (1987) was more successful. He implemented a multivariate cluster analysis. Among other things, he identified a major change around 750 BC in the structure of Greek funerary practices. He related this to the rise of the "polis ideology". From the examples above, it seemed that the way forward for cemetery analysis was the implementation of multidimensional analyses; firstly, because it included the multidimensional nature of cemetery material, and, secondly, because computer facilities alone defined the limitations of a symbolic approach.

Within the continental European tradition of archaeology, German researchers developed similar quantitative attitudes to the analysis of burials, independently of the discussion within the New Archaeology mentioned above (Härke 1992:30). Here, graves were assumed directly to *reflect* the status of the deceased. Also, it was assumed that graves reflected legal status. Thus, Veeck (1926) identified three male status groups of the row-grave (*Reihengräber*) cemeteries; those with swords were identified as free men, those with other weapons were semi-free, and the unfree were indicated by graves without weapons. This "legal" interpretation was later criticised within German scholarship, because it was a circular argument, projecting later Medieval sources onto the prehistoric archaeological record. There were two reactions to this criticism, one being rock-bottom positivism, which focused on the function and chronology of the artefacts. A more positive reaction was an attempt to refine the abovementioned method, which was pursued by Christlein (1975) and Steuer (1982). I shall discuss the latter reaction shortly. For a discussion of the East German tradition see Härke 1991, Beran 1996, Jacobs 1996.

Christlein's seminal work of 1975 was the most influential on burial analysis. He developed a hierarchy of status categories (*Qualitätsgruppen*) from A to D (Christlein 1975:157), where D was the highest status, belonging to the richest in an economic sense. Thus, he argued that graves could not reflect legal status, but instead reflected economic status. Many followed the ideas of Christlein, and his categories are still widely recognised within the German archaeological tradition. One criticism of Christlein's approach is his use of symbols, which on a one-to-one basis emphasised artefacts such as gold, silver and swords *per se*. Hence, less visible symbols and their *combinations* were ignored. His interpretations were still based on the assumption that graves were a *"mirror of life"*.

Steuer's (1982) rare synthesising approach recognised that there were other issues to consider concerning graves, but he did not pursue the consequences of this in full. He identified particular trends in cemeteries and settlements of the Migration Period in central and northern Europe, interpreting them as revealing a pattern, which he developed into a model for the social aspects of society. This model claims that cemeteries in a Migration Period context started out as family cemeteries, the oldest burial being the richest. Often, the graves have a group affiliation that may be interpreted as consisting of both rich and poor; the warlord, his family and his warriors within the farm unit. As there are varying groups, which in relative terms are differentiated, he concluded that between them the farm units had varying importance. Also, he argued from the changing burial rites of cemeteries, as well as settlement patterns, that Germanic society was a society of substantial geographical as well as social mobility, at least until the codification of Carolingian laws. The 3rd to the 7th centuries in particular experienced a development towards centralisation. He insisted that the presence or absence of weapons in graves was not direct evidence of the presence or absence of a warrior, as grave goods might also have reflected other aspects. Instead, we must look for the presence of artefacts holding a symbolic value which may be associated with a special person. Following Christlein, Steuer did not discuss in detail how to assess such a value.

In conclusion, most of German scholarship saw graves as *"mirrors of life"* in past society. One exception is Gebühr (1970, Gebühr & Kunow 1976, Härke 1997), who used multivariate analysis and correlated grave-goods with skeletal age and sex determinations in a study of Roman Iron Age cremation cemeteries. With this notable exception, most German archaeology ignored ritual, symbolic and ideological aspects of past society. In many ways this attitude, that graves are a reflection of society, is similar to the practice of New Archaeology in the Anglo-American world. This approach makes it straightforward to approach past society, because it means that the more objects are found in a grave, the richer was the deceased. In practice (e.g. Chapman et al 1981), processual archaeology and the general German approach were much alike.

A synthetic approach to burials

Härke's analysis of Anglo-Saxon weapon graves (1992), recognising the development both in German as well as in Anglo-Saxon scholarship, was innovative, because he combined the traditional data-oriented continental approach with a newer theoretically-conscious attitude in a positive way. In the history of burial analyses, he distinguished (1992:23) between

- A qualitative approach where, say, weapons are associated with categories of status, exemplified by Christlein,
- A quantitative approach where status is determined by means of quantitative analysis in similar fashion to processual archaeology,
- A multidimensional approach where variables are combined to form a less biased picture, exemplified by Morris and Pader.

Härke chose the multidimensional approach. He distinguished between

- Archaeological data, such as artefacts,
- Technical data such as grave size etc, both being intentional data, and
- Anthropological data, this being non-intentional data.

Härke established a convincing argument suggesting that weapons functioned as symbols of power and ethnic affiliation in the 5th to 7th centuries AD in Anglo-Saxon England.

A Scandinavian approach?

There is no unified Scandinavian archaeology. Swedish and Norwegian archaeology has often been more theoretically-oriented than Danish archaeology (Myhre 1991). The latter, which I shall focus upon here, was influenced mainly by German scholarship until the 1960s (Ravn 1997a), and Anglo-American scholarship thereafter (Ravn 1993). The attitude towards burials has shown a similar mixture. In the 1930s and 1940s the approach was to assess cultural provinces in an international perspective (Mackeprang 1943, Klindt-Jensen 1950), much like the German tradition, though without Nazi manipulation of the discipline. In the 1950s, most of the emphasis was on cataloguing and writing reports on the enormous number of finds which followed the post-war industrial revolution, a trend which continued into the 1960s and 1970s (e.g. Albrectsen 1954, Ramskou 1976). This trend has been termed "puritan Danish positivism" (Jensen & Nielsen 1997:10), because it focused exclusively on the material culture. It never approached the "Indian behind the artefact".

Apart from a few interesting initiatives which attempted social analysis of grave finds, such as Klindt-Jensen's analysis (1965) of the Lousgård cemetery on Bornholm and Kjærum's analysis of the megalith of Jordhøj (1970), it was via Sweden, and especially through the works of Malmer (1962, 1963), with their emphasis on methodology, objectivity and statistics, that a kind of New Archaeology was channelled into Danish archaeology. This inspired a number of scholars to pursue studies with a well-defined and articulate goal-definition, mainly with a chronological emphasis (e.g. Jensen 1978). An emphasis on statistics following the quantitative approach of the processual archaeology can be exemplified by Randsborg 1973. Randsborg's collaboration with Chapman and Kinnes (Chapman et al 1981) pulled Danish archaeology in a new and interesting direction in the 1980s.

Following this trend, Randsborg's student, Jørgensen (1988, 1990, 1992), applied more elaborate analyses to Migration Period graves on the Baltic island of Bornholm. Jørgensen developed a point score system which he suggested *reflected* status categories of the past community, as also assumed in the German tradition and processual archaeology. The score system was based upon the relative frequencies of artefact types in a grave sample. The results were seen as indicating status, rare types signalling exclusiveness and thus high status. This approach had its weaknesses, however, because quantitative methods in general are sensitive to variable preservation conditions. If a single artefact is missing, the picture may be biased. Explicit combination analyses were not undertaken in order to account for unique and symbolic aspects of graves, a fact that was mentioned by Sørensen (1979, 1987). Her studies were some of the first to include a symbolic approach in burial analysis in Scandinavia.

Hedeager (1978, 1990) initially drew on the methodology of the New Archaeology while she developed her interpretations in a Neo-Marxist direction. Her empirical approach was, however, initially the same as that of Jørgensen. She counted the number of artefact types (NAT) in the graves as an indicator of wealth. Thus, rich graves were those with the largest number and greatest variation of artefacts. As with Jørgensen's, Hedeager's method is easily biased by preservational factors. She did attempt combination analysis mainly of weapon graves, thus, establishing a relationship between her weapon group I and luxury goods (Hedeager 1990:118). In my view, a more convincing study, however, was Ringtved's analysis of Jutish graves in the Late Roman Iron Age and the Migration Period. Ringtved, employing a large body of data, examined both chronology and multidimensional combinations of material culture in graves and houses (1988). She established a regional partition of Jutland into a northern and a southern group on the basis of different artefact combinations, which she suggested had symbolic content in terms of regional identity.

Recently, the discussion of burial issues has been revived, resulting in a few major volumes on theory, method and practice (Iregren et al 1988, Stjernquist 1994, Hansen 1995, Jensen & Nielsen 1997). Here, some scholars call for the use of multivariate analyses, as well as a theoretically-conscious approach, seeing burials as ritual and ideological remains. I shall return to the discussion of this issue below.

Conclusions on the history of scholarship

In summary, the history of research in Britain, USA, Germany and Scandinavia may be summarised as presenting a problem when working with burial analyses; because what we see in the graves may not be a *direct reflection* of past society, as was originally suggested by Binford. I acknowledge this criticism and will in this paper try to present a better theory and method with which we may understand burials. My argument will be that in order better to understand burials, it is necessary to account for *the multidimensional nature of burials*, as well as *symbolic and ritual aspects*. Thus, it is necessary to discuss the theory and method behind burial studies, as well as the understanding of social structure and ritual in more detail. I suggest that a multivariate approach is the way forward for a better social understanding of burial material.

A synthetic approach

Thus I suggest that we follow Härke's (1992) distinction between archaeological data, technical data and anthropological data. Following Ian Morris I also suggest that, when studying burials, one must assume what may seem trivial, namely that a burial is an *intentional action* and thus meaningful. It seems equally trivial but important and reasonable to assume that *a burial results from a funeral,* and *a funeral is part of a set of rituals.* This hypothesis is based on elaborate research within sociology and anthropology, as well as archaeology, and seems to have stood the test of time over the last century (Hertz 1960, Huntington et al 1979, Bloch et al 1982, Morris 1992).

Assuming that a funeral is part of a set of rituals, questions about social, economic and religious issues in grave material must be approached from the perspective of *symbolic action* (Morris 1992:1, Näsman 1994:29). Another assumption, which is substantiated by social anthropology, is that *people use rituals as symbols to make social structure explicit* (Huntington et al 1979). Thus we need to discuss what we mean by the term social structure.

Social structure and social organisation

In contrast to social structure, social organisation is here seen as the *"empirical distribution of relationships in everyday experience"* whereas social structure, on the other hand, is defined as *"an ideal model, a mental template, of the relative placing of individuals in the world"* (Morris 1987:39). Social structure is created in dialogue between the individual and society by means of symbols and rituals to which funerals also belong (Leach 1954:15ff). Following Hodder:

> "If the symbolic structures are produced in the social realm then there is likely to be a close tie to social structures. By the latter I mean organised relations of kin, gender, age set, class etc, which are themselves often integrally related to divisions and

relations of production, reproduction and exchange." (Hodder 1990:13).

In other words, in order to understand social structure, we must work between the levels of social organisation and social structure, approaching it through the material symbols which are patterns of social practice. In the present case, this implies that besides looking at burials which are biased by ideology, one needs to include other, differently-biased find categories (e.g. skeletal evidence), as well as (where present) literary sources, in order better to test the hypotheses developed from burials. This is best done by implementing multivariate analysis to which I will return below. But first, we need to discuss briefly the nature of rituals and symbols.

Rituals and symbols

Ritual action seems to produce its own kind of symbolic knowledge. Social structure, since it is a set of internalised but constantly re-negotiated roles and rules, is closely interrelated with this symbolic knowledge (Morris 1992:9). But how should we understand symbols which seem to be used so elaborately in rituals? Here I follow Hodder's definition of symbols as being:

> "the secondary connotations evoked by the primary associations and uses of an object or word. These 'secondary meanings' refer to abstract and general concepts which tend to be organised into oppositional structures" (Hodder 1990:13).

Whether one agrees or disagrees it seems that the way to decipher patterns in the archaeological record is to look at temporal and spatial aspects in context with the depositional and typological unit. Hodder (1986) has proposed that it is the interrelationships of similarities and differences between these four entities, seen in an ideational context, that provides a better understanding of the meaning of the archaeological record. In this paper I endorse a "contextual archaeology", where "context" is defined as "the totality of the relevant environment" and where "relevant" refers to a significant relationship to the object (Hodder 1986:143). I suggest that significance be assessed by *multivariate statistical analyses*, to which I shall return below.

There seems to be four levels of *"relevant environment"* when we discuss symbolism in relation to graves. The first and largest is the location and landscape context (Lucy 1995, Huggett 1996). The second is grave form and monument. The third is grave goods and skeletons; and, lastly, the fourth is their relation to the decoration of the grave goods. My approach here will be to analyse the interrelationship between grave form, monument, grave goods, decoration and skeletal evidence. The landscape context is not included in this paper, because the example used makes it difficult to generalise about landscape context. My assumption is, following Richards (1987:27), that if an attribute is *unintentional*, then it will be *randomly distributed* throughout the artefacts and will not correlate with other attributes.

It may be concluded from the above discussion that I see burials as a meaningful category which is multivariate in nature. A way to identify symbolic action in burials is thus to establish *significant* patterns and groups in the burials by opening up a "dialogue with the dead" along the typological, temporal, as well as depositional and spatial, line. It is now possible to proceed to a discussion of the method with which I am going to attempt the identification of significant patterns in burials.

Methodological approach

In this example I shall only use multivariate analysis, although in my Ph.D. thesis I compared my results with traditional statistical analyses. A combination of the two enhances the study of qualitative symbolic aspects of past society. The multivariate method of analysis is one called by statisticians *exploratory multivariate data analysis* (EMA) of the specific type called Correspondence Analysis (CA).

Exploratory Data Analysis (EDA), according to the statistician Baxter, refers to "techniques that usually do not postulate an underlying model for the data and often have the ... aim of reducing data to a form which may be used to inspect the data for archaeologically useful structure ... in a compact form such as a two-dimensional plot" (Baxter 1994:1). Thus, I see the EMA as an inductive method.

The CA is part of a number of Exploratory Multivariate Analyses. It holds the potential of "revealing 'invisible' and qualitative patterns by relating more than two variables and units in a large body of material" (Madsen 1988:12). It works as illustrated in a simplistic way in the following example:

> "If you measure the IQ of all children in a school, and at the same time note their shoe numbers, then you are going to find a high degree of correlation between IQ and shoe numbers. The correlation is real enough, but it has no explanatory value. It is a third value, age, which correlates with both IQ and shoe number, and binds them together in logical dependence".
> (Madsen 1990:331).

Thus, the CA bears the potential of revealing more variables which in traditional statistical analyses are not identified as easily. In opposition to cluster analyses, the CA does not force the material into certain expected structures, because it also accounts for small amounts of material. The basic element of the CA is that it reveals the structural relationship between units/variables on the basis of their average similarity (Jensen and Nielsen 1997).

In short, the CA is an *experimental multivariate data analysis,* a way of handling a large body of material by *tuning in* on the structures hidden in the material. Thus, the limitations of the method are our interpretation of the CA, because we choose the variables for analysis. But if our choices "work", then our working hypothesis is substantiated.

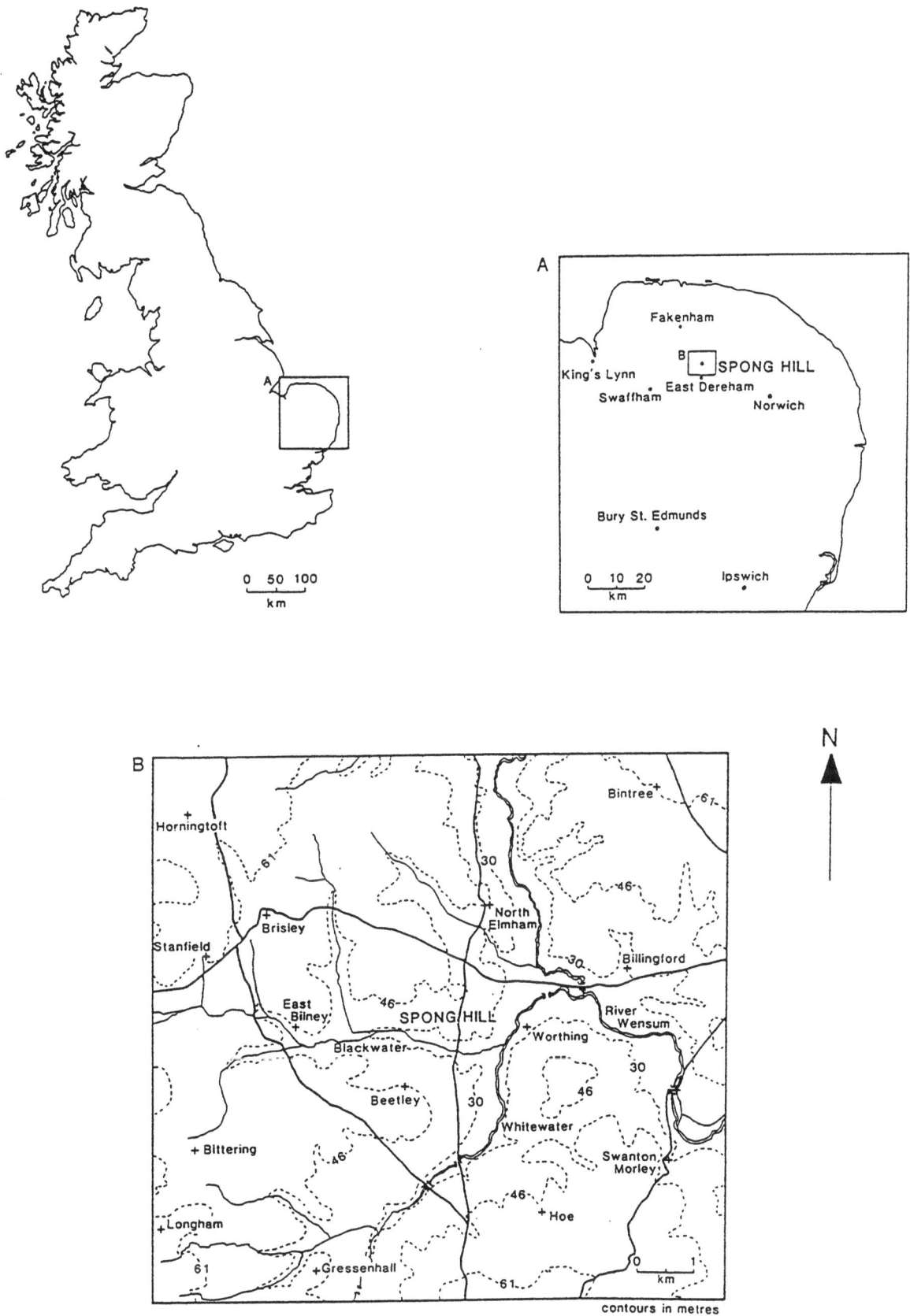

Fig. 27. *The location of Spong Hill. A) In relationship to major towns in the region. B) Contour map with rivers, roads and nearby settlements. (From Hills et al 1984.)*

Applying the method to data – an analysis of Spong Hill

In order to illustrate the potential of a multivariate method in the identification of symbolic aspects I will include parts of an analysis of an Early Anglo-Saxon cemetery consisting of both cremations and inhumations. Spong Hill offers an excellent opportunity for detailed analysis with advanced analytical tools, because it has been worked through by specialists and because it is totally excavated. Results may be compared with broader analyses carried out on larger and more representative samples in England (Richards 1987, Brush 1994, Härke 1992). Thus, the present analysis should be seen both as innovative and as a continuation and evaluation of earlier analyses.

The Spong Hill site is situated in Norfolk, East Anglia in England, 2 km south of North Elmham, which was probably the site of an Episcopal see from the end of the 7th century (fig 27). It is placed on a ridge about 40 m above sea level, north of the "Black Water River", south-west of the river Wensum, to the west of the Roman road between Worthing and Beetley. Prehistoric and Roman occupation was found in the area, preceding the cemetery site (Healy et al 1988, Rickett et al 1995). How big the settlement area was and how dense the Anglo-Saxon occupation around the Spong Hill cemetery cannot be assessed because intensive survey and excavation of the area could not be completed (ibid:158).

Between 1972 and 1984 excavations were carried out by the Norfolk Research Committee and thereafter by the Norfolk Archaeological Unit focusing mainly on the cemeteries. Results are presented in Hills 1977; Hills et al 1981, 1984, 1987, 1994; McKinley 1994; Rickett 1995 and Healy et al 1988. The entire cemetery is dated around the early Anglo-Saxon period of the 5th and 6th centuries. Thorough analysis of the chronology has been performed, e.g. by Hills (1976) and Nielsen (pers. comm.), but more work needs to be done. Generally speaking, however, pottery styles seem to develop from simple hanging arches via plastic decoration towards elaborate stamp decoration. The cemetery produced 2485 cremations and 57 inhumations making it one of the largest and to date best-recorded Anglo-Saxon sites of its type in Britain. The inhumations at the site seem relatively late, though there are cases of cremations cutting inhumations, and, judging from spatial distribution in the northeast of the site, otherwise post-dating the inhumations (Hills et al 1984:41).

In the following I will discuss some of the results which have been reached through analysis of the cremation graves at Spong Hill with reference to the deceased's sex. Due to limitations of space, I will not include the discussion of age issues. The analysis of other cremations and inhumations in England is also excluded from the discussion. I will move directly to the CA as it is this method that we will explore. To those who are interested in the details of a more elaborate social and chronological analysis, I refer to Ravn 1998b, Ravn in press a and Ravn in press b.

Artefacts and ornaments in significant relationship to gender in the Spong Hill cremations

The first CA ended up with 1334 graves and 50 types which could be used. Fig. 28 shows a tendency towards a separation into three clusters, a large group where mainly females occur together with among other things spindle whorls, and a gradual more male side where sexed male skeletons appear together with whetstones, playing pieces etc. The pattern is a tendency only, which is why the miniature artefacts, the third cluster clearly situated in the male side, were excluded in the further analysis.

Male group I

The cluster with miniature artefacts I shall call male group I. The spatial distribution of miniature artefacts spreads in even groups over the entire site (fig. 29), indicating that chronology is not the important dimension here. This is confirmed by the presence of both late and early ornamentation on the pottery. But there is no significant relationship with a certain age group, not even in a conventional analysis. The small number of graves justify exclusion in a further analysis. No ornaments or stamps could be associated with this group, pointing to a low symbolic activity on pots, as is also the case among the women. The relatively low number of graves, 36, as well as the low symbolic activity, implies that group I was either poor or special in other ways, as I shall discuss shortly.

Male group II

Excluding the miniature artefacts and a number of other badly defined variables, 994 graves and 32 types were suitable for analysis. Of these, in group II the number of graves with two or more attributes was 189. Now, three groupings appear among the variables (fig 30). In the second group called male group II, there are a number of artefacts associated with the clearly male-sexed skeletons (male); such as shears (shears), playing pieces (playpiec) and glass vessels (glsves); which also appear together with horse and sheep. Plain cordon (corplain) ornamentation as well as pottery stamp type XII are also associated with this group. Spatially, group II is distributed over the entire area. The following distribution maps are not of combinations (unless otherwise mentioned), but of presence/absence of the mentioned artefacts. The distribution of playing pieces points to around 4-5 major groups on site. Horse and sheep were distributed over the entire site. In comparison to the conventional analysis all of these artefacts belong to the group of adults, a fact which is not contradicted by the CA of age below.

Male group III

In the third group, male group III, the number of graves with two or more attributes was 231. In this group possibly male-sexed skeletons (male?) appear together with artefacts such as whetstones (honesto), bronze tweezers (twbron), bone beads (bonebead), and weapons (weap). A weapon is here defined as any martial implement, e.g. a scabbard, an arrowhead, a shield boss etc. Defined thus, the number of weapon graves is 11. A number of pottery

Correspondence Analysis of gender, artefacts and decoration
Type scores
X-Axis: 1. component Eigenvalue: 0.5445 (4.7% inertia)
Y-Axis: 2. component Eigenvalue: 0.5317 (4.6% inertia)

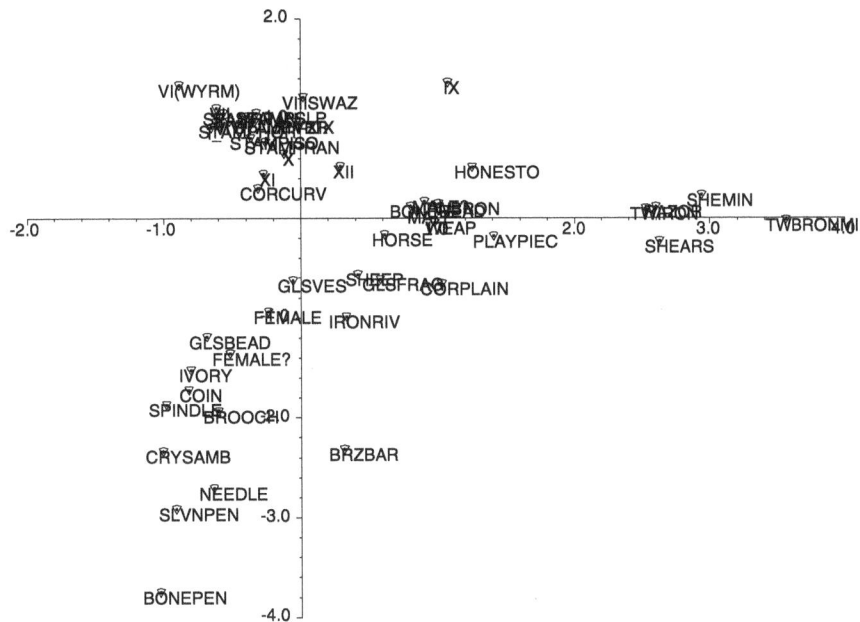

Fig. 28a. Spong Hill. Correspondence analysis of artefact types, pottery stamps and osteological sex with respect to the types. The miniature artefacts distinguish themselves in the right half of the scattergram.

Correspondence Analysis of gender, artefacts and decoration
Unit + Type scores
X-Axis: 1. component Eigenvalue: 0.5445 (4.7% inertia)
Y-Axis: 2. component Eigenvalue: 0.5317 (4.6% inertia)

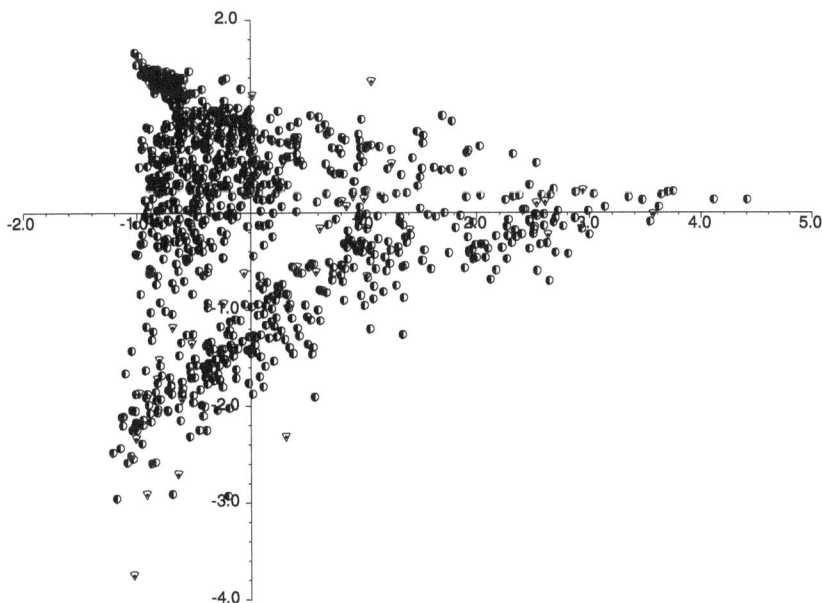

Fig. 28b. Spong Hill. Correspondence analysis of artefact types, pottery stamps and osteological sex with respect to the units. This picture is less clear due to the number of units in one plot.

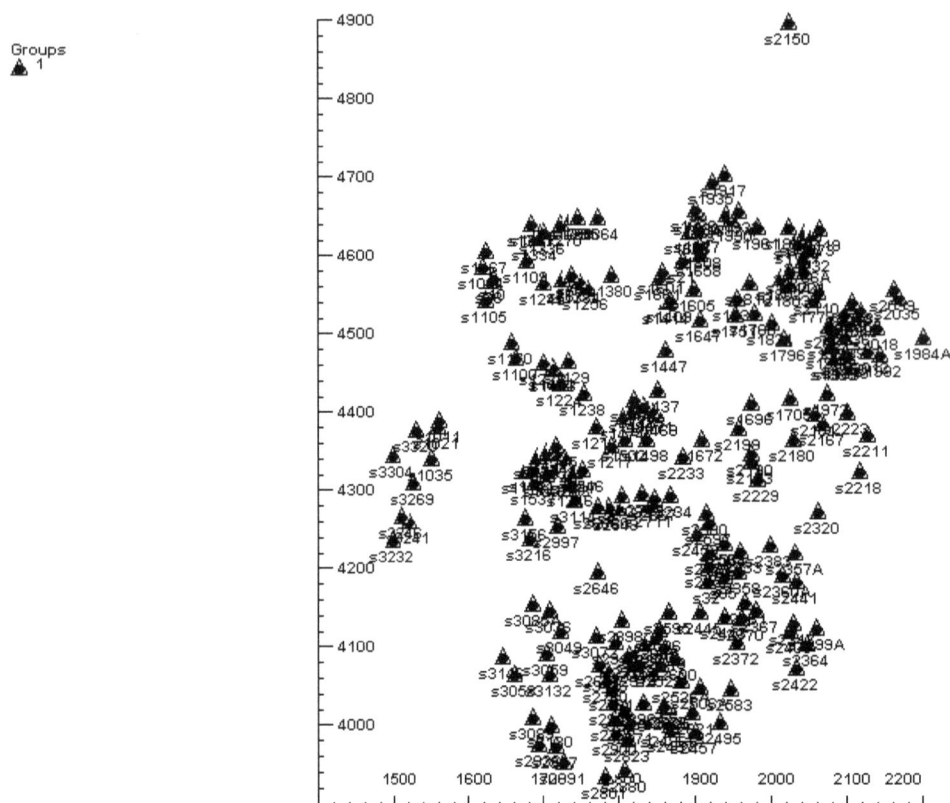

Fig. 29. Spong Hill. Spatial distribution of miniature artefacts.

stamps were also associated with this combination of artefacts; especially stamp types I, II, III, X, V, IV, VIII and XIII-XIX; and curved cordons (corcurv). Spatially, group III could not be clearly distinguished either.

The female group

At the other end of the diagram a distinct group of artefacts is associated with female-sexed skeletons (female) and possibly female-sexed skeletons (female?), clearly supporting McKinley's identifications. The artefact associations were coin, glass bead (glsbead), ivory, spindle whorls (spindle), silver pendants (slvpen), and crystal & amber (crysamb). The spatial distribution shows that these categories are distributed over the entire site in a similar way as among the males.

Thus, this pattern points to *no clear internal division* among females in contrast to the males. Maybe this lack of internal social division and competition explains the absence of pottery stamps and ornamentation in the grave assemblages of women, as suggested in ethnographic field studies where Hodder only identified ornamentation where an internal and external competition was present (Hodder 1982b). In general, the spatial distribution of sexed skeletons in the sample points to an even distribution, meaning that females and males were buried next to each other in family groups.

Interpreting the groups

In sum, the structures found from the CA of the cremation graves and the conventional analysis cannot be interpreted as chronological. Neither was it possible to trace any clear-cut ethnic patterns. Of the male groups, I suggest group I to be the least socially prominent one. This contention is based, partly *ex silentio*, upon the absence of a significant relationship between ornaments and partly, upon the presence of two other male groups which, judging from the quality of the material, were more prominent. Male group I is, however, not the poorest group, as the poorly equipped graves excluded from the analysis must have belonged to less prominent persons.

Male group II has symbolic content in terms of sex and age in that it is dominated by adult males. That they were adults is supported in analyses which are excluded from this paper, but which can be found in my Ph.D. thesis (Ravn 1998b). The conclusion of symbolic content is based upon the coincidence of playing pieces and bronze tweezers in the gendered group, as well as in the aged group of the CA. The meaning of playing pieces might be that games had connotations similar to that of chess in the High Medieval Period, symbolising intelligence, flair for strategic thinking and the ability to lead a battle.

Correspondence Analysis of gender, artefacts and decoration
Type scores
X-Axis: 1. component   Eigenvalue: 0.5464 (5.4% inertia)
Y-Axis: 2. component   Eigenvalue: 0.4479 (4.4% inertia)

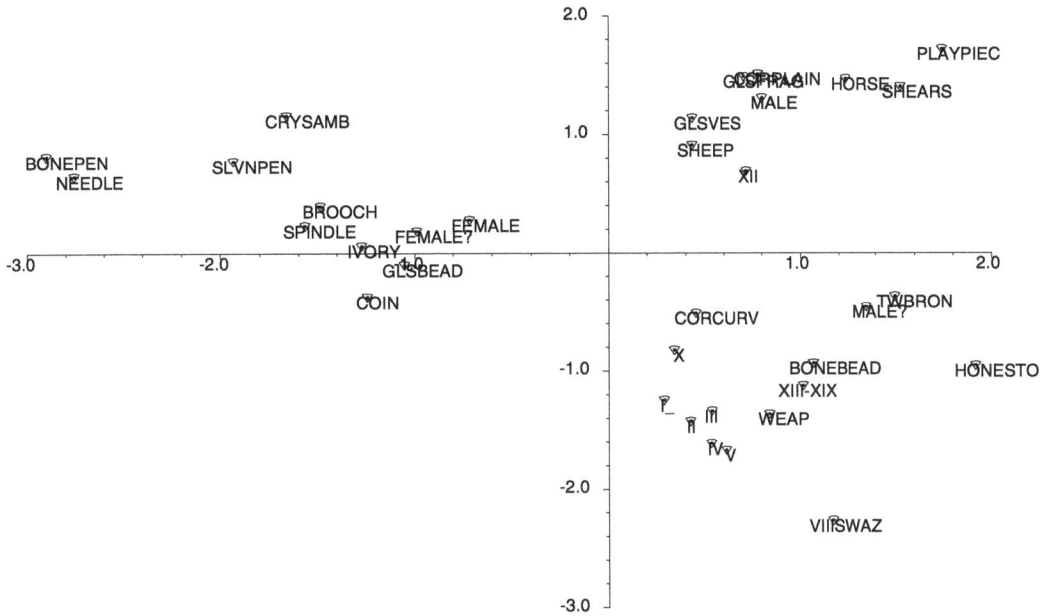

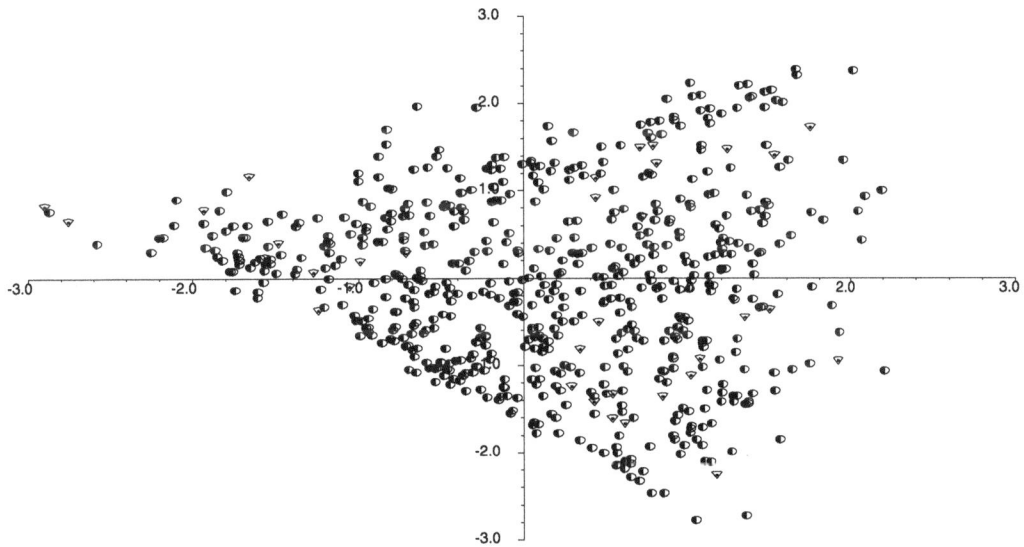

Correspondence Analysis of gender, artefacts and decoration
Unit + Type scores
X-Axis: 1. component   Eigenvalue: 0.5464 (5.4% inertia)
Y-Axis: 2. component   Eigenvalue: 0.4479 (4.4% inertia)

Fig. 30. Spong Hill. Correspondence analysis of artefact types, pottery stamps and osteological sex; excluding the miniature artefacts etc. a) With respect to the types. b) With respect to the units.

Correspondence Analysis of age, artefacts and decoration
Type scores
X-Axis: 1. component   Eigenvalue: 0.4765 (12.3% inertia)
Y-Axis: 2. component   Eigenvalue: 0.4590 (11.8% inertia)

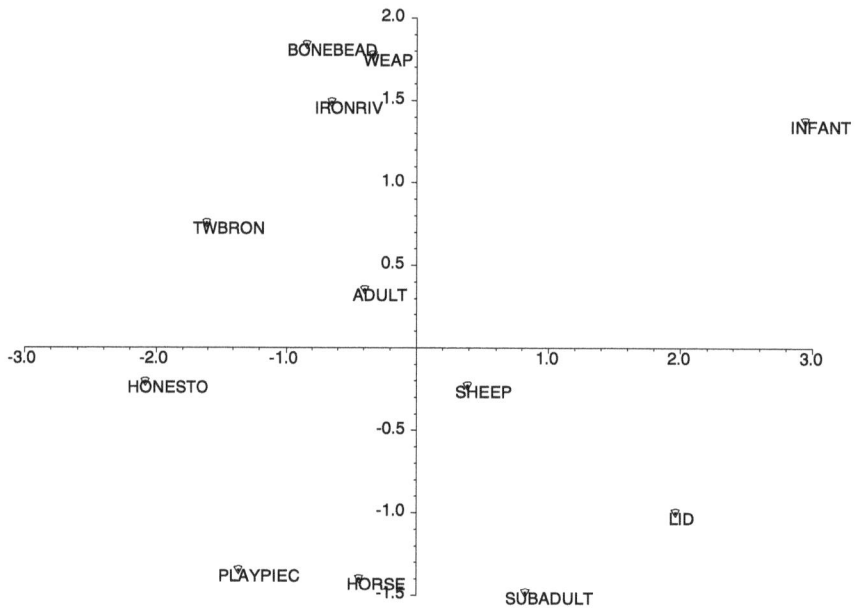

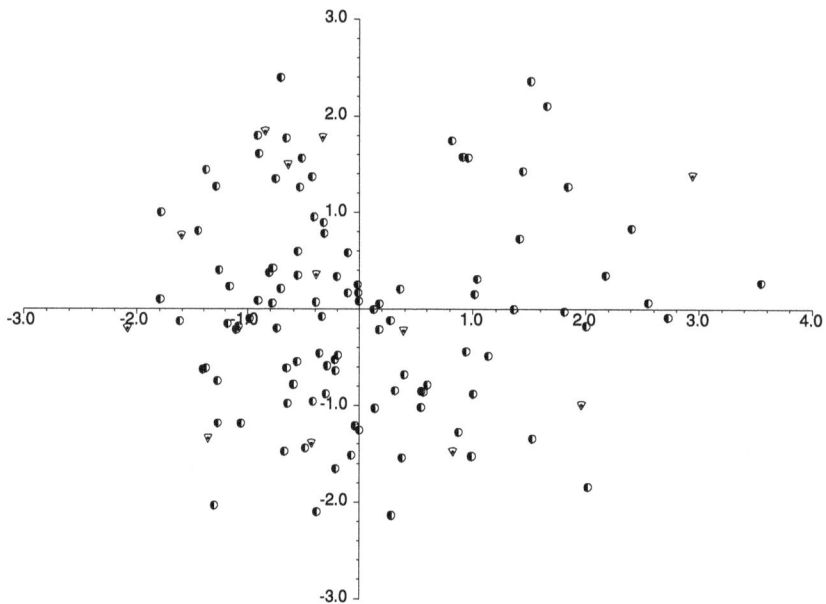

Correspondence Analysis of age, artefacts and decoration
Unit + Type scores
X-Axis: 1. component   Eigenvalue: 0.4765 (12.3% inertia)
Y-Axis: 2. component   Eigenvalue: 0.4590 (11.8% inertia)

Fig. 31. *Spong Hill. Correspondence analysis of artefact types, pottery stamps and osteological sex; excluding the miniature artefacts etc. This is how the picture changes when two children's graves (1217 and 1227) are also excluded. a) With respect to the types. b) With respect to the units.*

Interesting in that connection is the significant association with animal burials, especially horses, an association which is also seen in conventional analyses throughout Anglo-Saxon England (Crabtree 1995). Does this, as has been shown for earlier Roman Iron Age weapon offerings in Denmark (Ørsnes 1988), North German cemeteries (Gebühr & Kunow 1976, Weber 1996:172) and Gotland in the Migration Period (Jensen & Nielsen 1997:56 – I am very grateful to Karen Høilund Nielsen for drawing my attention to this fact), indicate that older prestigious men were the war lords who lead battles from horseback (see also Steuer 1982)? In any case there is a significant relationship between adult men, horses and playing pieces at Spong Hill and between older men and horses on the Continent pointing to a relationship between high status, mobility and warfare. Only one pottery stamp type, type XII and plain cordons, can be associated with this group. Stamp type XII may be interpreted as a phallic symbol (e.g. Hills et al 1994, fig. 97:x357, 2877 etc) which would fit with an ideal of power and potency.

The zoomorphic pottery stamp type IX could not be associated in a significant way with either group II or III, but certainly it belonged to males as was also the case with the Wyrm design (type VI). Hills (1983:100) suggests that the few animal designs often occur in relationship with swastikas which explains why they could not be placed in either group. Though the sex of only one of these graves could be assessed as male and the rest as adults, I suggest on the basis of the CA that the six pots with both types of designs belonged to a number of special members of the family, probably leading adult males. The small number of graves makes it difficult to substantiate or explain the importance of this tendency further; but the presence of both animals, swords and miniature artefacts in some of them points to the fact that they were important, but did not belong to any of the three groups. Nor can their position at the site support an alternative explanation as a special family spread over six generations, since they are scattered towards the south, west and north of the site (Hills 1983:101) with few grouped together. The animal design being found both in Angeln (Capelle 1987) and on the Gallehus horns in Denmark (Brøndsted 1960:324), as well as in the later Viking period (Roesdahl 1992:14), suggests an interregional connection, and supports the importance of animals, especially horses, in the Anglo-Saxon and Nordic world-view.

In male group III, a large number of pottery stamp types were associated with tweezers of bronze, bone beads, whetstones and weapons. The two former could positively be associated with adults, whereas weapons as previously mentioned could also be associated with children. The question then arises what an association between weapons and children means. The multivariate analysis of age was surprising in that here was also a connection between children and weapons, a fact that is supported in the conventional analysis. A closer look suggests, however, that more than half of the graves (i.e. graves 1105, 2851a, 2892, 3145, 3234) were adult graves and only graves 1051, 1217, and 1227 were children's graves containing arrowheads; whereas graves 1211 and 3271 were sub-adults' graves and grave 3114 that of a person of unknown age. Excluding children's graves 1227 and 1217 from the

analysis changes the picture dramatically in that weapons then clearly are associated with adults (fig. 31). Thus, the two children's graves with arrowheads may have been so unusual that they bias the entire analysis, meaning that the real picture clearly associated weapons with a family of both children and adult males, as identified among inhumation graves (Härke 1992:187).

The general pattern of the analysis of both age and gender supports the contention that all were buried in family groups, different sexes next to each other, the old leading male, the weapon group and the groups with miniature artefacts together with females and children, as suggested by McKinley (1994). A similar pattern is identified by Weber (1996:174) for Issendorf in Germany. This picture supports the overall idea of a *family-based* cemetery with internal social division *within* a farmstead.

Concluding discussion on cremations in England

In general, there are many similarities between the material analysed at Spong Hill and the Anglo-Saxon cremations analysed earlier by Richards (1987). On that basis I find it reasonable to conclude that the pattern at Spong Hill can be expected to be found at other cremation cemeteries in England, with a number of regional variations on the theme. At Spong Hill four ideal status groups among the men were identified in the cremation graves.

1) The first, and I suggest the most prestigious, is group II where playing pieces symbolised the ability to lead a battle, glass vessels had connotations in terms of external relations and animals symbolised prosperity and power. Shears might symbolise well-groomed looks and the connection between power and hair as known among contemporary Frankish warriors and seen for example on Childeric's signet ring. His burial is dated between AD 481 and 486 (Wood 1994:41), but the ring is slightly older. The power of hair is outlined also in Beowulf as well as among ethnographic cases (Leach 1958, Hallpike 1969). Most of the shears seem too small for shearing sheep, which would have been an alternative explanation.

Group II were mainly men who led battles, a pattern also identified in the Germanic graves of the Continent from the Roman Iron Age (Gebühr & Kunow 1976). It is interesting also that the association of playing pieces evokes associations to Odin and his wisdom (Davidson 1964:45). Furthermore, the presence of the horse in this group leads the thought towards Odin's horse, Sleipnir (Davidson 1964:41). That horses must have been meaningful in burial ritual and did not just reflect economic aspects is substantiated by the fact that the presence of horses and dogs is much higher at Spong Hill than for instance at settlement sites such as West Stow (Crabtree 1995:24). The presence of glass suggests that it is a symbol of the drinking rituals so well-known e.g. from the Beowulf poem.

2) Group III were the warriors, or retainers, who distinguished themselves towards the end of the span of the cremation cemetery, possibly developing into the warrior ideal expressed so clearly in the later inhumations. This group shows a number of pottery stamps suggesting that its

members were in a negotiating position between the rich and the poorer, trying to legitimate their power, not only through their weapons but also through a religious relationship to the warrior god, Thor. I suggest that Thor may be associated with the presence of whetstones and swastika symbols, both known to be related to fire, the swastika symbolising his hammer. At least, this association is known from later sources (Davidson 1964, Simpson 1979). The presence of these symbols in combination has also been noted at other Anglo-Saxon cremation cemeteries which were analysed on an intuitive basis (Reynolds 1980). This stamp group from Spong Hill is, however, to my knowledge the first in Anglo-Saxon archaeology which has been identified through stringent methodology and on statistically significant grounds.

3) The least distinct of the three groups in social terms may be group I, buried with iron miniature artefacts. I cannot from the archaeological evidence prove anything but that they were less well placed than the two other groups in relative terms. The group spreads over all age-groups meaning that they cannot be an age-group of children as suggested by Richards (1987).

4) The least prestigious social group, I suggest, is represented by the 1151 poorly furnished or unfurnished graves, which were excluded at an early stage from the CA due to insufficient or lacking variables. If this is true, the less prominent group constituted 40-46% of the entire population at the Spong Hill cemetery. The actual percentage is 46% (1151 / 2485 x 100), but the true number is probably lower, as at least 5 % of the graves were excluded from the analysis due to insufficient co-ordinates, disturbance and grave robbery.

The female group showed no subgroupings, and thus no hierarchy can be established.

East Anglian social structure

As outlined above it is possible to distinguish four male groups. The female group is homogenous and this points to an internal division at the micro-level only among men, whereas at the macro-level, women, being more heterogeneous, were the carriers of "ethnic identity" between various regions, as also indicated from brooch types in general and from inhumation graves (Brush 1994:253).

The site generally suggests a much larger size of the settlements or catchment area than may be seen in, say, contemporary Vorbasse in Denmark (Hvass 1983). Alternatively, the cemetery has been used by several settlements in the area, a pattern which is different from that most common in Scandinavia and southeast Europe (Ravn 1998b:151 ff).

In other words, the social division seen in the burial custom acts *within* the individual family. In a family household, the lord, the primary spouse, the warriors and the servants lived and slept in the same house together and were seen as a unit with an internal division. This is substantiated by the fact that there is no central group of rich graves among the cremation graves distinguishing

themselves before the inhumations appear. In the cremation graves a growing group within the family increasingly expressed its warrior ideology and relation to Thor through the use of whetstones and a number of pottery stamps, especially the swastika (Davidson 1964, Simpson 1979, Reynolds 1980).

Playing pieces are observed in some inhumation graves (Härke 1992:161), pointing to a continuation from cremation to inhumation of the use of playing pieces as a symbol of political leadership. Although the use of horses, and animals in general, decreases significantly in the inhumation ritual, the presence of horse gear (Härke 1992:161) indicates a continuation of the prestigious relationship between horse and power though the symbols had changed. A recently excavated example of this phenomenon is seen in a male grave with horse and sword from Lakenheath, East Anglia.

Although some of the differences between inhumations and cremations might possibly be explained by different conditions of preservation, I suggest that cremations in general had another symbolic meaning, as seen especially in the plentiful presence and selection of ornamentation on pots and the absence of similar ornamentation on pots from inhumations. Inhumations and cremations, being partly coexistent, suggest that neither chronological nor preservational factors can have been the explanation for that difference.

In short, the special nature as well as the relatively late date of the inhumation graves point to a high-ranking group having distinguished itself, socially and religiously, from other less "rich" farmsteads where the families still cremated their dead. This contention is supported by the fact that the 57 inhumation graves at Spong Hill cluster in the northeast corner of the cemetery, separately from the cremations (for a detailed analysis of the Spong Hill inhumations see Ravn 1998b:216ff). It may mean that those families saw themselves as belonging to a more powerful group of society, perhaps the lineage of the local leaders, and that they tried to monopolise their interpretation of religion by interring their dead in another way. Ritually and religiously, inhumation burial may indicate that more emphasis was placed upon the actual burial than on the rites that preceded it (McKinley 1994).

I would further suggest that the poorly furnished graves occurring among the cremations were those of less important individuals living on the farms, as seen also in Scandinavia. This means that even the less important people at a farmstead were considered part of the family and its religion.

Thus, a scenario materialises where a small social elite monopolises the interpretation of religion, possibly by emphasising a warrior ideology connected to the Aesir in the 5th century, as suggested also by gold and weapon hoards from contemporary Scandinavia (Hauck 1987, Fabech 1991:300, Hedeager 1997). This interpretation does not contradict Härke's (1992a:218) suggestion, but stresses more than earlier that a Germanic identity is not exclusively related to inhumations. I have shown that cremations are just as "Germanic" as inhumations in terms of symbolism. The difference between cremations and inhumations, not being one of chronology nor regionality, suggests to me that the difference is one of social and religious identity.

Conclusion

In sum, I suggest that CA is a good method for revealing structures in raw data, whether social, chronological, or symbolic. Since it is a multivariate method of analysis, it also confronts the problem of multidimensionality which the history of research has showed us to be a recurring issue in burial analysis. With a theoretical approach which takes into account the relationship between intentional and functional data in graves, and the symbolic meaning of ritual in funerals, I believe that CA is the method which at present may most likely help us to reveal and understand qualitative aspects of past society. As mentioned above, naturally, we need to include more and other finds and other find categories in our final interpretation in order to account for biases.

My analysis in this paper is an attempt to contribute to the discussion of the social significance of burial material by analysing the Spong Hill cremations in depth. By applying a different theoretical outlook and previously not used techniques such as multivariate CA, statistically significant combinations of material culture in graves could be identified. These are interpreted as symbolic reflections of sex, age, social status and ethnic identity. The artefact combinations were supported by the concurrence of sexed skeletons which appeared with a number of specific artefacts in the CA. The analysis shows that material culture was selected and used conspicuously as symbols of social status, ethnic identity, age and gender in different rituals and in various ways to express an internal division within the community – whether real or unreal will not be assessed here. But the difference may be of less importance since people live their identity as reality, as expressed by Bourdieu (1977).

The CA has proved a useful tool which may help us unravel some of the inherent meaning of that selective material expression. The identification of material form, function and symbolic meaning is essential not only for the identification of patterns in time and space, but also for the identification of social significance. Malmer´s thesis: "From a random variation no conclusions can be drawn, but a non-random variation implies a pattern of some sort presumably in time or space or most likely both" (1963:27, my translation) is not untrue. But from the discussion above it may be pertinent to add that a non-random pattern is likely to embody variations in ideology and social and ethnic identity *as well* as variation in time and space.

Acknowledgements

This paper is an elaboration of one presented at the EAA Annual Meeting, Gothenburg 1998, to which I was kindly invited by Martin Rundkvist. The paper is based on research carried out at Cambridge University for my Ph.D. thesis, submitted in February 1998. Funding for my research has kindly been provided by the Danish Research Academy and Århus University, to both of which I am very grateful. A more elaborate version of this paper may also be found in a volume to be published at the University of Lund (Ravn in press a). I thank Dr. Catherine Hills for giving me access to her updated database, and for her useful comments on the Spong Hill cemetery and Anglo-Saxon archaeology in general. Furthermore, Professor Ulf Näsman is thanked for his useful comments on Scandinavian archaeology during my doctoral research. The text was submitted for publication in November 1998.

References

Albrectsen, E. 1954. *Fynske jernaldergrave II. Førromersk jernalder.* Copenhagen.

Ariés, P. 1974. *Western attitudes towards death – from the Middle Ages to the present.* The Johns Hopkins symposia in comparative history. Baltimore.

Ariés. P. 1981. *The hour of our death.* London.

Baxter, M.J. 1994. *Exploratory multivariate analysis in archaeology.* Edinburgh University Press.

Beowulf. Alexander, M. 1973. *Beowulf. A verse translation.* London.

Beran, J. 1996. On social psychology and the professional self-assessment of the last generation of East German archaeologists. *Journal of European Archaeology* (1996) 4, pp 39-44. European Association of Archaeologists. Aldershot.

Binford, L.R. 1972. Mortuary practices: their study and their potential. *An archaeological perspective,* pp 208-239. London. Reprinted from *American Antiquity* (1971) 36, pp 6-29.

Bloch, M. 1977. The past and the present in the present. *Man* 12 (n.s.), pp 278-292. Royal anthropological institute of Great Britain and Ireland. London.

Bloch, M. 1982. Death, women and power. See Bloch & Parry 1982:211-230.

Bloch, M. & Parry, J. (eds.). 1982. *Death and the regeneration of life.* Cambridge University Press.

Bourdieu, P. 1977. *Outline of a theory of practice.* Cambridge studies in social anthropology 16. Cambridge University Press.

Brush, K. 1994. *Adorning the dead.* Unpublished Ph.D. dissertation. University of Cambridge.

Brøndsted, J. 1960. *Danmarks Oldtid III. Jernalderen.* Copenhagen.

Capelle, T. 1987. Animal stamps and animal figures on Anglo-Saxon and Anglian pottery. *Medieval Archaeology* 31, pp 94-96. The society for Medieval archaeology. London.

Chapman, R.; Randsborg K. & Kinnes, I (eds.). 1981. *The archaeology of death.* New directions in archaeology. Cambridge University Press.

Christlein, R. 1975. Besitzabstufungen zur Merowingerzeit im Spiegel reicher Grabfunde aus West- und Süddeutschland. *Jahrbuch des Römisch-Germanischen Zentralmuseums Mainz, 20 Jahrgang 1973,* pp 147-180.

Crabtree, P.J. 1995. The symbolic role of animals in Anglo-Saxon England: Evidence from burials and cremations. Ryan, K. & Crabtree, P.J. (eds.). *The symbolic role of animals in archaeology.* MASCA research papers in science and archaeology, vol 12, pp 20-26. Museum Applied Science Center for Archaeology, Museum of Archaeology and

Anthropology, University of Pennsylvania. Philadelphia.

Davidson, H.R. Ellis. 1964. *Gods and myths of northern Europe*. Middlesex.

Fabech, C. 1991a. Social organisation, religiøse ceremonier og regional variation. Fabech, C. & Ringtved, J. (eds.). *Samfundsorganisation og regional variation. Norden i romersk jernalder og folkevandringstid*, pp 283-301. Jysk Arkæologisk Selskabs Skrifter XXVII. Århus.

Flannery, K.V. & Marcus, J. 1996. Cognitive archaeology. Hodder, I. & Preucel, R.W. (eds.). *Contemporary archaeology in theory. A reader,* pp 350-363. Social archaeology. Oxford.

Gebühr, M. 1970. Beigabenvergellschaftungen in mecklenburgischen Gräberfeldern der älteren römischen Kaiserzeit. *Neue Ausgrabungen und Forschungen in Niedersachsen* 6, pp 93-116. Hildesheim.

Gebühr, M. & Kunow, J. 1976. Der Urnenfriedhof von Kemnitz, Kr. Potsdam-Land. *Zeitschrift für Archäologie* 10, pp 185-172. Zentralinstitut für alte Geschichte und Archäologie. Akademie der Wissenschaften der DDR. Berlin.

Geertz, C. 1973. *The interpretation of cultures – selected essays*. London.

Gennep, A. Van. 1960 [1909]. *The rites of passage*. London.

Giddens, A. 1984. *The constitution of society – outline of the theory of structuration*. Cambridge.

Goldstein, L. 1981. One-dimensional archaeology and multidimensional people – spatial organisation and mortuary analysis. See Chapman, Kinnes & Randsborg 1981:53-70.

Goody, J.R. 1962. *Death, property and the ancestors. A study of the mortuary customs of the Lodagaa of West Africa*. Stanford.

Härke, H. 1991. All quiet on the western front? Paradigms, methods and approaches in West German archaeology. Hodder, I. (ed.). *Archaeological theory in Europe. The last three decades*, pp 187-222. London.

Härke, H. 1992. *Angelsächische Waffengräber des 5. bis 7. Jah-hunderts*. Zeitschrift für Archaeologie der Mittelalters. Beiheft 6. Bonn.

Härke, H. 1997. The nature of burial data. Jensen, K.C. & Nielsen, K.H. (eds.). *Burial and society. The chronological and social analysis of archaeological burial data*, pp 19-27. Århus University Press.

Hallpike, C.R. 1969. Social hair. *Man* 4 (n.s.), pp 256-264. Royal anthropological institute of Great Britain and Ireland. London.

Hansen, U.L. 1995. *Himlingeøje – Seeland – Europa. Ein gräberfeld der jüngeren römischen Kaiserzeit auf Seeland, seine Bedeutung und internationalen Beziehungen*. Nordiske Fortidsminder serie B band 13. Det Kongelige Nordiske Oldskriftselskab. Copenhagen.

Hauck, K. 1987. Gudme in der Sicht der Brakteaten-Forschung. *Frühmittelalterlichen Studien. Jahrbuch des Instituts für Frühmittelalterforschung der Universität Münster* vol 21, pp 147-181.

Healy et al. 1988. *The Anglo-Saxon cemetery at Spong Hill, North Elmham. Part VI. Occupation during the seventh to second millennia BC*. East Anglian Archaeology, report no. 39. Norwich.

Hedeager, L. 1978. A quantitative analysis of Roman imports in Europe north of the Limes and the question of Roman-Germanic exchange. Kristiansen, K. & Paludan-Müller, C. (eds.). *New directions in Scandinavian archaeology*, pp 191-216. Studies in Scandinavian prehistory and early history 1. Copenhagen.

Hedeager, L. 1990. *Danmarks jernalder. Mellem stamme og stat*. Århus University Press.

Hedeager, L. 1997. *Skygger af en anden virkelighed. Oldnordiske myter*. Copenhagen.

Hertz, R. 1960 [1907]. *Death and the right hand*. Aberdeen.

Hills, C.M. 1976. *The results of the excavations at the Anglo-Saxon cemetery at Spong Hill, North Elmham, Norfolk, with reference to cultural and chronological contexts*. Unpublished. Ph.D. dissertation. University of London.

Hills, C.M. 1980. Anglo-Saxon cremation cemeteries, with particular reference to Spong Hill, Norfolk. Rahtz, P. et al. (eds.). *Anglo-Saxon cemeteries 1979. The fourth Anglo-Saxon Symposium at Oxford*, pp 161-170. British Archaeological Reports, British Series 82. Oxford.

Hills, C.M. 1983. Animal stamps on Anglo-Saxon pottery in East Anglia. *Studien zur Sachsenforschung* 4, pp 93-110. Urgeschichts-Abteilung. Niedersächsisches Landesmuseum Hannover.

Hills, C.M. et al. 1977. *The Anglo-Saxon cemetery at Spong Hill, North Elmham. Part I. Catalogue of cremations*. East Anglian Archaeology, report no. 6. Norwich.

Hills, C.M. et al. 1981. *The Anglo-Saxon cemetery at Spong Hill, North Elmham. Part II. Catalogue of cremations*. East Anglian Archaeology, Report no. 11. Norwich.

Hills, C.M. et al. 1984. *The Anglo-Saxon cemetery at Spong Hill, North Elmham. Part III. Catalogue of inhumations*. East Anglian Archaeology, Report no. 21. Norwich.

Hills, C.M. et al. 1987. *The Anglo-Saxon cemetery at Spong Hill, North Elmham. Part IV. Catalogue of cremations*. East Anglian Archaeology, Report no. 34. Norwich.

Hills, C.M. et al. 1994. *The Anglo-Saxon cemetery at Spong Hill, North Elmham. Part V. Catalogue of cremations*. East Anglian Archaeology, Report no. 67. Norwich.

Hodder, I. 1980. Social structure and cemeteries: a critical appraisal. Rahtz, P. et al. (eds.). *Anglo-Saxon cemeteries 1979. The fourth Anglo-Saxon Symposium at Oxford*, pp 161-170. British Archaeological Reports, British Series 82. Oxford.

Hodder, I. 1982a. *The present past – an introduction to anthropology for archaeologists*. London.

Hodder, I. 1982b. *Symbols in action – ethnoarchaeological studies of material culture*. New studies in archaeology. Cambridge University Press.

Hodder, I. 1986. *Reading the past – current approaches to interpretation in archaeology*. Cambridge.

Hodder, I. 1990. *The domestication of Europe – structure and contingency in Neolithic societies*. Social archaeology. Oxford.

Hodder, I. & Preucel, R.W. 1996. Material symbols. Hodder, I. & Preucel, R.W. (eds.). *Contemporary* archaeology in theory. A reader, pp 299-314. Social archaeology. Oxford.

Huggett, J.W. 1996. Social analysis of Early Anglo-Saxon inhumation burials – archaeological methodologies. Journal of European Archaeology (1996) 4, pp 337-365. European Association of Archaeologists. Aldershot.

Huntington, R. & Metcalf, P. 1979. Celebrations of death – the anthropology of mortuary ritual. Cambridge University Press.

Hvass, S. 1983. Vorbasse. The development of a settlement through the first millennium AD. Journal of Danish archaeology 2, pp 127-136. Odense University Press.

Iregren, E.; Jennbert, K. & Larsson, L. (eds.). 1988. Gravskick och gravdata. Rapport från arkeologidagarna 13-15 januari 1988. Institute of Archaeology, report series no. 32. University of Lund.

Jacobs, J. 1996. Zur Wissenschaftsstrategie in der Deutschen Archäologie seit 1990. Journal of European Archaeology (1996) 4, pp 45-54. European Association of Archaeologists. Aldershot.

Jensen, J. 1979. Oldtidens samfund. Tiden indtil år 800. Dansk socialhistorie 1. Copenhagen.

Jensen. C.K. & Nielsen, K.H. 1997. Burial data and correspondence analysis. Jensen. K.C. & Nielsen, K. H. (eds.). Burial and society. The chronological and social analysis of archaeological burial data, pp 29-62. Århus University Press.

Jones, S. 1997. The archaeology of ethnicity. Constructing identities in the past and present. London.

Jørgensen, L. 1988. Family burial practices and inheritance systems. The development of an Iron Age society from 500 BC to AD 1000 on Bornholm, Denmark. Acta Archaeologica 58 (1987), pp 17-53. Copenhagen.

Jørgensen, L. 1990. Bækkegaard and Glasergaard. Two cemeteries from the Late Iron Age on Bornholm. Copenhagen. Arkæologiske studier 8. Institute of prehistoric archaeology, University of Copenhagen.

Jørgensen, L. 1992. Castel Trosino and Nocea Umbra. A chronological and social analysis of family burial practices in Lombard Italy (6th-8th cent. A.D). Acta Archaeologica 62 (1991), pp 1-58. Copenhagen.

Kjærum, P. 1970. Jættestuen Jordhøj. KUML 1969, pp 9-66. Jysk Arkæologisk Selskab. Copenhagen.

Klindt-Jensen, O. 1950. Foreign influences in Denmark's Early Iron Age. Acta Archaeologica 20 (1949), pp 1-229. Copenhagen.

Klindt-Jensen, O. 1965. Befolkningsgrupper, fundhorisonter og stiltræk i sen jernalder. KUML 1964, pp 52-61. Jysk Arkæologisk Selskab. Copenhagen.

Leach, E. R. 1954. Political systems of highland Burma – a study of Kachin social structure. London.

Leach, E. R. 1958. Magical hair. Journal of the Royal Anthropological Institute 88 (2), pp 147-164. London.

Lucy, S. 1995. The Anglo-Saxon cemeteries of East Yorkshire. Unpublished Ph.D. dissertation. University of Cambridge.

Mackeprang, M.B. 1943. Kulturbeziehungen im nordischen Raum des 3.-5.Jahrhunderts. Hamburger Schriften zur Vorgeschichte und germanischen Frühgeschichte, Band 3. Leipzig.

Madsen, T. 1990. The use of multivariate statistics in Scandinavian archaeology. Bock, H. & Ihm, P. (eds.). Classification, data analysis, and knowledge organization – models and methods with applications – proceedings of the 14th annual conference of the Gesellschaft für Klassifikation e.V., University of Marburg, March 12-14, 1990, pp 330-342. Berlin.

Malmer, M.P. 1962. Jungneolitische Studien. Acta Archaeologica Lundensia, series in octo, no. 2. Lund.

Malmer, M.P. 1963. Metodproblem inom järnålderns konsthistoria. Acta Archaeologica Lundensia, series in octo, no. 3. Lund.

McKinley, J. I. 1994. The Anglo-Saxon cemetery at Spong Hill, North Elmham. Part VIII. The cremations. East Anglian Archaeology, report no. 69. Norwich.

Miller, D. 1985. Artefacts as categories – a study of ceramic variability in central India. New studies in archaeology. Cambridge University Press.

Morris, I. 1987. Burial and ancient society. The rise of the Greek city state. New studies in archaeology. Cambridge University Press.

Morris, I. 1992. Death ritual and social structure in classical antiquity. Key themes in ancient history. Cambridge University Press.

Myhre, B. 1991. Theory in Scandinavian archaeology since 1960 – a view from Norway. Hodder, I. (ed.). Archaeological theory in Europe. The last three decades, pp 161-186. London.

Myres. J.L.N. 1969. Anglo-Saxon pottery and the settlement of England. Oxford.

Näsman, U. 1988. Analogy in Nordic Iron Age archaeology. A contribution to the development of a Nordic historical ethnography. Rasmussen, B.M. & Pedersen, P. (eds.). Fra stamme til stat i Danmark 1. Jernalderens stammesamfund, pp 123-140. Jysk Arkæologisk Selskabs Skrifter 22. Århus.

Näsman, U. 1994. The Iron Age graves of Öland – representative of what? See Stjernquist 1994.

Ørsnes, M. 1988. Ejsbøl. Waffenopferfunde des 4.-5. Jahrhundert nach Chr. 1. Nordiske fortidsminder Serie B 11. Det Kongelige Nordiske Oldskriftselskab. Copenhagen.

Pader, J. 1982. Symbolism, social relations and the interpretation of mortuary remains. British Archaeological Reports, International Series 130. Oxford.

Parker Pearson, M. 1982. Mortuary practices, society and ideology – an ethnoarchaeological study. Hodder, I. (ed.). Symbolic and structural archaeology, pp 99-114. Cambridge seminar on symbolic and structural archaeology. Cambridge University Press.

Patrik, L. 1985. Is there an archaeological record? Advances in archaeological method and theory 8, pp 27-57. New York.

Radcliffe-Brown, A. 1922. The Andaman islanders. Cambridge University Press.

Ramskou, T. 1976. Lindholm Høje. Gravpladsen. Nordiske fortidsminder Serie B 2. Det Kongelige Nordiske Oldskriftselskab. Copenhagen.

Randsborg. K. 1973. Wealth and social structure as reflections in Bronze Age burials. Renfrew, C. (ed.). The explanation of culture change – models in prehistory – proceedings of a meeting of the Research seminar in archaeology and related subjects held at the University of Sheffield [December 14-16, 1971], pp 565-570. London.

Ravn, M. 1993. Analogy in Danish prehistoric studies. *Norwegian Archaeological Review* vol. 26, no. 2., pp 59-90. Oslo University Press.

Ravn, M. 1997a. Til aftenselskab med Sophus Müller i Glyptoteket. *Aarbøger for nordisk Oldkyndighed og Historie* 1995, pp 153-171. Det Kongelige Nordiske Oldskriftselskab. Copenhagen.

Ravn, M. 1997b. Fra Gotland til Byzans. *Tidskriftet SFINX*, 1997, nr. 3, pp 130-135. Århus.

Ravn, M. 1998a. Review of Siân Jones: The archaeology of ethnicity. Constructing identities in the past and present. *Archaeological review from Cambridge* 14:2, pp 170-172.

Ravn, M. 1998b. Germanic social structure (c. AD 200-600). A methodological study in the use of archaeological and historical evidence in Migration Age Europe. Unpublished Ph.D. thesis. University of Cambridge.

Ravn, M. In press a. The use of symbols in burials in Migration Age Europe. To be published by the University of Lund.

Ravn, M. In press b. Kan vi erkende religion i forhistoriske grave ? Christensen, L. Bredholt & Sveen, S. (eds.) To be published by Århus University Press.

Ravn, M. & Britton, R. (eds.). 1997. History and archaeology. *Archaeological Review from Cambridge*, 14:1. (1995).

Renfrew, C. 1994. Towards a cognitive archaeology. Renfrew, C. & Zubrow, E. (eds.). *The ancient mind – elements of cognitive archaeology*, pp 3-12. New directions in archaeology. Cambridge University Press.

Reynolds, N. 1980. The king's whetstone – a footnote. *Antiquity* 54, pp 232-37. Cambridge.

Richards, J.D. 1987. *The significance of form and decoration of Anglo-Saxon cremation urns.* British Archaeological Reports, British Series 166. Oxford.

Rickett, R. et al. 1995. *The Anglo-Saxon cemetery at Spong Hill, North Elmham. Part VII. The Iron Age, Roman and Early Saxon settlement.* East Anglian Archaeology, Report no. 73. Norwich.

Roesdahl, E. 1992. Princely burial in Scandinavia at the time of conversion. Kendall, C.B. & Wells, P.S. (eds.). *Voyage to the other world – legacy of Sutton Hoo*, pp 155-170. Medieval studies at Minnesota, vol. 5. University of Minnesota Press. Minneapolis.

Schjødt, J.P. 1993. Det "hellige" i religionsvidenskaben. *Themata* 5, pp 4-13. Department of Religious Studies, University of Århus.

Shanks, M. & Tilley, C. 1987. Social theory and archaeology. Oxford.

Sørensen, M.L.S. 1979. Living and dead – problems and possibilities. *Kontaktstencil* 16, pp 148-166. Århus.

Sørensen, M.L.S. 1987. Material order and cultural classification – the role of bronze objects in the transition from Bronze Age to Iron Age in Scandinavia. Hodder, I. (ed.). *The archaeology of contextual meanings*, pp 90-101. New directions in archaeology. Cambridge University Press.

Simpson, J. 1979. The king's whetstone. *Antiquity* 53, pp 96-101. Cambridge.

Sperber, D. 1975. *Rethinking symbolism.* Cambridge studies in social anthropology 11. Cambridge University Press.

Steuer. H. 1982. *Frühgeschichtliche Sozialstrukturen in Mitteleuropa – eine Analyse der Auswertungsmethoden des archäologischen Quellenmaterials.* Abhandlungen der Akademie der Wissenschaften in Göttingen. Philologisch-historische Klasse F. 3, 128. Göttingen.

Stjernquist, B.J. 1994. (ed.). *Prehistoric graves as a source of information.* Konferenser 29. Kungliga Vitterhets Historie och Antikvitets Akademien. Stockholm.

Thompson, J. B. 1984. *Studies in the theory of ideology.* Cambridge.

Veeck, W. 1926. Der Reihengräberfriedhof von Holzgerlingen. *Fundberichte aus Swaben* n.F. 3, pp 154-201. Stuttgart.

Weber, M. 1996. *Das Gräberfeld von Issendorf, Kreis Stade. Kulturgeschichtliche Studien an Brandgräbern in der Zeit der angelsächsischen Landname.* Unpublished Doctoral Dissertation. University of Hamburg.

Wood, I. 1994. *The Merovingian kingdoms 450-751.* Singapore.

Placing the dead: investigating the location of wealthy barrow burials in seventh century England.

Howard M.R. Williams, Department of Archaeology, University of Reading

Introduction

When we think of data obtained from archaeological excavations of burial sites, we envisage the information derived from artefacts and human bones. While these remain the traditional focus of archaeological study and interpretation, a great deal of information can be derived from studying the positioning of burial sites. This paper presents a case study in this research by identifying principles behind the location of high status burial sites in early Anglo-Saxon England dated to the late sixth and seventh centuries AD. The landscape context of graves can provide important insights into the social and symbolic role of burial places during a period of political and religious transformation. It is during the seventh century AD that we can begin to discern the emergence of historically attested kingdoms and the conversion of the Anglo-Saxon elite to Christianity. An understanding of the types of location chosen for the final resting places of selected members of these elite groups might reveal a great deal about their social status and ideologies and their relations with the wider populations of southern and eastern England. The paper focuses upon one Early Medieval burial site at Lowbury Hill in Oxfordshire, southern England, and proceeds to compare this site with other high status burial sites from Wessex and the Upper Thames region. Firstly, let us discuss a theoretical and methodological base for addressing the subject.

Mortuary landscapes

The landscape context of burial sites of the first millennium AD has received relatively little and intermittent treatment by scholars until very recently (see Bonney 1966, 1976; Reynolds 1997; Williams 1997b; Lucy 1998; Semple 1998). Traditional studies of landscape tend to focus upon settlement patterns and land use with limited consideration of mortuary practices and their material remains (e.g. Hooke 1998). Studies of burial location in this period tend to be descriptive rather than interpretative. Where studies of burial location take place, they usually focus upon single variables such as relationships with ancient monuments or boundaries rather than all the full range of elements likely to influence the placing of the dead (e.g. Bonney 1966, 1976; Goodier 1984; Williams 1997b, 1998).

In order to consider the placing of high status burial sites of the seventh century, we can take the lead from the work of Christopher Tilley (1994, 1996), John Barrett (1994) and Richard Bradley (1997, 1998). These scholars and others have applied social theory and phenomenological approaches to space and place in investigating the settings of ritual sites and monuments. Studies have incorporated a variety of approaches by investigating the relationships of archaeological sites with the natural topography, proximity and associations with inherited monuments, patterns of intervisibility with other sites and axes of movement through the landscape. These perspectives emphasise the materiality and elemental nature of place and often discuss the mythical and symbolic qualities invested in sacred sites and the wider landscape. Also, there has been interest in the ways by which monumental architecture and monument location can structure the movement and experience of people. The spatial ordering of practices and rituals at these sites is thought to influence the construction and reproduction of social relations in the past (Barrett 1994; Tilley 1994, 1996; Bradley 1997).

These studies encourage us to imagine new approaches to the study and interpretation of Early Medieval cemeteries. Graves and cemeteries during the first millennium AD were never regarded as dots on maps or as site plans in the way that archaeologists consistently portray them. Burial sites had to be encountered at times of emotional stress and social insecurity. Their significance lay in the ways they were engaged with and experienced during rituals but also during less formalised encounters within daily life (Williams in press). Funerals are important events in traditional societies. The procession to the burial site and rituals conducted at the grave-side could have been important public gatherings and "fields of discourse" during which social and political strategies and relations were played out (Barrett 1994). Subsequent to the funeral, graves could become enduring features of the cultural landscape and potentially the focus of further burials, ancestor rites and other forms of formal meeting. Graves can have a continuing role in the social life of a community; they might be viewed as places of mediation between the living and the dead, as well as being the dwelling places of malign spirits and/or the community of ancestors.

Funerary rituals and the use of burial sites involve the physical and symbolic transformation of the corpse, soul and the mourners into new social categories and identities (Hertz 1906, Huntingdon & Metcalf 1991). Sometimes these transformations manifest themselves in the spatial translation of the dead and the placing of burial sites (e.g. Århem 1989, Kan 1989). This is supported by the knowledge that symbolic and ideological factors make an equally strong contribution to practical considerations in choosing the place of burial in many societies (e.g. Bloch 1974, Kan 1989, papers in Meyers 1993, Williams 1997). As the points where long and complex rituals culminate and reach a partial conclusion, burial sites can become invested with powerful emotional and social ties for the living. The use of a communal burial place and the repeated association of the dead with particular locales can contribute to the creation of an idealised social order that structures ideas of kinship and group solidarity (Bloch 1974, Bloch & Parry 1982, Meyer 1993, Warren 1993, Williams in press). The spatial elements of performances, gestures and actions during funerary rituals can be seen as "technologies of the self"; they are means by which individuals and groups understand their place in the world and sense of identity (Bloch 1982, Foucault 1988). The landscape context of burial sites might not only embody the ideals and beliefs of the living, but may also have actually influenced these very concepts through their use and repeated visits. Inhabiting and experiencing burial places would have contributed towards their changing symbolism and significance for past populations. Hence we might consider the use of place and space during mortuary practices as recursively related to ideologies and relationships between the dead and the living in past societies.

High status burial sites in England during the late sixth and seventh centuries AD

Armed with these theoretical themes we are in a position to construct methodologies to investigate patterns in the placing of "high status" graves in England during the late sixth and seventh centuries AD. These burial sites are well known in the archaeological literature due to the splendour of the grave goods found at sites such as Sutton Hoo, Broomfield, Benty Grange and Taplow. Their interpretation has a central place in our understanding of the changing nature of Anglo-Saxon society during the period (Welch 1992, Carver 1998). They represent a distinctive, if heterogeneous, group of wealthy graves, and this wealth has overshadowed investigations of their landscape context (e.g. Arnold 1988).

These graves include both male and female individuals; usually they are found singly and spatially segregated from contemporary "communal" cemeteries (Boddington 1990; exceptions exist in the southeast where large "barrow cemeteries" are known, Shephard 1979, Eagles & Struth in press). Graves often contain large quantities of high quality artefacts including rich weapon assemblages, gold and silver jewellery and a range of vessels. Sometimes graves have elaborate structures including ship burials, chambers and beds (Speake 1989, Carver 1995). They are placed beneath sizeable barrows or inserted into ancient monuments (Carver 1998, Van de Noort 1993, Williams 1998). During the seventh century, cremation rites disappear and "final phase" cemeteries rarely include cremation burials (Boddington 1990, Geake 1992). The occasional use of cremation to dispose of the dead among high status graves reflects a further distinctive element of these burial sites. Perhaps the use of cremation was a symbol of mythical status and links with a past in which cremation rites were more common (Williams 1997a, 1999). Despite the difficulties inherent in interpreting status from grave wealth (James 1989), it is plausible to interpret these burials as representing a variety of high status "royal" and "noble" groups. They indicate members of leading households holding power over the rapidly evolving patchwork of kingdoms and tribal groupings that existed across England during the seventh century (Arnold 1988:115, Bassett 1989, Yorke 1990, Dumville 1997, Carver 1998).

A methodology for investigating the location of Early Medieval burial sites

Wealthy burial sites were visited and their surrounding landscapes traversed on foot, by bicycle and by car as a starting point in the interpretation of their landscape context. This was combined with a thorough study of maps as well as archaeological and historical evidence for the locality of each burial site. It might be suggested that observations made in visiting these sites today are hopelessly subjective and intuitive, biased by modern aesthetics and perceptions of the landscape (e.g. Johnston 1998). These difficulties can be countered by implementing a systematic methodology. There are four main strands to such a methodology for Early Medieval burial sites. Firstly, we can justify our observations with reference to ethnographic and anthropological evidence for the significance of grave location in many societies (see above). Secondly, we can compare and contrast the qualities of high status burial sites with the locations of other Early Medieval burial sites. In this way it is possible to identify the selectivity in grave location by mourners and how their choices differed from other "lower status" burial sites. Prehistoric round barrows were frequently reused as Early Medieval burial sites and therefore represent the most important "control" against which to describe the location of high status graves (Williams 1997b, 1998). In this way we can begin to understand why certain locations were reused, while other prehistoric barrow sites available in the landscape were not selected.

Thirdly, we can combine environmental, historical and place name evidence as a control for observations. These sources can reveal aspects of vegetation, land use and the socio-political organisation of the landscape. Therefore they help in securing the validity of interpretations revealed by field observations. Often, we cannot "prove" the exact vegetation cover for a site, and hence understand its view-shed. Equally, given the denuded state of many barrows and the presence of woodland, we cannot fully identify from which parts of the landscape the barrow would have been visible. However, we may be able to assume that if a visual interrelationship was important, it would have been preserved by vegetation clearance.

Lastly, place name and literary evidence can inform us concerning the way people perceived the landscape in the Medieval period (Osborn & Overing 1994, Semple 1998). For example, there is some independent corroboration for the significance of barrow location in the description of the hero's funeral in the Anglo-Saxon poem *Beowulf*. Composed in the later, Christian Anglo-Saxon period, the poem derives from existing oral traditions. It might incorporate elements of idealised expectations for the placing of a high status barrow burial originally derived from the perspectives of the Anglo-Saxon elite of the seventh and eighth centuries. Beowulf dies fighting to defend his kingdom from a dragon. The monster is described as residing in an ancient tomb situated on a high, flat moor, on a headland and close to the sea (Alexander 1973:120, lines 2211-2; 121, lines 2241-2). The tomb was constructed by an ancient people and contained a hoard of treasure (Alexander 1973:121, lines 2215-7; 131, lines 2546-7). The cremation of Beowulf and the raising of the barrow took place on the headland, perhaps nearby this ancient monument (Alexander 1973:150-1, lines 3137-49, 3156-68). Beowulf's funeral and barrow seem to be associated with the physical and territorial boundary of the Geatish kingdom formed by high ground and the sea. The barrow was placed in a "liminal" location. Routes of movement also seem important in the location of the grave. It is explicitly stated that the barrow became an important landmark observed by seafarers (Alexander 1973:151, lines 3156-58). The funeral and the barrow were evidently located to be seen from afar and perhaps also to view routeways. These clear references to the landscape context of Beowulf's barrow in a mythical and imaginary landscape may have important implications for the criteria deemed important in locating real Anglo-Saxon high status barrows. It may tell us about the ways barrow placing was expected to be interpreted during the funeral and afterwards.

While these approaches cannot secure an "objective" and unambiguous interpretation of the placing of the dead, it helps us to situate field observations within an interpretative framework. The use of GIS (Geographical Information Systems) was not selected for this preliminary study, although the use of computer-aided studies of Early Medieval burial sites holds great potential for future research. Yet even if computer studies were utilised, they are not a replacement for observations made in the field when subtle features of the landscape can be recognised more clearly than through computer analysis. Indeed, this study provides a clear example of the limitations of GIS for such studies (*pace* Llobera 1996). At Lowbury Hill, a GIS program was employed to identify the tracts of the landscape intervisible with the Saxon barrow (Fulford & Rippon 1994). However, this analysis did not identify the subjective but potentially significant *experience* of viewing the landscape from the barrow (see below).

It became evident from visiting high status burial sites that four factors contribute towards a description of their landscape context:

1. Inherited monuments of prehistoric and Roman date
2. Topography & view-sheds
3. Routes – both roads and water courses
4. Boundaries and settlement patterns

Derived from field observation, these criteria provide the best starting point to discussing wealthy grave locations of the seventh century.

Lowbury Hill

Let us now pursue a single case study for this approach by investigating the location of the Saxon barrow on Lowbury Hill in southern England (NGR SU 541823). The barrow lies close to the modern county boundary between Oxfordshire and Berkshire and has been excavated twice this century by teams from Reading University, in 1914 and 1992 (Atkinson 1916, Fulford & Rippon 1994, fig. 32). A concise description of the Saxon barrow's location in the 1994 excavation report provided a valuable starting point for this study (Fulford & Rippon 1994, Härke 1994).

Heinrich Härke's discussion of this site remains the first clear attempt to *interpret,* rather than simply describe, a high status barrow burial in terms of its landscape context.

The grave contained the skeleton of a male of over 45 years of age (Fulford & Rippon 1994). The skeleton lay supine and orientated with the head to the south. The burial was covered by a primary barrow which is now in a very denuded state from plough damage and erosion. Accompanying the skeleton were a sword, spear, knife, sugar-loaf style shield boss, shears, comb, bronze and iron buckles, and a bronze hanging bowl with enamel escutcheons (Atkinson 1916:19-23, Fulford & Rippon 1994). The assemblage seems to date broadly to the later seventh century AD (Arnold 1988, Hawkes 1986:91).

Monument reuse

Anglo-Saxon burial sites frequently reuse ancient and abandoned monuments of both prehistoric and Roman date throughout southern and eastern England (Williams 1997b, 1998; Semple 1998). At Lowbury the barrow is adjacent to the visible ruins of a probable Romano-Celtic temple (Atkinson 1916; fig. 32, 33). The temple continued in use during the fourth century AD (Fulford & Rippon 1994:201). By the seventh century it is likely that the temple was abandoned and ruinous but remained an enduring feature in the landscape. Monument reuse for burial at Lowbury seems to have extended beyond the spatial proximity of the Saxon barrow to the Roman structure. Härke has suggested that soil and Roman artefacts were deliberately taken from within the Roman temple and used in the barrow construction as a means of emphasising links with the ancient ruins (Fulford & Rippon 1994:202, Härke 1994:204). The barrow was placed on the eastern side of the temple (Fulford & Rippon 1994; fig. 32, 33)., immediately outside of, and controlling the entrance into, the rectangular temenos enclosure. Had the entrance to the temple still been visible in the seventh century, the location of the barrow would have fundamentally altered the way people approached, and entered the Roman structure. The reuse of the site is further emphasised by an Early Medieval female grave found during Atkinson's excavations inserted into the temenos ditch at the southwestern corner of the temple (Atkinson 1916). Lastly, the systematic destruction and robbing of the temple could have taken place in the seventh century and may have been related to the funerary activity on the site (Fulford & Rippon 1994:202). The enduring relationship is recognised between the Roman and Saxon structures in the Anglo-Saxon name for the hill: "Lowbury". The name seems to combine the Old English words *hlaew* meaning barrow, and *burh* meaning enclosure or camp (Gelling 1974:512).

We cannot know if local traditions retained aspects of the temple's use and associations between its abandonment in the fourth/early fifth century and its reuse in the late seventh century. Nor can we be certain whether the site remained a cult focus in the sub-Roman period or whether it took on a different function. Either way, the siting of the Saxon grave directly infringed upon the experience and use of the ruinous temple complex. The funerary ritual and the

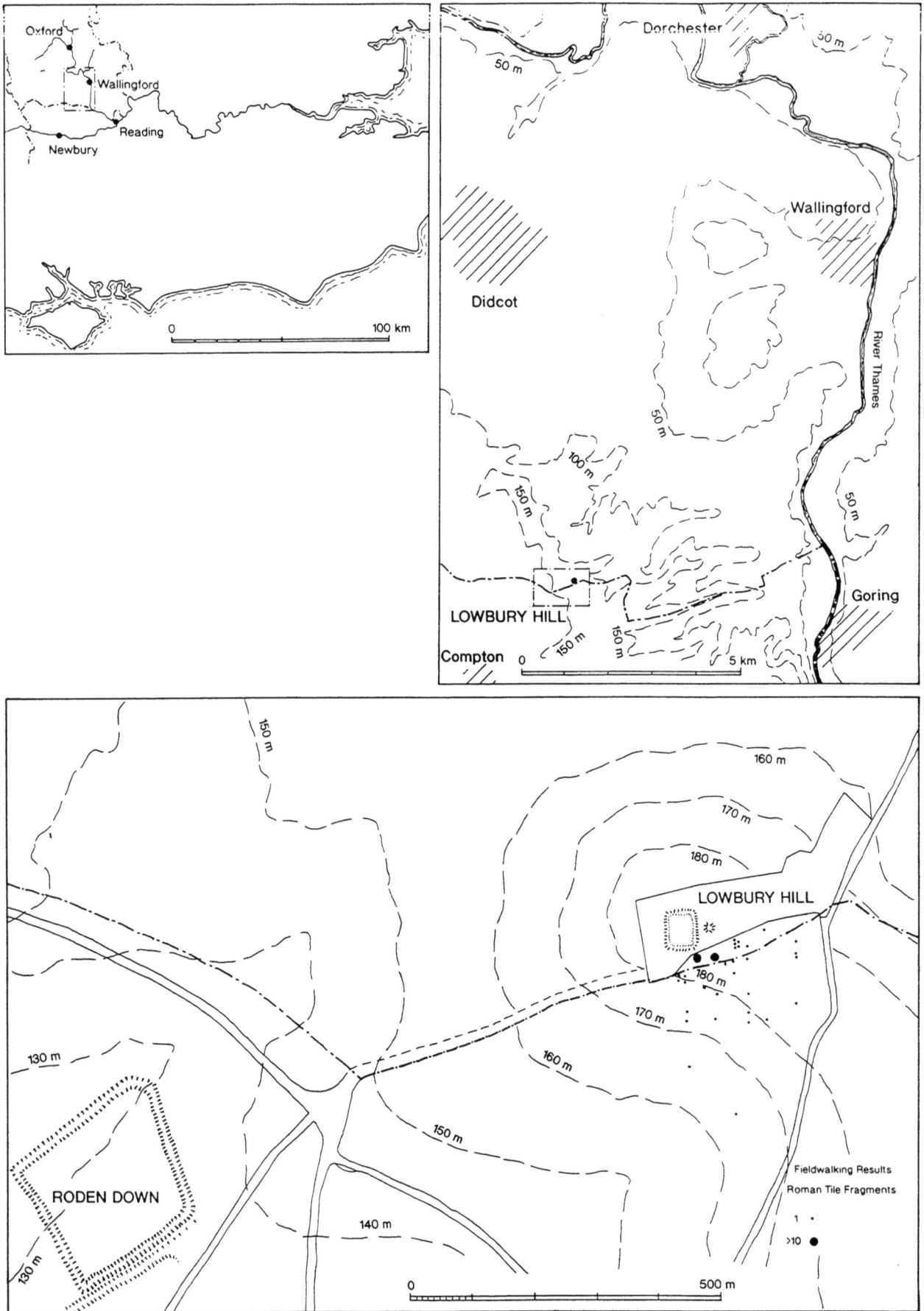

Fig. 32. *The regional and local context of the Lowbury Hill barrow burial showing its relationship to the probable Romano-Celtic temple (after Fulford & Rippon 1994).*

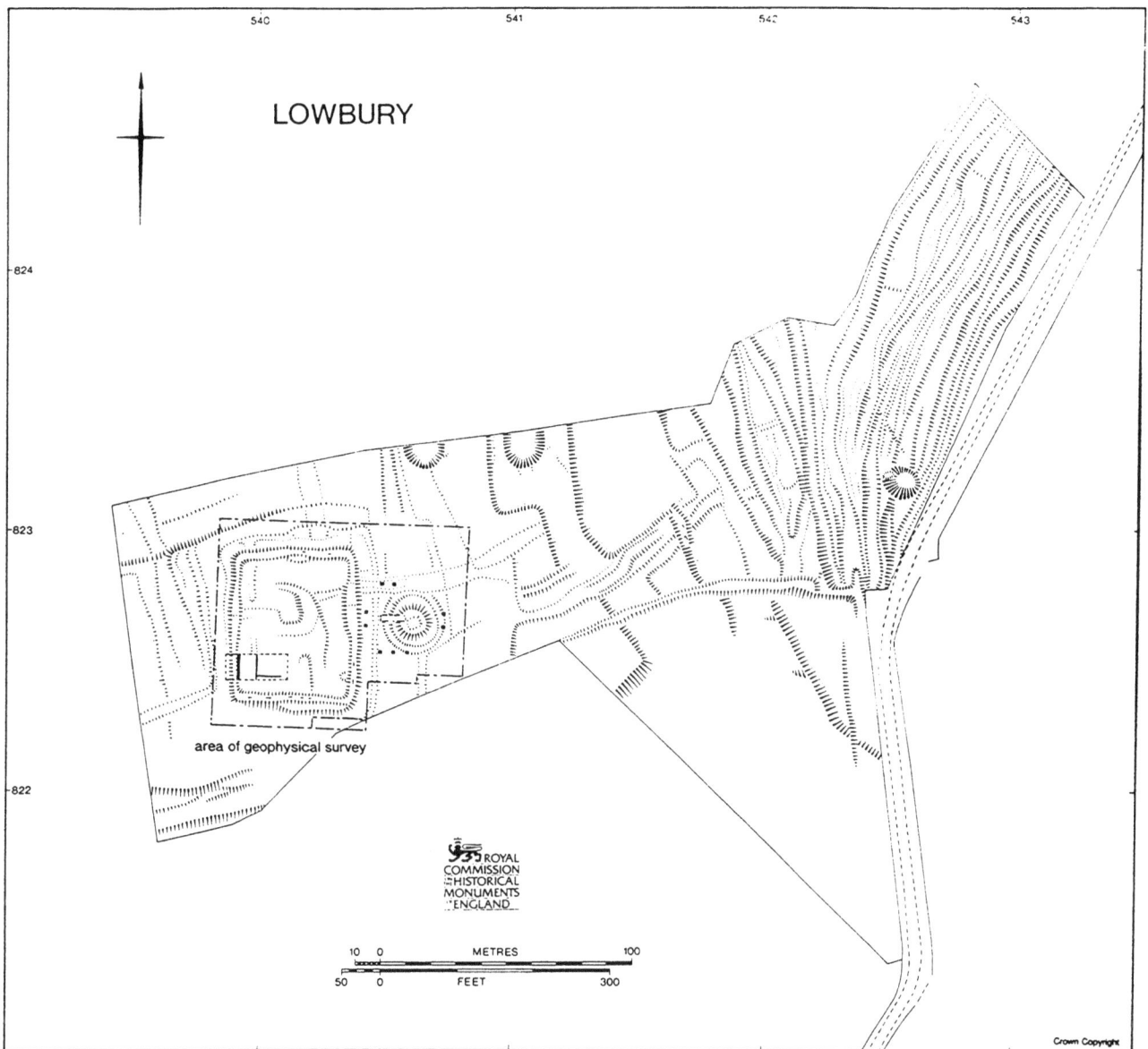

Fig. 33. RCHM Earthwork survey of Lowbury Hill showing both Saxon barrow and Romano-Celtic temple and the geophysical survey and areas excavated by Reading University in the early 1990s (after Fulford & Rippon 1994).

building of the Saxon barrow may have involved a reinterpretation of the ruins, giving them fresh meanings as a focus of elite mortuary rites.

Monument reuse is commonplace in southern and eastern England between the late fifth and seventh centuries in England. Early Medieval burial sites in the upper Thames region frequently reuse prehistoric monuments including henges, linear earthworks, hillforts, round and long barrows (Williams 1997b). This practice continued into the late Anglo-Saxon period when the prehistoric barrow at Scutchamer Knob on Cuckhamsley Hill was reused as the meeting place for the shire-court of Berkshire. The place name Cuckhamsley is thought to derive from "Mound of Cwichelm" which suggests that the prehistoric monument became associated with the West Saxon kings (Peake 1937, Meaney 1964:45-6, Gelling 1974:481-2, Hawkes 1986, fig. 34). A similar royal association with an ancient monument (possibly a Neolithic grave described in a 13th century source) has been suggested for the place name "Cutteslowe" north of Oxford (Dickinson 1974, Hawkes 1986:89). The use of Roman structures as Early Medieval

burial sites is also well attested in the region. There are well known cases of early and middle Saxon burial sites inserted into or adjoining Roman villas, burial sites, temples and other structures (Williams 1997b). Therefore, the reuse of an ancient monument at Lowbury reflects a continuation and elaboration of existing and widespread practices in Early Medieval burial location rather than a novel association made by high status graves (Williams 1998).

We can gain some possible insights into the motivations and meanings behind this relationship. Ancient and abandoned remains could have held associations with ancient peoples and were places of contact between past and present, the living and the dead. In this context, the placing of the grave may have been a symbol of elite control of supernatural knowledge, power and meanings bound within the ancient monument. Once the barrow had been situated on the site, the kin of the Saxon individual buried at Lowbury could claim exclusive access to the Roman structure and its significance through the graves of the dead. Whether the ancient remains were seen as the

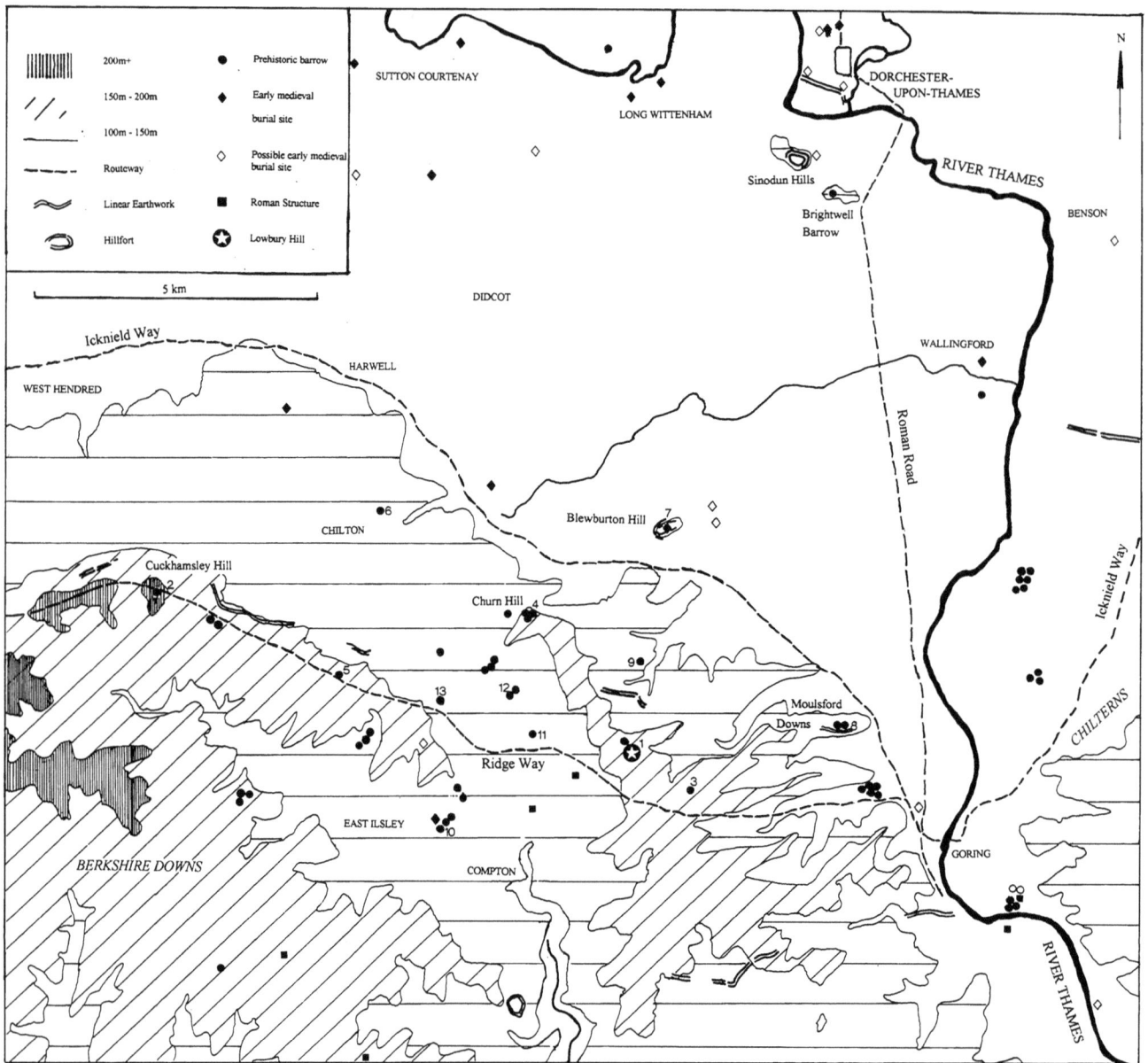

Fig. 34. *Lowbury Hill and its environs. 1 = Lowbury; 2 = Scutchamer Knob; 3 = Town Copse; 4 = Churn Knob; 5 = Gore Hill, West Ilsley; 6 = Hagbourne Hill; 7 = Blewburton Hillfort; 8 = Lingley Knoll; 9 = Aston Upthorpe; 10 = Cross Barrows, East Ilsley; 11 = Lower Chance Farm; 12 = Churn Farm; 13 = Fox Barrow.*

works of gods, ancestors, "Roman" or "British" groups, the barrow may have been situated to portray the high status group as the legitimate heirs to the power and authority of the past. This ritual association with a distant past may have helped to legitimise claims over land, people and resources (Bradley 1987; Härke 1994; Härke & Williams 1997; Williams 1997, 1998; see below).

Topography and view-sheds

The placing of the grave can also be described by considering topography and views from the site. Lowbury Hill is one of the highest points on the Berkshire Downs and the Saxon barrow is situated on the summit of the hill at 186 metres O.D. (Atkinson 1916, Fulford & Rippon 1994, Härke 1994:203, fig. 32 & 34). The selected location affords commanding long distant views in most directions. This can be demonstrated in a panorama based upon

photographs taken from the hilltop (fig. 35) and the estimated greatest distances visible from the hill in every direction (fig. 37). Northwards one looks into the Upper Thames valley towards the Sinudon Hills over Dorchester-upon-Thames, Boar's Hill west of Oxford and the hills east of Oxford around Garsington and Cuddesdon. The scarp of the Chilterns can be seen to the northeast. Prospects to the southeast are the most restricted but southwards observers have extensive long distance views to the Kennet valley and the North Downs over twenty eight kilometres away. Westwards, views extend over the northern scarp of the Berkshire Downs towards Cuckhamsley Hill (fig. 34 & 35).

A GIS study of the land visible from the hill gives the impression of a very partial intervisibility with the surrounding landscape (fig. 36, Fulford & Rippon 1994), yet this does not correspond with the perception of the view-shed when one visits the site. While prospects are relatively restricted to the east and southeast the *impression* is of a "balanced" and commanding panorama in all directions (fig. 35 & 37). Had the barrow been placed tens of metres from its actual location this effect would have been impeded and prospects in certain directions would have gained precedence over others. For example, this would have been the case had the Saxon barrow been placed within the temenos of the Romano-Celtic temple to the west of the summit.

Fieldwork demonstrates that other hill summits in the region around Lowbury do not afford similar all-round and extensive views. Only a high-point (187 m O.D.) near Warren Farm one kilometre southeast of Lowbury Hill might have offered a similar view-shed and summit location. Perhaps this site was not chosen because there was no ancient monument at this point while Lowbury Hill offered both summit location with all-round views as well as the ruins of the Roman structure. Early Medieval burial sites in the locality, including Aston Upthorpe, Blewburton, East Ilsley, Harwell, Upton, Wallingford and West Hendred (Meaney 1964, Dickinson 1976, Hamerow 1993), do not share the summit location and extensive views of the Saxon barrow at Lowbury (fig. 34, 37).

Prehistoric round barrows are numerous in the locality (Grinsell 1934, Richards 1978) and a representative sample were selected and visited for comparison with the Saxon barrow on Lowbury. An impression of the view-sheds available from these barrows can be gained by measuring the furthest distance intervisible with the site in each direction (fig. 38-42). Most of these barrows have different topographical positions from the Saxon grave. They are situated on spurs, breaks-of-slope, hillsides and valley bottoms. Many of these barrows have restricted or directed views over localised basins from which they are often "false-crested" (fig. 38-40, table 1, see also Richards 1978:35). The Bronze Age barrow cemeteries found north and east of Lowbury in the Thames valley are usually located in low-lying positions with relatively restricted views (e.g. Benson & Miles 1974, Gates 1975, Allen 1995:123-5).

There are a few barrows with long distant and broad panoramas comparable with Lowbury. These include the barrows at Churn Knob on Churn Hill northwest of Lowbury Hill and Gore Hill, West Ilsley (fig. 41). Despite the impressive views from these mounds, they only afford prospects northwards over the Thames valley. For example, vistas southwards from Churn Knob are blocked by the summit of Churn Hill. Therefore the experience of views from these sites is very different from the Lowbury barrow site.

Of all the sampled prehistoric round barrows in the vicinity, only two in the locality offer similar topographical locations and view-sheds to the Lowbury barrow (fig. 42). At Town Copse (southeast of Lowbury Hill), the barrow was placed on a hilltop but away from the highest point of the hill. This location afforded distant views south, north and east but this is at the expense of views to the west. Consequently this barrow does not fully achieve the "all-round" views of Lowbury. Scutchamer Knob on

Cuckhamsley Hill (west of Lowbury) is located on a hilltop summit with long distant views in most directions. In particular, Scutchamer Knob has views southwards towards the North Downs which are comparable to Lowbury. Yet there remain subtle differences from the Lowbury barrow. While the North Downs are visible to the south, much of the view is obscured by high ground close by both to the south and west. Therefore, in addition to the association with the Romano-Celtic temple, the topography and views from the Lowbury barrow provided a unique setting for the funeral and subsequent encounters with the Saxon grave. These qualities are shared by few other sites in the region.

Routeways

We must now consider the ways in which the barrow may have been perceived by those moving through the landscape. Fieldwork suggests an important association with the Ridge Way path traversing the scarp of the Berkshire Downs and passing close to Lowbury Hill immediately to the south (fig. 34). The path may have been used throughout the Early Medieval period, although its precise route and exact antiquity remain obscure (Atkinson 1916, Gelling 1978, Melpas 1987:33, Richard Bradley pers.comm., Andrew Reynolds pers.comm.) The line of the modern by-way may define approximately this ancient line of movement across the downs (Atkinson 1916). Even though the barrow is today heavily denuded, it remains sky-lined from the Ridge Way. In the Early Medieval period, when the barrow was presumably far higher and perhaps marked by a timber post or other mortuary structure, it would have dominated the northern skyline. For an observer approaching along the scarp of the Berkshire Downs from the west, Lowbury Hill first comes into view near Scutchamer Knob on Cuckhamsley Hill. Lowbury then remains in view for nine kilometres (fig. 43). Before being eroded and denuded, the barrow would have been visible for much of this route, passing out of view only for the short distance that the Ridge Way ascends towards Lowbury. For those approaching from the east, the Lowbury barrow is revealed to the observer after a long and gradual ascent from the Thames valley.

The dry valley immediately west of Lowbury Hill describes an important north-south routeway through the Berkshire Downs passing Compton where a minster church was founded in the later Saxon period (Blair 1994:57, fig. 34). In addition to the relationship with the Ridge Way, it may be significant that the Lowbury barrow would have been sky-lined from this route of movement as well. Approaching Lowbury from Blewburton hillfort to the north over the foothills of the downs, the barrow is sky-lined from the tops of rises even in its modern denuded state. Similarly, approaching from the northeast along the "Fair Mile" the barrow would have dominated the approach to the downs. Such routes may hold great antiquity, being used by people moving between the arable and grazing on the downs and lowland meadows (Hooke 1985:141-2). It can be demonstrated by fieldwork that no other hilltop, Early Medieval burial site or prehistoric barrow site could have afforded such a dominant location in relation to routes of movement through the landscape.

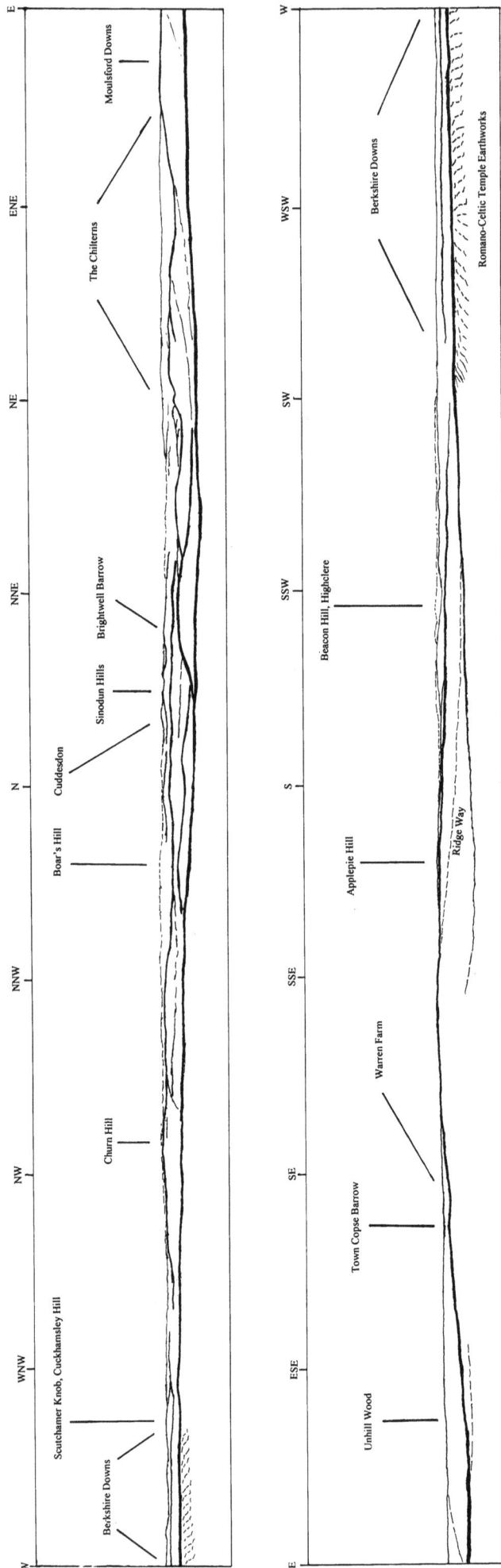

Fig. 35. *Panorama from Lowbury Hill showing the long distant and 'balanced' nature of the view. Drawn from photographs by the author.*

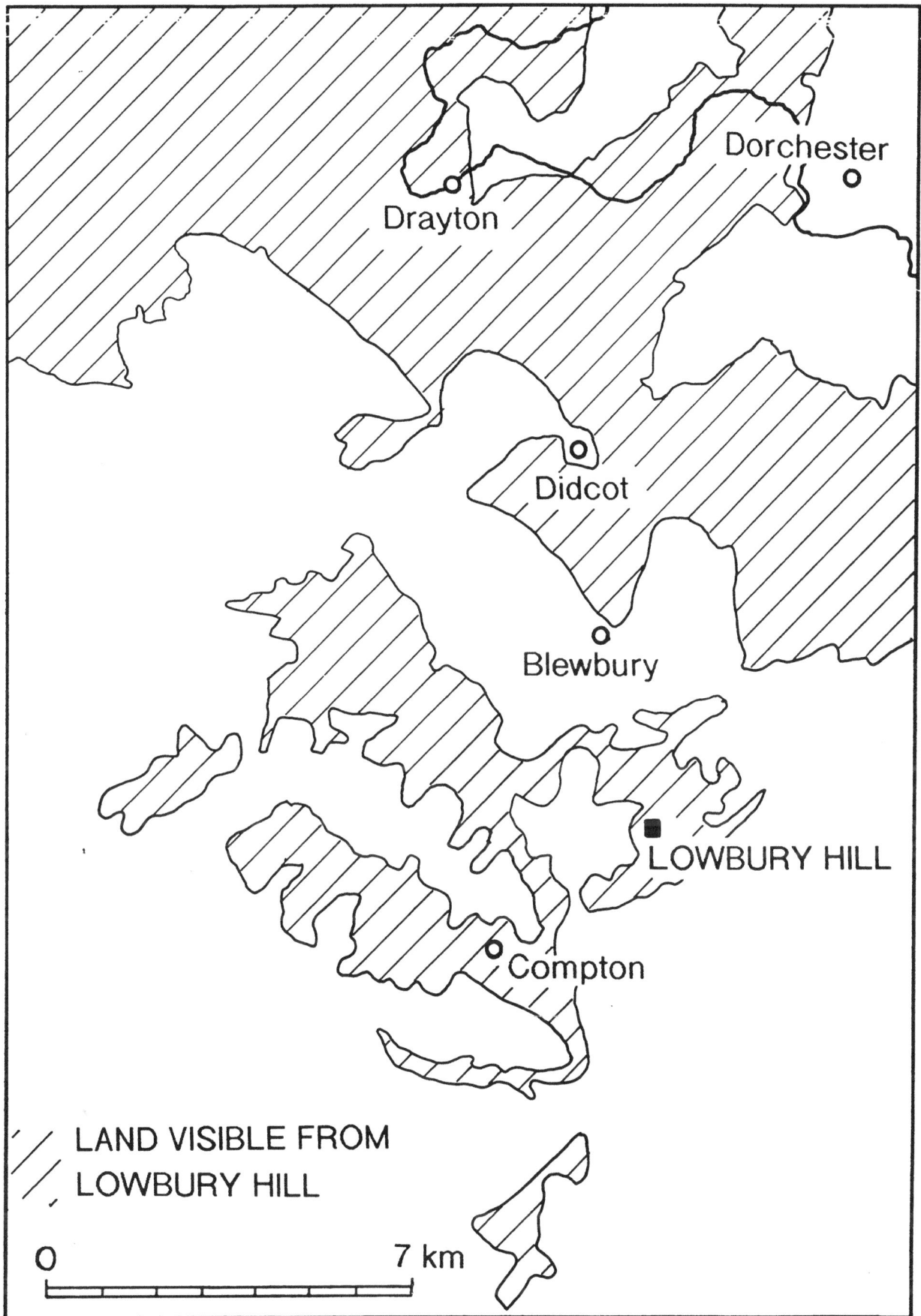

Fig. 36. *A GIS study showing land visible from Lowbury Hill (after Fulford & Rippon 1994).*

Lowbury Hill

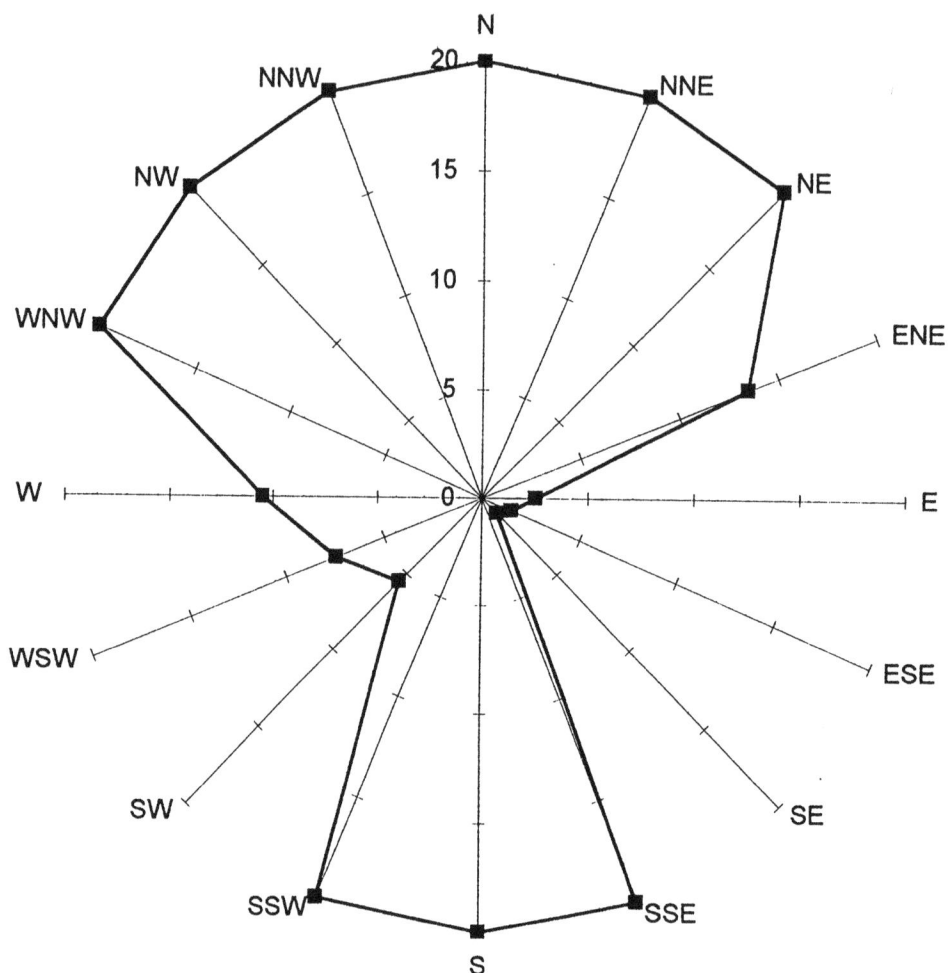

Fig. 37. *The extent of views (in kilometres) from Lowbury Hill.*

For example, by comparing the length of the Ridge Way intervisible from Lowbury with that of prehistoric barrows, a clear contrast can be observed (fig. 43).

From other routes in the Thames valley (fig. 34), Lowbury Hill would have been visible for many kilometres. Although we cannot tell whether the barrow itself could be seen from such distances given its denuded state, the small bushes on Lowbury Hill can be clearly discerned for up to ten kilometres within the Thames valley. Presumably a sizeable barrow with a modest mortuary structure or timber post would have been highly visible from the north when newly built. For example, had there been an Early Medieval east-west route connecting the ford of the Thames at Wallingford with the Icknield Way around Harwell, Lowbury Hill would have been clearly visible (if not prominent) for many kilometres on the southern sky-line.

However, the hill and barrow would have been invisible from long sections of other routes passing closer to Lowbury. This is the case for the important routes described by the river Thames and the Roman road from Dorchester-upon-Thames to Silchester passing through

Streatley (for the route of road see Margary 1969:150-152, Melpas 1987). The Saxon barrow was close to the Icknield Way that passed along the base of the downs to the north of Lowbury. (Atkinson 1916; Gelling 1978, 1979; Melpas 1987). However, Lowbury Hill would have been obscured from view for travellers moving along the Icknield Way by the foothills of the downs. It seems as if the barrow's location was selected to be extremely visible from routes passing through the Berkshire Downs at the expense of others traversing the Thames valley.

This investigation of routes of movement highlights a further aspect of the relationship between Lowbury and ancient monuments. As we have seen, Lowbury hill is surrounded by prehistoric barrows (fig. 34). While approaching Lowbury from any direction, travellers would have passed by these structures en route to the summit. It is tempting to suggest that these encounters with ancient monuments and distant views of the Saxon barrow sky-lined on the hill-top may have combined to encourage relationships and distinctions between the Saxon monument and the vestiges of the ancient past.

Blewburton Hillfort Rampart: Anglo-Saxon Cemetery

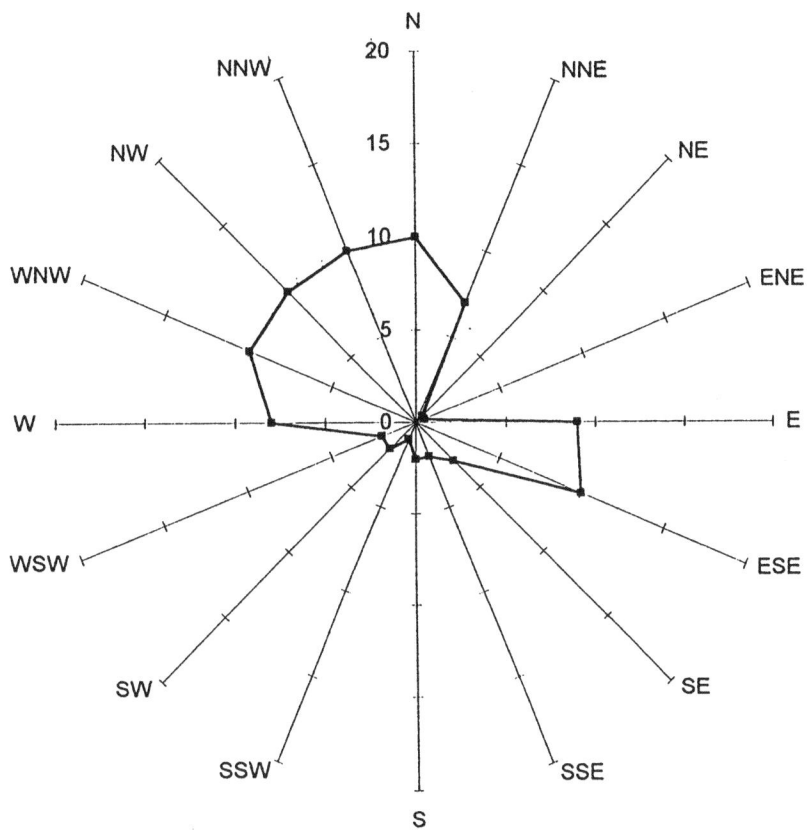

East Ilsley barrows and Anglo-Saxon burial

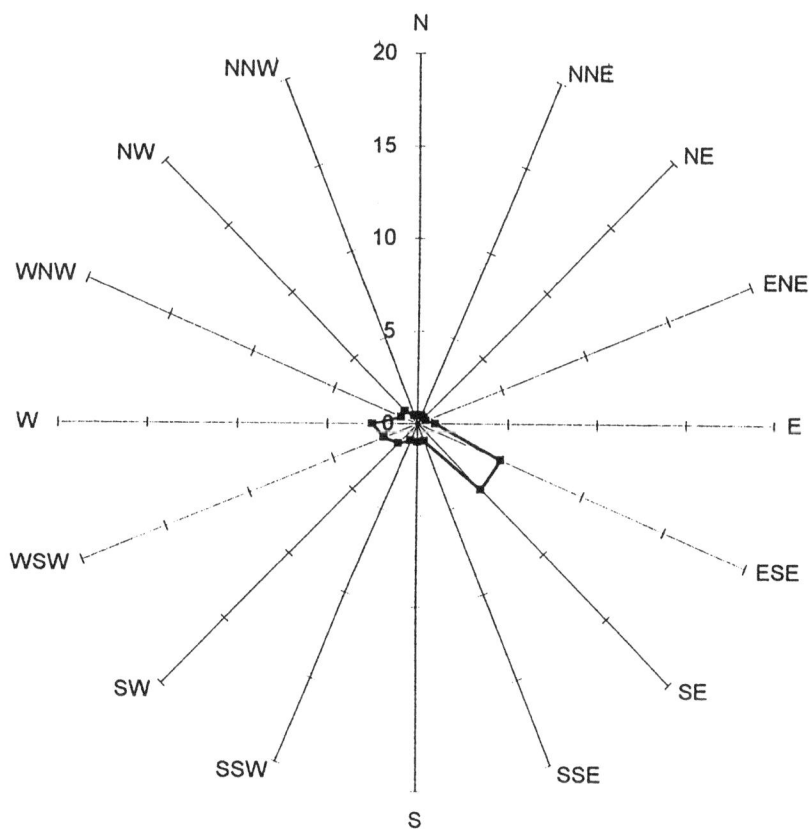

Fig. 38*. The extent of views (km) from (a) Blewburton Hill Anglo-Saxon cemetery and (b) the barrows and Early Medieval burials of Cross Barrows, East Ilsley.*

Lower Chance Farm

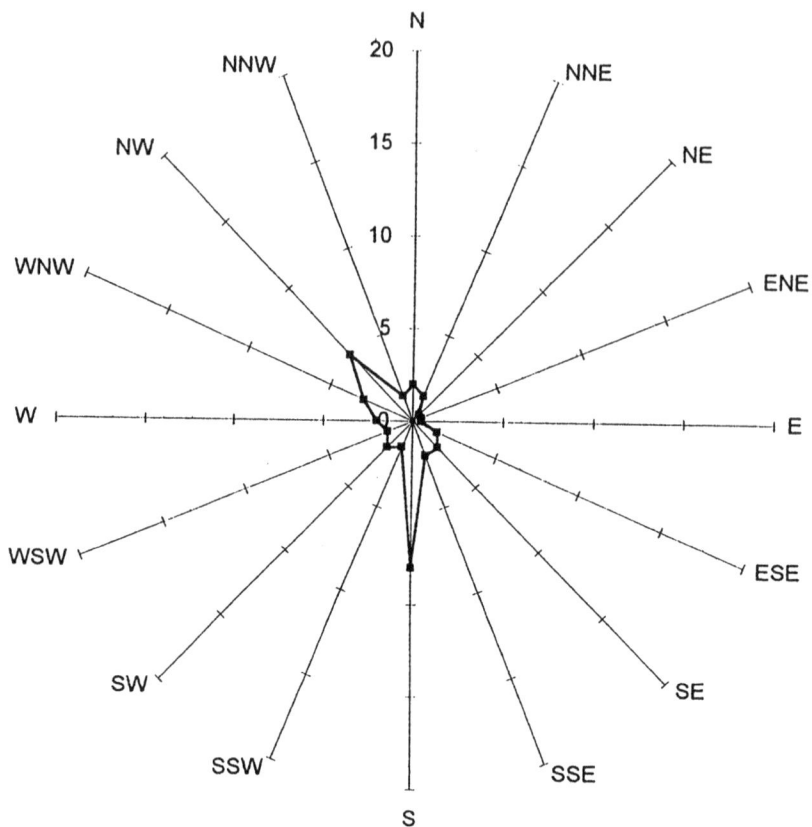

Churn Farm Barrow

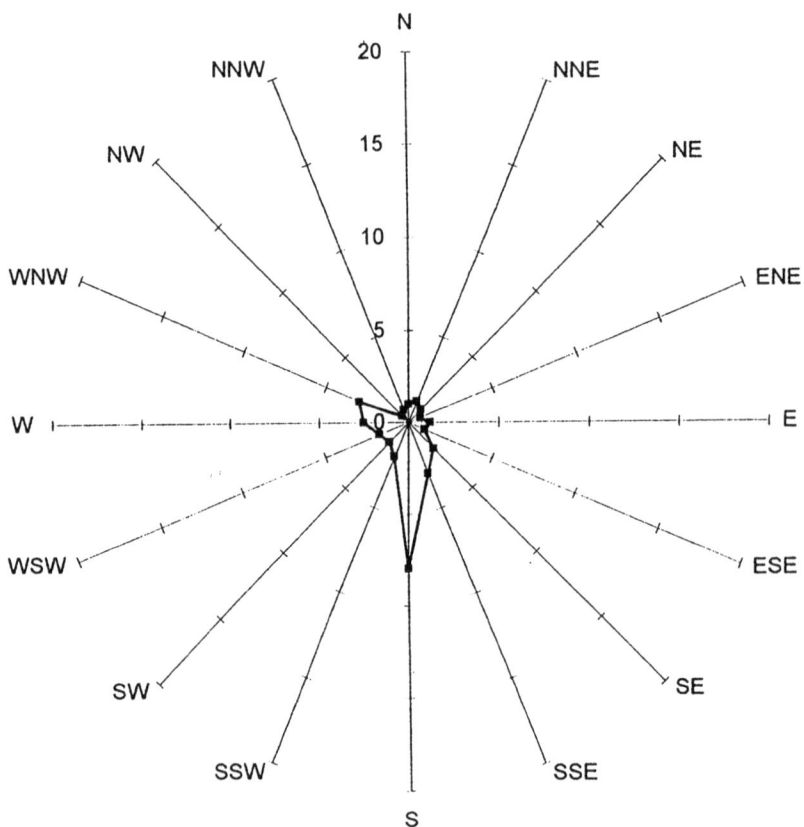

Fig. 39. *The extent of views (km) from barrows located on valley bottoms; (a) Lower Chance Farm and (b) Churn Farm.*

Aston Upthorpe Disc Barrow

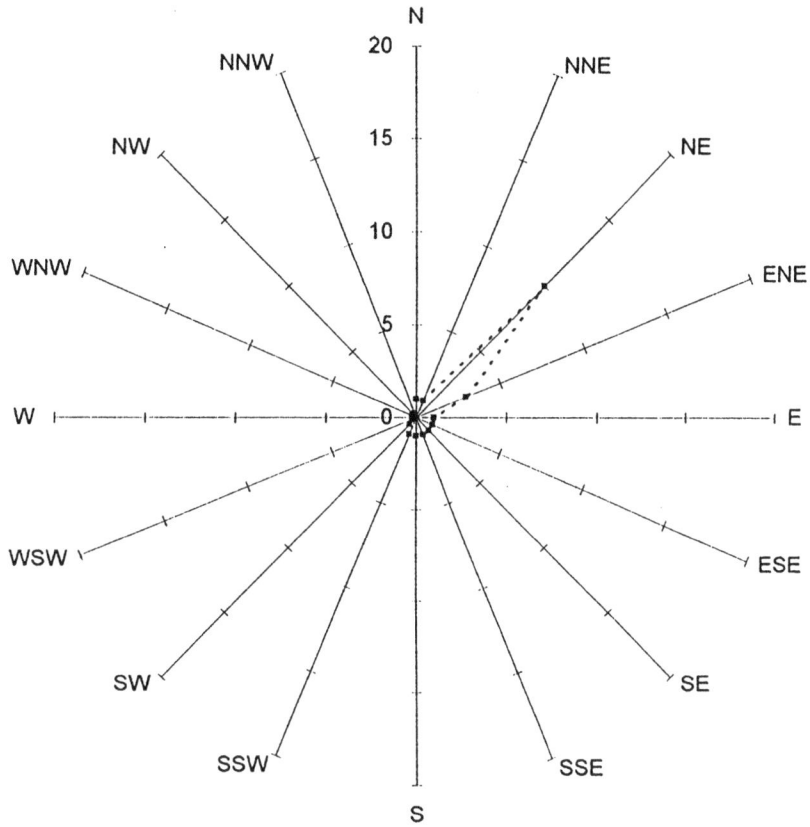

Fox Barrow

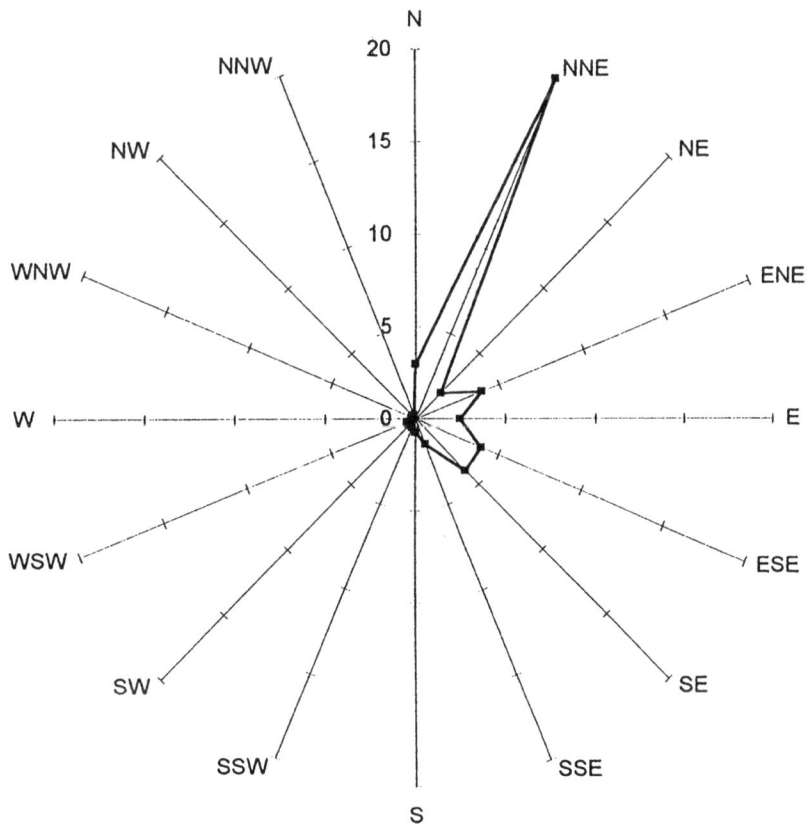

Fig. 40. The extent of views (km) from barrows located on (a) hillsides (Aston Upthorpe) and (b) spurs (Fox barrow).

Hagbourne Hill

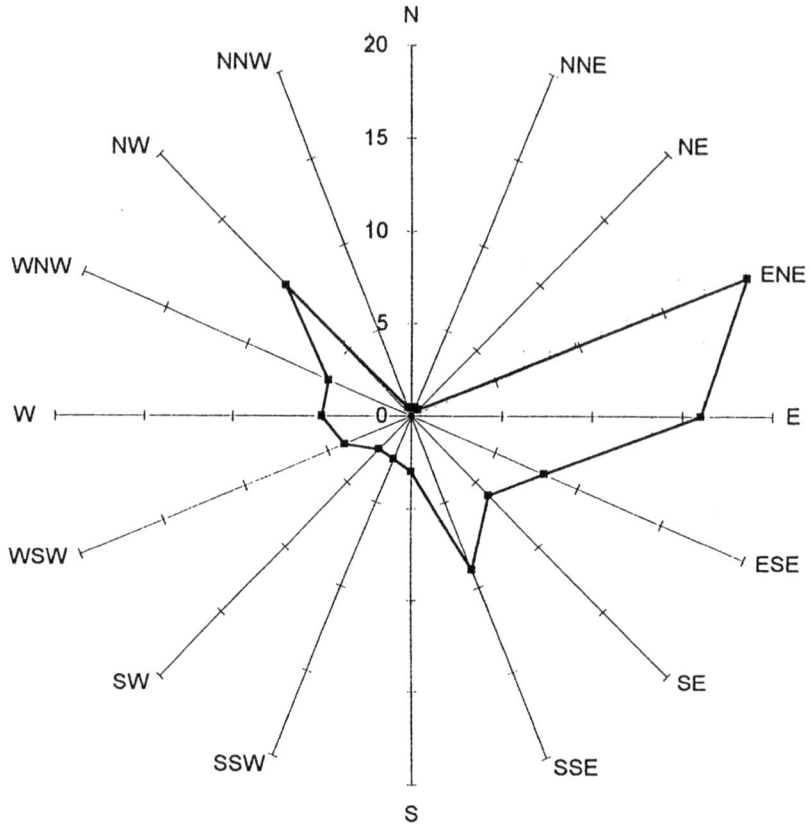

Fig. 40 (contd) *. The extent of views (km) from barrows located on (c) spurs (Hagbourne Hill).*

Gore Hill, West Ilsley

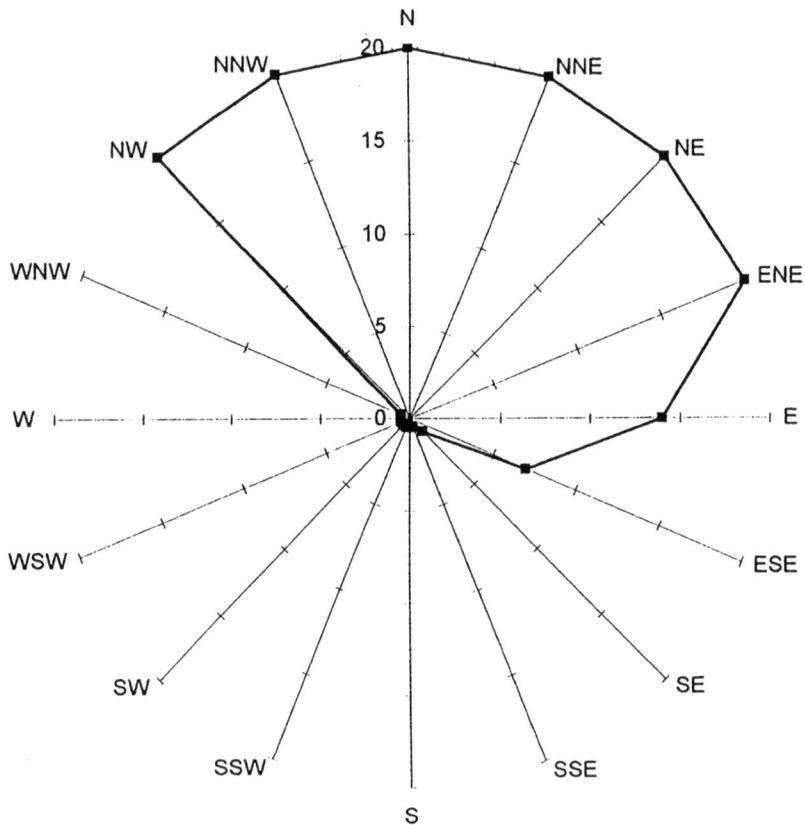

Fig. 41. *The extent of views (km) from barrows located (a) on breaks of slope (Gore Hill, West Ilsley).*

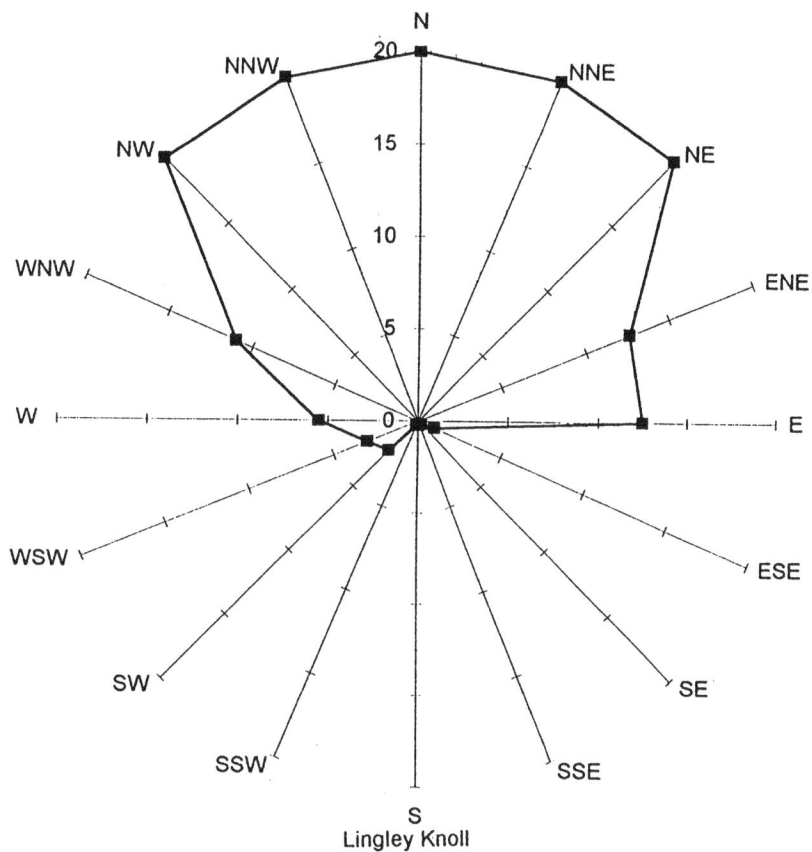

Fig. 41 (contd.). *The extent of views (km) from barrows located (b) on breaks of slope (Churn Knob) and (c) on ridges (Lingley Knoll).*

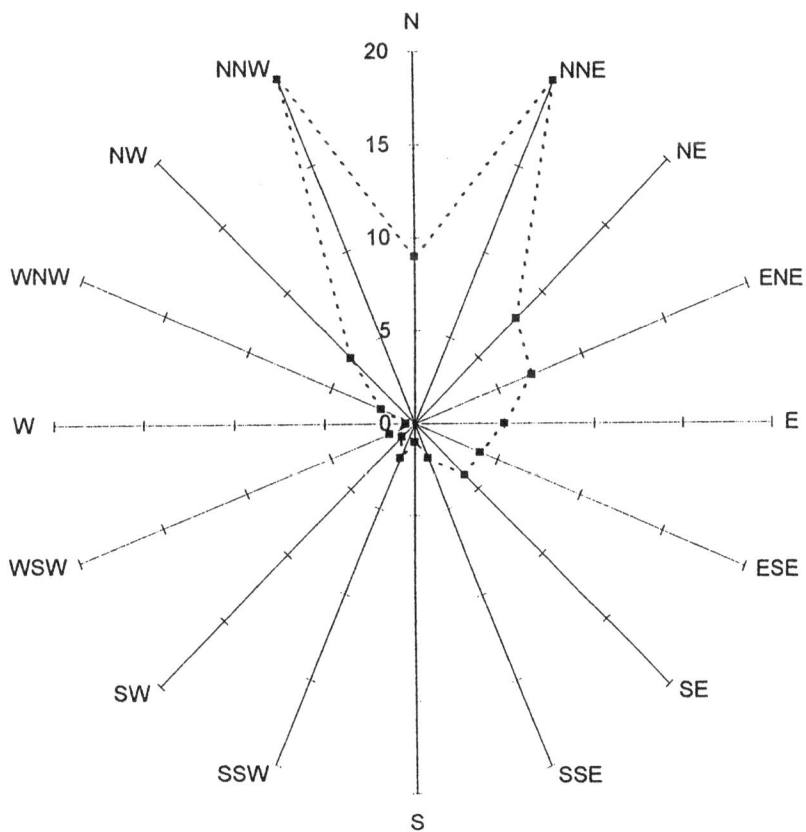

Town Copse

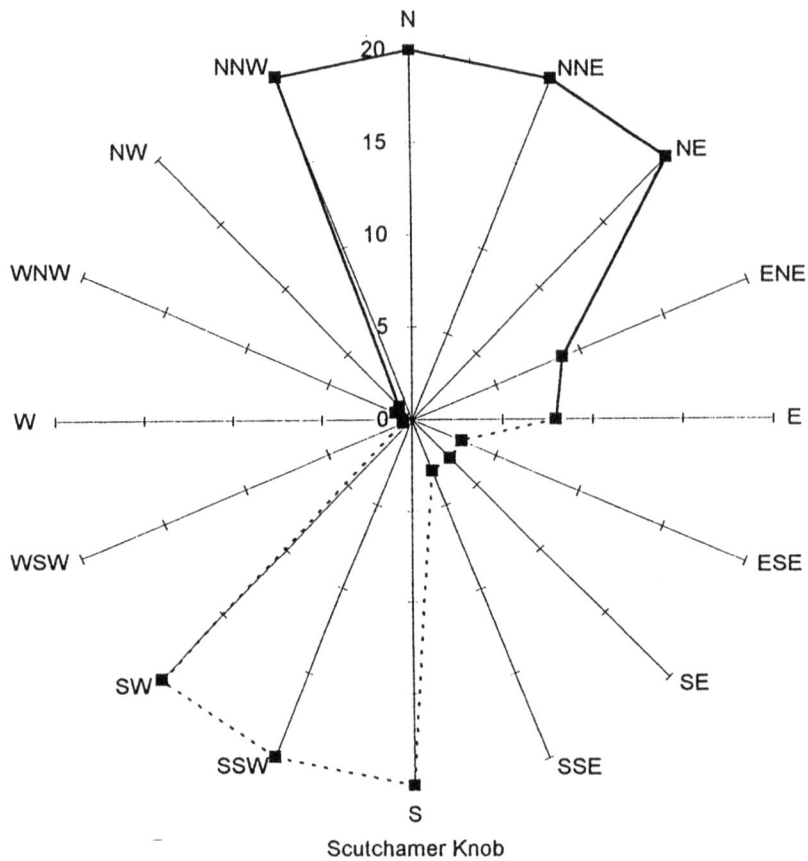

Scutchamer Knob

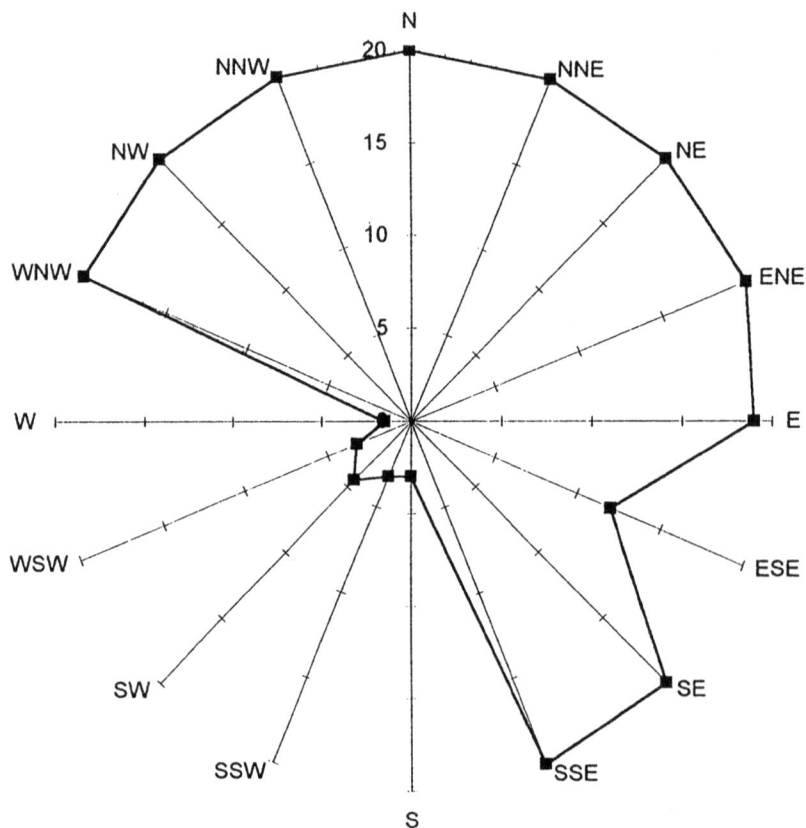

Fig. 42. *The extent of views (km) from barrows located on hilltops (a) off-summit (Town Copse) and (b) on-summit (Scutchamer Knob).*

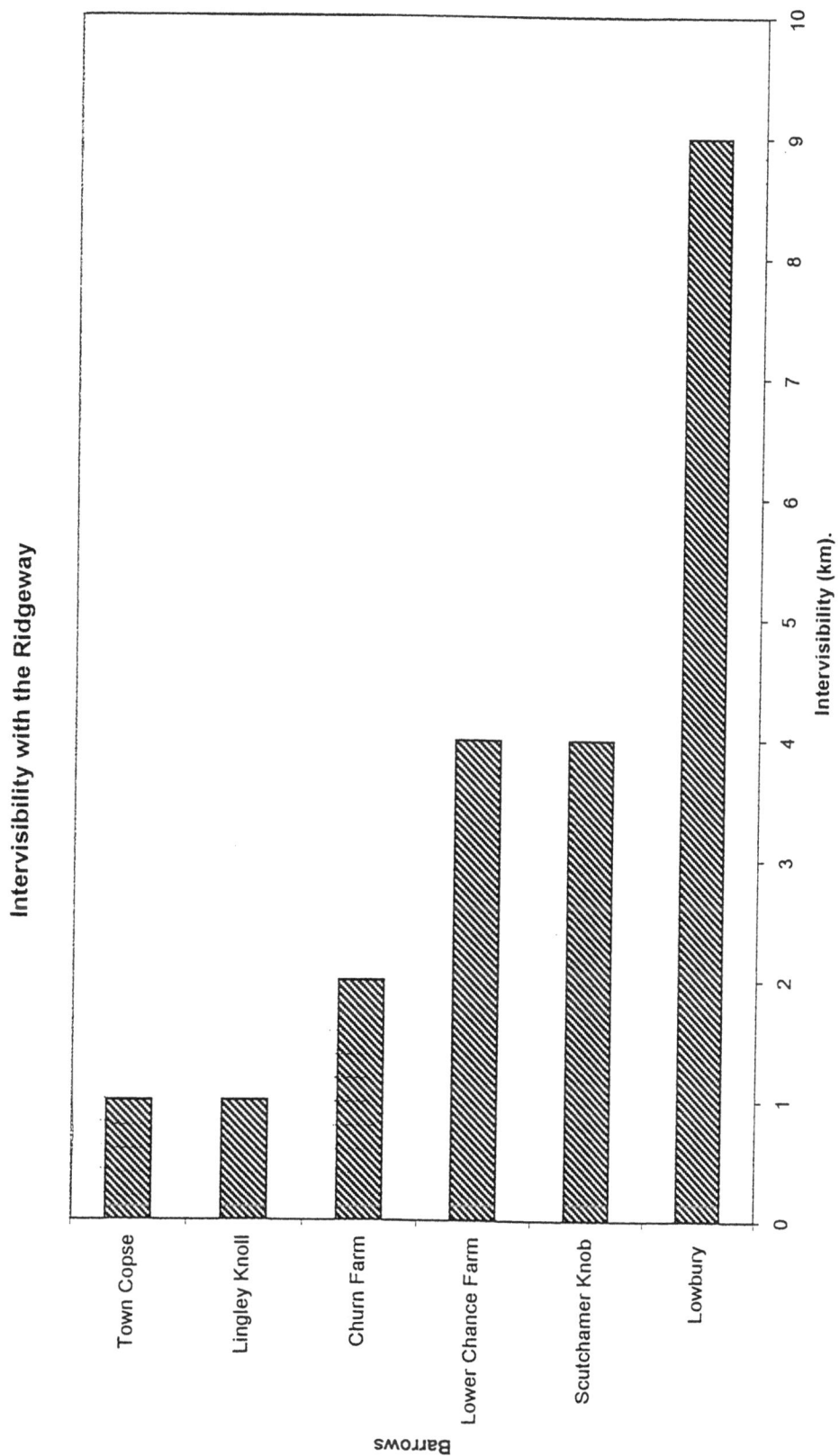

Fig. 43. The lengths of intervisibility (km) between barrows and the Ridge Way demonstrating the dominant location of Lowbury in relation to the route.

	Monument type	Early medieval burial	Early medieval place name/reference	Topography	Views	Intervisible with ridgeway	Distance from ridgeway (km)	Distance of ridgeway intervisibility (km).	Intervisible with Blewbury estate boundary	Distance from Blewbury boundary (km)
Lowbury	Bowl barrow	Y	Y	Summit	All round, distant	Y	0.6	9	Y	0.1
Scutchamer Knob	Bowl barrow	?	Y	Summit	All round, distant	Y	0.1	4	N	4.2
Town Copse	Bowl barrow	?	N	Hilltop, off summit	Wide, long	Y	0.4	1	Y	0.7
Lingley Knoll	Bowl barrow	?	N	Ridge top	Wide, long	Y	1.3	1	Y	2.0
Hagbourne Hill	Bowl barrow	?	N	Spur, BS	Wide, long	N	2.8	0	Y	1.7
Cross Barrows, East Ilsley	Bowl barrows (3)	N	N	Spur	Directed, short	N	0.9	0	N	1.6
Fox Barrow	Bowl barrow	?	Y	Spur	Directed, short	N	0.7	0	Y	0
Aston Upthorpe	Disc barrow	?	N	Hillside	directed, short	N	2	0	N	1.5
West Isley	Bowl barrow	?	N	Hillside, BS	directed, short	N	0.1	0	Y	0.6
Churn Knob	Bowl barrow	?	N	Hillside, BS	Wide, long	N	2.4	0	Y	1.4
Blewburton hillfort	Hillfort	Y	N	Hillside, BS	Wide, short	N	4.1	0	Y	1.4
Churn Farm	Bowl barrow (2)	?	N	Valley Floor	Restricted	Y	0.9	2	Y	0.9
Lower Chance farm	Bowl barrow	?	N	Bottom of hill	Restricted	Y	0.2	4	Y	0.2

Table 1. *A summary of information on the location of Lowbury Saxon barrow and comparison with neighbouring prehistoric sites and Early Medieval burials.*

The main axes of movement through the landscape would have been important for the builders of the Lowbury barrow, since they structured the ways in which the barrow would be seen, experienced and interpreted. Perhaps such routes were incorporated into the funeral procession in some way. Travellers passing along the Ridge Way would find it difficult to avoid referencing or acknowledging the presence of the barrow, either as a marker on the journey or as a known grave of a powerful individual. The situation of the grave suggests a desire for the identity, status and authority of those that placed the grave on Lowbury Hill to be recognised and respected by all those moving through the landscape.

Territory and settlement

Finally, we need to consider the Saxon barrow on Lowbury Hill in terms of its relationship to territorial units and settlement patterns. By the late Saxon period, Lowbury Hill lay at the southern extent of Blewbury Hundred and the charter bounds have been reconstructed by Margaret Gelling (Gelling 1978, 1979). Other than Lowbury, no prominent hilltops are incorporated into the route of the boundary and only two other barrows (Fox barrow and Lower Chance Farm) are as close to, and intervisible with, the Blewbury estate boundary. Neither barrow is situated in a prominent position (table 1).

There are well known difficulties of interpreting relationships between burial sites and later boundaries and a number of different interpretive scenarios are possible (Bonney 1966, 1976; Goodier 1984; Hooke 1985:132). For example, territories may have changed between the seventh and tenth centuries and the boundary may have only incorporated the hilltop once the barrow was centuries old. However there is circumstantial evidence that might support the validity and social significance of the association of the barrow and boundary. Many scholars believe that late Saxon estates were not created *de novo*. Della Hooke has suggested that some of the estates on the northern scarp of the Berkshire Downs could have been created as part of a gradual process during the middle Saxon period, while others see them having much greater antiquity (Hooke 1988:127-141, see also Richards 1978:53, Tingle 1991:70). The distribution of burial sites provides some supporting evidence for such assertions. Blewbury estate is named after, and focuses upon, an Iron Age hillfort (Gelling 1978, Semple 1998:116) re-used during the late fifth and sixth centuries for a mixed-rite Anglo-Saxon cemetery (Collins & Collins 1959, Williams 1997, Semple 1998). A concentration of early Anglo-Saxon burial sites is known from around Blewburton Hill. The hillfort may have been a focus for settlement and communal gatherings as well as burial. If so, it seems possible that the Lowbury barrow burial lay in a peripheral and "liminal" location in relation to this settlement and burial activity. This may have been the case already in the seventh century. In this regard it is interesting to note the association with the Iron Age earthwork Grim's Ditch runs along the base of the Berkshire Downs immediately north of Lowbury. This ancient boundary is incorporated into the bounds of the Blewbury estate near Fox barrow (Gelling 1978). Therefore we have strong hints that the Lowbury

barrow may have been close to the contemporary boundary of an "archaic hundred" or "multiple estate" centred on Blewburton hillfort (for other examples, see Hooke 1995).

There are hints that boundaries in middle and late Anglo-Saxon charters were defined as much by ritual procession as by the written documents in which they are recorded (Kelly 1990:44, 46). The peripheral location of the Lowbury barrow can be related to this evidence. The funeral procession, burial rites, barrow building and other rituals could have held an important role in defining boundaries in order to legitimise control of land and other resources (Charles-Edwards 1976, Shephard 1979, Carver 1998).

On a regional level the barrow also seems peripheral (fig. 32 & 34). Our knowledge of Anglo-Saxon settlement patterns in the Upper Thames region is strongly biased towards the gravel terraces (Scull 1992:264-268), yet it seems clear that the focus of settlement was upon the terraces along the Thames and its major tributaries (Dickinson 1976, Hawkes 1986, Hamerow 1992, Blair 1994). During the seventh century, Dorchester-upon-Thames became the first episcopal see of the West Saxon kingdom and later received Mercian patronage (Dickinson 1974, Hawkes 1986:88, Blair 1994). Close by there appears to be a number of early royal or high status sites such as Benson. At Drayton substantial halls have been recognised from aerial photography (Benson & Miles 1974:60-2; Hawkes 1986:88-89; Hooke 1988:125; Blair 1988, 1994). Abingdon was another possible seventh century foundation (Hooke 1995:85-6). By Domesday, the upper Thames region focused upon Abingdon and Dorchester was one of the most densely populated regions in England (Hooke 1988:124-6, Blair 1994).

In contrast, there is limited evidence of Anglo-Saxon settlement on the Berkshire Downs (Richards 1978:51-55). This is not to say that the landscape around Lowbury was uninhabited or sparsely settled, since Anglo-Saxon pottery found in low densities may still represent land-use and settlement (Gaffney & Tingle 1989:145, Tingle 1991:71, pace Härke 1994:203). However, it does appear that the barrow marked an area that was relatively peripheral in the Early Medieval period, away from concentrations of settlement and political authority. It may be significant that the hilltop affords views over the Dorchester region, and from the Thames valley Lowbury Hill frames the southern horizon as part of the northern scarp of the Berkshire Downs. These visual relationships may have contributed to the significance of the hilltop. As well as forming a political or social boundary, the hill marked the visual boundary of the Upper Thames region. In this way the barrow acted as a symbolic and physical marker of territory. Could it be relevant that the inhumation was orientated with the head to the south, so that the dead would "look out" to the north over the Thames valley? The barrow may have created or maintained links between a high status social group and an important physical and political boundary marked by the southern edge of the upper Thames region. Equally the grave may have marked the northern extent of the estates on the eastern Berkshire Downs (Hawkes 1986, Eagles 1994).

On an inter-regional scale, the Upper Thames region and the local territory around Dorchester-upon-Thames was also "liminal" (Morris 1993:21), because the region became a focus for conflict and changing boundaries between the West Saxon and Mercian kingdoms during the later seventh century (Blair 1994). Indeed, Ashdown and the area around Lowbury Hill may have marked the northernmost extent of the West Saxon kingdom for some time during the later seventh century (Eagles 1994:25). The relationship of the Lowbury barrow to these shifting territories at a number of nested levels appears complex and ambiguous, but may have been important in selecting the location of the grave.

Summary

In summary, the specific location chosen for the Lowbury barrow may have been associated with important route-ways, and placed on the edge of a local and regional territory away from concentrations of settlement. It is argued that the grave was placed to emphasise an association with the material remains from the distant past in the form of the Romano-Celtic temple. Furthermore the barrow was placed on the summit of one of the highest hills in the region. This situation afforded extensive vistas over the surrounding landscape. These characteristics are

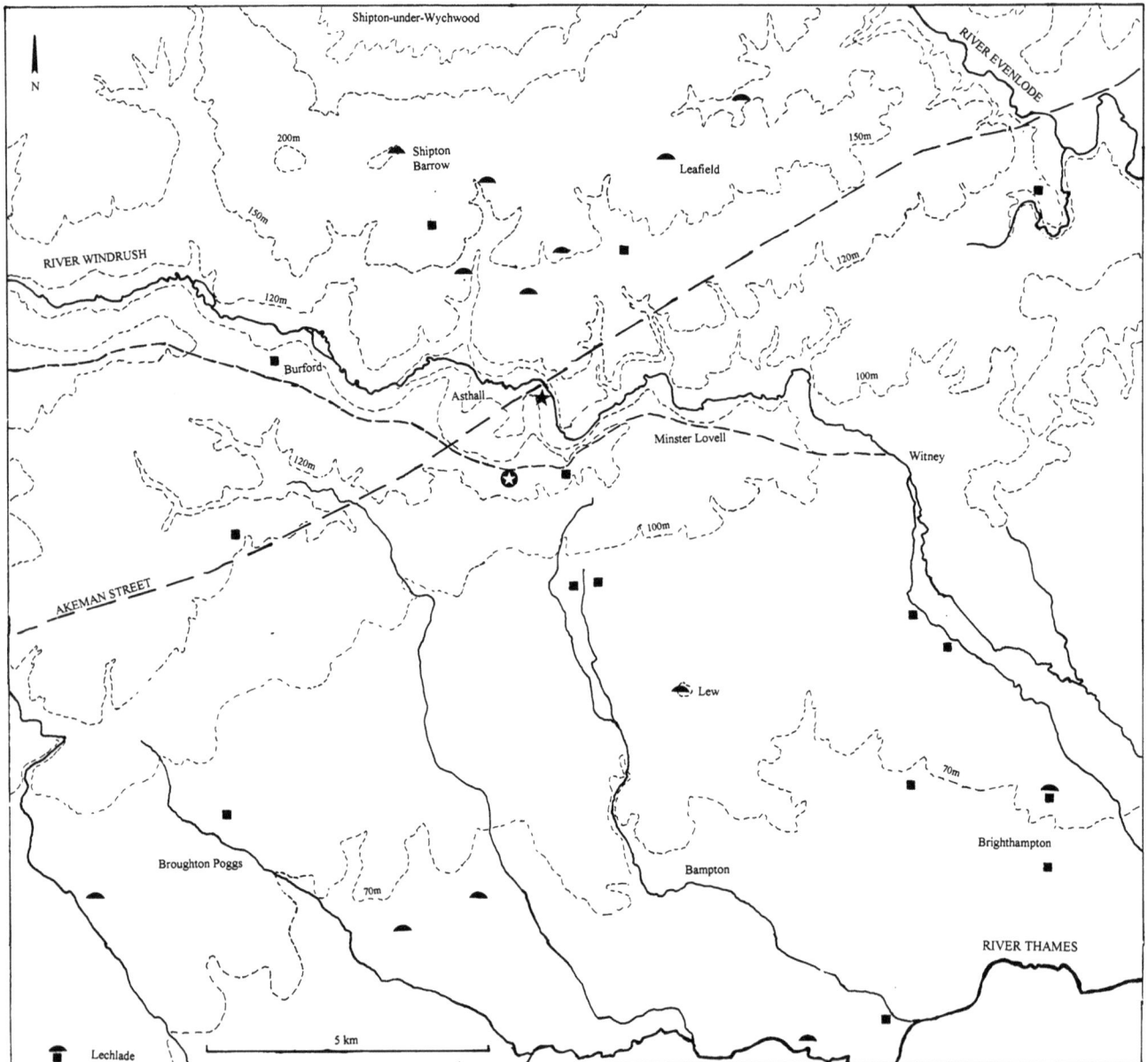

Fig. 44. The region around Asthall barrow in north Oxfordshire showing relationships with route-ways, ancient monuments and other Anglo-Saxon burial sites. Star in circle = Asthall barrow. Black star = Asthall Romano-British small town. Black semi-circles = Single round barrows and round barrow cemeteries. Black squares = Anglo-Saxon burial sites.

not shared by other locations in the environs. Individually these aspects do not explain the location of the Saxon barrow. For example, it is difficult to explain the barrow's situation solely in terms of monument reuse (*pace* Härke 1994; Härke & Williams 1997; Williams 1997, 1998). Instead it is the combination of factors that begins to suggest a logic behind the grave's placing in the landscape.

Other high status burial sites

In addition to a detailed study of the placing of the Saxon barrow at Lowbury, it is important to consider whether comparable principles of location apply to other high status burial sites across southern and eastern England.

Asthall

Within the Upper Thames region, similar patterns were identified by fieldwork around the early seventh century cremation barrow burial at Asthall (NGR SP 290101: see also Dickinson & Speake 1992, fig. 44 & 45). The barrow was placed on a ridge-top, close to the Roman road Akeman Street (Hawkes 1986:91, Dickinson & Speake 1992). The barrow would have been sky-lined along this route in antiquity. Another important and ancient west to east route from Minster Lovell to Burford and Gloucestershire passes directly by the barrow (Grundy 1933, fig. 46). In later centuries, the barrow was close to a salt road from Droitwich in the west Midlands into the upper Thames region (Blair 1994). The location affords vistas in all directions, but especially southeast over the Thames valley towards Dorchester. In the far distance, the Berkshire Downs define the southern horizon. The barrow is some distance from the concentrations of seventh century burial sites, presumably reflecting concentrations of settlement, found to the southeast near the confluence of the River Thames and the River Windrush (Dickinson 1976, fig. 44). Also, the monument is close to hundred-boundaries; the intersection of the territories of minster churches established at Bampton, Minster Lovell and Shipton (Blair 1994:70). This boundary is very important because it defines the edge of Wychwood. This is thought by some scholars to mark the ancient boundary zone between the kingdoms of the *Gewissae* (the "West Saxons in the upper Thames region") and the Hwicce of the southwest Midlands during the seventh century (Leeds 1939:359, Dickinson & Speake 1992, Blair 1994, Hooke 1998).

Barrows in the vicinity of Asthall are largely undated, and many have been suggested as Saxon in date (Leeds 1939:365, 367; Hawkes 1986; Dickinson & Speake 1992, Blair 1994:45). There is no direct evidence to support this assertion and it has long been realised that the date of barrows cannot be ascertained from form and size alone (Grinsell 1934, *pace* Hawkes 1986:91). It therefore seems more appropriate to assume a prehistoric date for most of them, and this view is supported by evidence from antiquarian excavations (Leeds 1939:243-44). The views and topography of these undated barrows vary considerably; but many are on hillsides with restricted views overlooking narrow valleys in contrast to the Asthall monument. A few large barrows are placed on high summits with wide and distant views at Shipton, Leafield and Lew. The view-sheds from these summit barrows are comparable to Asthall although they do not appear as closely related to boundaries and routes of movement.

Early Medieval burial sites of the local region around Asthall are not found in comparable locations. At Burford and Minster Lovell (Leeds 1939:366-7, Kennet 1969, Dickinson 1976), burial sites are situated on hillsides south of the Windrush valley like Asthall. However, observations suggest that these sites do not afford comparable all-round views in the manner of the Asthall barrow. Furthermore, these burial sites are not associated with Akeman Street or the intersection of hundred-boundaries. The vast majority of other Early Medieval burial sites in the region (Meaney 1964, Dickinson 1976, Dickinson & Speake 1992) are placed on valley floors, terraces and hillsides rather than on ridge tops and summits of hills. Like Lowbury, the location of Asthall stands out from surrounding barrows and Early Medieval burial sites.

However, there are slight differences between the locations of Lowbury and Asthall. While some Roman pottery was incorporated into the barrow material (Dickinson & Speake 1992) and Neolithic material has been recovered close by (Leeds 1939:242; NMR 917740, 332376), there is no definite evidence for a pre-existing and visible monument close to the Asthall barrow. In the environs, there are well attested cases of Early Medieval monument reuse for burial at Lyneham long barrow (Conder 1896) and the Standlake Down round barrow cemetery (Dickinson 1973, Williams 1997). There is also tentative evidence that the minster at Bampton was founded on a Bronze Age barrow cemetery (Blair 1998, Semple 1998). It appears that the Saxon barrow is set apart from concentrations of prehistoric barrows to the north and southeast (Barclay et al 1996) but may have referenced the material remains of the past in a different way. From the Asthall barrow, the Leafield and Lew barrows, and possibly also the Shipton barrow would have been sky-lined. Additionally, the barrow overlooks the remains of the Roman small town near the Medieval village of Asthall. Few other locations can command these visual references with prominent ancient sites. These patterns of intervisibility combined with the physical similarity of the Asthall barrow to the nearby prehistoric mounds may have created links between past and present in an equivalent manner to the reuse of an ancient site.

Lowbury and Asthall differ in another way. In contrast to Lowbury, the Asthall barrow is placed slightly north of the highest point of the hill (fig. 45). This may have been a deliberate feature of the barrow's location because this situation facilitates views into the Windrush valley, the Roman road and Roman small town to the north without losing views in other directions. Even though the ground rises to the summit of the hill immediately south of the barrow, extensive views south and southeast over the Thames valley towards the scarp of the Berkshire Downs are maintained. Therefore the positioning of the barrow slightly north of the hilltop may have been a compromise that created a "balanced" view similar to the placing of the Lowbury barrow.

Taplow

The wealthy male burial at Taplow Buckinghamshire (NGR SU 906822) is dated to the early seventh century. The monument is situated on a chalk promontory with wide and distant views over the Thames valley (Smith 1905, Stocker & Went 1995). The barrow is not placed on the break-of-slope, but instead it is set back in a slightly higher situation that encourages wide views. The barrow was placed within the perimeter of an earthwork fortification of prehistoric date (Smith 1905). There are hints of prehistoric and Roman material incorporated into the barrow's construction (Smith 1905). The site is adjacent to, and intervisible with, the River Thames. The Thames may have been an important boundary between the territories of the Middle Saxons and a postulated tribal territory identified as the *Sunningas* (Gelling 1974, Blair 1991). Downstream from Taplow, the Thames forms the boundary between the kingdoms of the Middle Saxons and Surrey (Blair 1991). The barrow was close to the early monastic foundation upstream at Cookham (Gelling 1979, Hooke 1995:86). Furthermore, the river valley would have been an important route for water and land traffic (Stocker & Went 1995). All travellers moving by water along the Thames or by land along its banks would have seen the barrow sky-lined from great distances downstream (fig. 47). Once again fieldwork demonstrates that nearby prehistoric barrows (e.g. Cock Marsh barrows: Grinsell 1934:49-50) and Early Medieval burial sites (e.g. Cock Marsh, Cookham, Bourne End: Grinsell 1934:49-50, Meaney 1964, Farley 1987) do not occupy similar topographical locations, view-sheds or relations with routes and boundaries.

Cuddesdon

The fourth high status burial in the Thames valley is situated upon a prominent hilltop at Cuddesdon (NGR SP 599032). The wealth of the grave goods retrieved from this site suggests the presence of a barrow burial of the early seventh century although evidence for a barrow was not found (Dickinson 1974). The wealthy burial was situated on the highest point of the hill with wide and distant views in most directions. A Roman villa is known to have existed on the hill-top and the grave may have been situated in relation to the ruins in a manner comparable with the Lowbury barrow's association with the Roman temple (Dickinson 1974, Hassal 1939:100). The grave would have been peripherally placed but intervisible with the Anglo-Saxon centre of Dorchester-upon-Thames (see above). The location utilises the nearest prominent landmark to the hundred-boundary and in many ways the situation of the site is directly comparable to Taplow, Asthall and especially Lowbury. Although relationships with important route-ways are more elusive, the barrow (assuming one was present) would have been sky-lined from lower ground to the east and south and would have been a commanding landmark for people moving through the Upper Thames valley.

Discussion: the Thames Valley high status burials

The fact that four high status barrow burials within the Thames valley display similar criteria for location might not seem surprising until we realise just how few Early Medieval burial sites in the region can be regarded in a comparable way. While monument reuse by Early Medieval burial sites appears commonplace, few are on ridges or summits of hills with extensive all-round views, associated with boundaries and routes of movement. In contrast to high status graves which appear to be placed with reference to regional territories on prominent hill-tops, it could be argued that lower status communal burial sites were closely associated with contemporary patterns of settlement and land-use even when reusing ancient structures.

Wessex

Outside the Thames valley similar locations were chosen for high status graves. In Wiltshire, the extremely wealthy female bed burial on Swallowcliffe Down, and the weapon burials from Maiden Bradley and Coombe Bissett (Meaney 1964, Bonney 1976, Speake 1989, Eagles 1994) follow identical patterns to those suggested for the Thames Valley sites. For example, the Swallowcliffe bed burial reused a large Bronze Age barrow and the grave cut, destroying the primary prehistoric interment (ST 967254: Speake 1989). The reuse and appropriation of an old monument is apparent. The barrow selected for reuse was on a high point of the downs with extensive views in every direction. There are numerous other prehistoric barrows in the neighbourhood (Grinsell 1957), but few have similar topographical locations and comparable views. The ridge-top is followed by a west-east ridge-way recorded in the tenth century charter (Grundy 1919:259, Speake 1989: 120). Walking along the modern line of the ridge top route, the barrow would have been sky-lined for a considerable distance. The site lies on the boundary of the Swallowcliffe estate and very close to the boundary of Chalk hundred. Although hundreds are not recorded before the tenth century (Yorke 1994), Chalk hundred may represent an earlier territorial unit defined by natural frontiers formed by the downs long before it was recorded in a charter of AD 955 (Grundy 1919:25). Bruce Eagles has observed the significance of this boundary in relation to a hypothetical British territory surviving around Tisbury to the north of Swallowcliffe (Eagles in press). This evidence suggests that the Swallowcliffe bed burial was deliberately situated upon an early territorial division. Therefore, the Swallowcliffe grave was located in a comparable manner to the Upper Thames graves.

The Maiden Bradley wealthy weapon grave found on Rodmead Down dates to the late seventh century and may have been secondary in a prehistoric barrow. The vast majority of prehistoric barrows in the vicinity are situated on valley bottoms, breaks of slope and prominent spurs, but the barrow selected for reuse was on the summit of the hill. The location is close to a territorial boundary of Early Medieval date formed by Selwood to the west of Rodmead Down. Perhaps this was an ancient pre-Saxon territorial boundary (Hooke 1998, Eagles in press) and the barrow is close to a Roman road passing over this division. The weapon grave at Coombe Bissett near Salisbury appears to have been inserted into a prehistoric barrow on a ridge-top with extensive all-round views. The location was adjacent to the Roman road Ackling Dyke at the convergence of the boundaries of three hundreds (Meaney 1964; Eagles 1994:25, in press). In both the cases of Maiden Bradley and Coombe Bissett the location chosen for the high status graves contrasts with the majority of prehistoric barrows and Early Medieval burial sites nearby.

The remaining high status burial sites from Wessex – female graves at Woodyates and Roundway Down and male weapon graves at Ford Laverstock and Oliver's Battery – also adhere to some, but not all, of the criteria discussed above (Andrew 1934, Meaney 1964, Musty 1969, Bowen 1990). For example, all appear to reuse prehistoric monuments, and many are close to Roman roads and possible early boundaries. Some might be regarded as peripheral while maintaining intervisibility with early centres of power. However, none are on the highest tops of hills with all-round views. It seems as if these affordances could not be reconciled with these other criteria. For example, the wealthy female grave inserted into a long barrow at Woodyates selected the monument closest to both the important territorial division formed by the line of the Bokerley Dyke and the route of the Roman road Akerling Dyke. Yet such a position could not allow a hilltop location with extensive views, and indeed, the line of the Bokerley Dyke completely obscures views eastwards while views west and north are extremely restricted. The two weapon graves from Ford Laverstock were placed adjacent to the Roman road between Winchester and Old Sarum, one inserted into a prehistoric barrow, the other under a primary mound. The site is quite low down with restricted views, although two hillforts and at least two barrow groups are sky-lined from the location. It appears that sometimes burial sites had to "make do" with far from ideal conditions while trying to fulfil a number of conflicting strategies.

These relationships are more significant when we realise how few Early Medieval burial sites from Wiltshire share these attributes. As with the upper Thames region, monument reuse is widespread among the Early Medieval burial sites of Wiltshire. Many burial sites are close to parish boundaries (Bonney 1974), but very few are on the summits of hills and adjacent to Roman roads. The high status graves of Wessex stand out from other Early Medieval burial sites in both their wealth and their location in the landscape.

These themes have been discussed in terms of high status graves in Wessex and the Upper Thames region (table 2). High status sites from other regions might employ aspects of these location strategies. The early seventh century barrow burial at Caenby in Lincolnshire seems to have reused the site of prehistoric barrows associated with at least two important route-ways (Everson 1993). At Benty Grange in the Peak District, the primary Saxon barrow was located on a prominent hill spur with spectacular views in most directions. The site is immediately adjacent to the Roman road between Buxton and Little Chester that forms the modern parish boundary. The site lies among a high concentration of prehistoric monuments. It is intervisible with numerous prehistoric barrows in comparable locations and the Neolithic henge at Arbor Low.

The Sutton Hoo barrow cemetery in Suffolk (Carver 1998) might be interpreted in a similar way, situated on a ridge overlooking the River Deben with views in all directions. The river would have been an important route of movement that may have included water-borne traffic moving upstream from the North Sea towards the royal centre at Rendlesham. The location is strikingly similar to the Taplow barrow. However, evidence for monument

High Status burial	Monument Reuse	Boundary, hundred, estate or natural frontier	Topography	Views	Routes
Lowbury	X	X	Summit	All-round, long distance	X
Asthall		X	Ridge	All-round, long distance	X
Taplow	X	X	Spur	All-round, long distance	X
Cuddesdon	X	X	Summit	All-round, long distance	
Oliver's Battery	X	?	Hilltop; off summit	Wide, short distance	
Swallowcliffe Down	X	X	Summit	All-round, long distance	X
Roundway Down	X	X	Hillside	All-round, short distance	?
Coombe Bissett	?	X	Ridge	All-round, long distance	X
Rodmead Down	?	X	Summit	All-round, long distance	?
Ford, Laverstock	X		Hillside	Directed, short distance	X
Bokerley Dyke	X	X	Hillside	Restricted	X

Table 2. A summary of information on the location of high status Anglo-Saxon barrows of the seventh century in Wessex and the Upper Thames region.

reuse is ambiguous at Sutton Hoo and the site may not be completely peripheral given the evidence for settlement and a possible pagan temple adjacent to the barrow cemetery.

Discussion and conclusions

During the seventh century AD, high status graves appear to have been placed in the Anglo-Saxon landscape according to clearly defined strategies. Their location created explicit links with the remains of the ancient past, often on hill-tops with wide and distant views, close to important routeways, on the edges of local and regional territories and some distance from concentrations of Anglo-Saxon settlement and centres of power. Admittedly, not all high-status barrows follow this practice, and lowland examples such as Broomfield in Essex are well known. But the combination of location criteria seems to represent a general trend in their location that cannot be found among many other Early Medieval burial sites.

Interpretations of wealthy or "princely" barrow burials have focused on their association with a warrior elite with national or even international contacts. These wealthy burials are thought to relate to social and political stress and competition in this period as well as to changing patterns of inheritance and concepts of land tenure (Shephard 1979). They are regarded as an expression of the increasing political power and authority of this emerging warrior elite and their attempts to establish hegemony over rivals (Arnold 1982, Scull 1993). Many authors regard these themes as central to the process of kingdom formation. From a wider perspective, it has been argued that these graves incorporate overtly pagan rites as an ideological form of resistance to Christianity and Merovingian expansion (Carver 1989, 1998; Van De Noort 1993). In contrast, others see the grave goods in some barrow burials as expressions of a Christian elite identity in death (e.g. Yorke 1995). While these themes place the graves within a broad historical framework, the evidence from fieldwork presented above suggests that interpretations must first address the burials in their local environments. It is within their landscape settings that we can appreciate the ways in which they would have been encountered and experienced by people living and travelling during the Early Medieval period. Only once this is established can we begin to speculate concerning the significance and impact of the choices of grave goods, mode of interment and the selection of barrows as a monument form in seventh century society.

More than anything else, isolated high status graves are marked by the amount of expenditure and "conspicuous consumption" of resources that must have formed a dramatic and theatrical funerary display at the grave side. This investment of wealth appears focused on the spatial and physical treatment, alteration and reconstitution of the dead body into a new form. This was achieved by the elaborate inhumation of the dead or by cremation. This socially constructed "image of death" is usually assumed by archaeologists to directly reflect (in an uncomplicated way) the status of the deceased and mourners. However, the treatment of the dead may have had a further purpose.

High status individuals were being portrayed with a highly engendered and stylised identity in death. Burial rites portrayed the deceased in new images that may have reflected mythical and heroic ideology and their continued relationship with the living.

In other words, placing artefacts with the dead, raising a barrow and other aspects of the rituals surrounding death may have sought to establish the dead with a new status and identity as ancestors with links to a mythical past (Williams 1998, 1999). Moreover, perhaps the elaborate burial rites of selected individuals were thought to re-enact some mythical archetype for a funeral of a god, hero or ancestor (Eliade 1954). From this perspective, we might view the artefacts, corpse and funerary monument as mnemonic devices. They simultaneously constructed an ancestral identity for the deceased and propagated a mythical history that linked the past and the dead with the present and the living. Graves may have acted like chronicles and genealogies by constructing links between the present and an imagined past (Hunter 1974, Bradley 1987, Geake 1997, Härke 1997, Carver 1998). However, in contrast to written documents, this was a version of "history" and group identity constructed through ritual practices. While written histories would be largely restricted to a literate Christianised element of the elite in Early Medieval Britain, funerals had the potential of extending elite discourses to the wider population. They were public and communal events. By observing and participating in their funerals, and by encountering the barrows raised over wealthy graves, large numbers of people could be made aware of the mythical histories and ideologies claimed by high status groups. In this way, these few wealthy or "princely" graves may have held important messages for the groups that built them, and the wider society over which they held political and military power. Graves were material expressions of the past and the dead, serving in the reproduction of social memories, identities and inequalities.

The placing of graves may have been implicated in this funerary symbolism. The wealth and monumentality of the graves explicitly emphasised the presence of the dead in the landscape. It carved out a region of sacred space and time for the dead, simultaneously situated in the past and the present, in both the world of the living and extra-terrestrial realms. The translation of the dead to ancient monuments on territorial boundaries and prominent hill-tops with extensive panoramas intervisible with major routes of movement may have combined to situate the grave in a unique and liminal place in the Early Medieval landscape. Equally such locations would require long funerary processions and make the grave-side rites highly visible; this would serve to ensure as wide an audience as possible.

We must also understand the placing of the dead in terms of the belief that the spiritual elements of the deceased continue to reside at, or close to, their tomb (Williams 1997b, 1998; Semple 1998). In such prominent locations the dead may have been thought to influence and oversee the living, protecting and defending the land of kin and subjects within the view-shed of their graves. Rather than barrows acting in functional terms as "territorial markers", the inhabitants of these barrows may have been believed to protect descendants and ward off enemies (Charles-Edwards 1976:86-87 for Welsh and Irish examples, Ellis 1943:100-105 for Scandinavian parallels). The grave was the place of contact and mediation between the living and the dead. Yet, also, they where the places from which the dead commanded and dominated the lives of those dwelling in and moving through the landscape. On another level, placing the dead during mortuary practices may have established the living as the heirs of a "pre-Saxon" or "Roman" past while simultaneously constructing "conceptual links" with ancestral homelands and myths of Germanic origin (Williams 1998).

While the location of graves might represent aspects of elite sacred geography, they may also have served an explicitly political purpose to construct and legitimise the ritual discourses of these powerful groups. During the seventh century, elite authority and succession was far from stable (Yorke 1990). Leaders may have been mobile, moving from place to place extracting tribute from local populations (Charles-Edwards 1989). In this context the graves of "noble" individuals may have been an important means of emphasising the control over land, territory, people and resources by the survivors (Shephard 1979). In this scenario, the dead would be "fixed" to the land more permanently than their mobile and transient living counterparts. The location of graves may have contributed to disputes over succession and inheritance when the authority, property rights and prestige of a high status group was ambiguous, disputed or threatened. Alternatively, the placing of elite burials may have asserted rights over newly conquered territories or resisted the claims over land made by rival groups. The graves of the dead may have "cosmicised" or "consecrated" newly claimed territory (Eliade 1954:10). Ritual practices may have been weapons at least as valuable as military victories in asserting and legitimising the status of elite groups over others. Groups and individuals excluded from the meanings and symbolism of the barrow burial would have had to contend with encountering these graves when moving through the landscape. Even if they rejected and disputed the authority and power invested in the graves, these monuments may have made it difficult for others to make similar statements through the funerary use of landscape.

In conclusion, we can now perceive a view of the landscape context of high status graves in relation to their extravagant deployment of symbolism, labour and wealth. Through their distinctive locations and their monumentality, these graves may have been involved in the active transformation of the meanings and associations of the landscape and the histories embedded in it. Funerals would have articulated narratives that provided deceased individuals and mourners with explicit and visual links with a distant past. Graves were appropriating, altering and disturbing ancient monuments and the wider landscape in a visible way. It seems likely that such activities would have formed part of the creation of new histories but also the "forgetting" of alternative pasts. Thus, by placing the dead, Anglo-Saxon elite groups may have been trying to ideologically and politically re-shape and re-place the past with their own visions of society, history and identity.

Acknowledgements

Numerous thanks to Philip and Susan Williams for continuing support and encouragement.

I would like to express gratitude to Aaron Watson for numerous discussions and observations concerning the location of prehistoric monuments and Anglo-Saxon burial sites.

Thanks to Martin Rundkvist for inviting me to speak at the 4th EAA meeting at Gothenburg in September 1998. I appreciate the contribution of the session organiser and the many other archaeologists who asked questions and discussed my paper at the Gothenburg conference. Thanks also to Andrew Reynolds, Sarah Semple, Richard Bradley, Helen Geake, and others for their comments concerning a version of this paper presented at the session "Remembering and forgetting: exploring the past in the past" organised by Richard Hingley and the author at the Theoretical Archaeology Group conference in Birmingham, December 1998.

I am grateful to Karin Altenberg, John Blair, Hella Eckardt, Heinrich Härke and Aaron Watson for commenting on earlier drafts of this paper. All errors, field observations and interpretations remain the sole responsibility of the author. Thanks to Bruce Eagles for positive comments and access to articles in press. A great debt is owed to Helen Ullathorne, Aaron Watson and Philip Williams who made transportation available and accompanied me to Anglo-Saxon burial sites and other monuments in Wessex, the Upper Thames region, Cumbria and the Peak District during the research for this paper. Finally, thanks to the staff of the Royal Berkshire Hospital for treating and operating on a fracture sustained during fieldwork for this paper.

Fig. 45. The Asthall barrow viewed from the west. Today the barrow (diam c. 17 m) is surrounded by a stone wall and covered by trees. In antiquity it would have been wider and taller. The mound covered a primary wealthy cremation burial of the early seventh century. The ground rises to the south of the barrow on the right of the picture, yet the site retains exceptional views in most directions. Photograph: the author.

Fig. 46. View from the northeast approaching Asthall barrow along the road from Minster Lovell towards Burford. The monument dominates the skyline along this route that could have been in use in Saxon times. Photograph: the author.

Fig. 47. View of the location of the Taplow barrow on its hilltop taken from a location immediately east of the River Thames. Before the building of Taplow Court (the building on the hilltop), the barrow would have been skylined from the River Thames for many kilometres. Photograph: the author.

References

Allen, T.G. 1995. *Lithics and landscape: archaeological discoveries on the Thames Water pipeline at Gatehampton Farm, Goring, Oxfordshire 1985-1992.* Oxford University Committee for Archaeology. Oxford.

Alexander, M. (translation) 1973. *Beowulf: a verse translation.* London.

Andrew, W.J. 1931. Report on the first excavations at Oliver's Battery in 1930. *Hampshire Field Club & Archaeological Society* 12, pp 5-10. Winchester.

Århem, K. 1988. Into the realm of the sacred: an interpretation of Khasi funerary ritual. Cederroth, S; Corlin, C. & Lindström, J. (eds.). *On the meaning of death: essays on mortuary rituals and eschatological beliefs*, pp 257-299. Uppsala.

Arnold, C. 1982. Stress as a factor in social and economic change. Renfrew, A.C. & Shennan, S. (eds.). *Ranking, resource and exchange*, pp 124-131. Cambridge University Press.

Arnold, C. 1988. Territories and leadership: frameworks for the study of emergent polities in early Anglo-Saxon southern England. Driscoll, S.T. & Nieke, M.R. (eds.). *Power and politics in Early Medieval Britain and Ireland*, pp 111-127. Edinburgh University Press.

Atkinson, D. 1916. *The Romano-British site on Lowbury Hill in Berkshire.* Reading University College.

Barclay, A.; Bradley, R.; Hey, G. & Lambrick, G. 1996. The earlier prehistory of the Oxford region in the light of recent research. *Oxoniensia* 61, pp 1-20. Oxford.

Barrett, J. 1994. *Fragments from Antiquity: an archaeology of social life in Britain, 2900-1200 BC.* Oxford.

Bassett, S. 1989. In search of the origins of the Anglo-Saxon kingdoms. Bassett, S. (ed.). *The origins of the Anglo-Saxon kingdoms*, pp 3-28. Leicester University Press.

Benson, D. & Miles, D. 1974. *The upper Thames Valley – an archaeological survey of the river gravels.* Oxfordshire Archaeological Unit. Oxford.

Blair, J. 1989. Minster churches in the landscape. Hooke, D. (ed.). *Anglo-Saxon settlements*, p 35-58. Oxford.

Blair, J. 1991. *Early Medieval Surrey.* Stroud.

Blair, J. 1994. *Anglo-Saxon Oxfordshire.* Oxford.

Blair, J. 1998. Bampton: an Anglo-Saxon minster. *Current Archaeology* 160, pp 124-130. London.

Bloch, M. 1974. *Placing the dead – tombs, ancestral villages and kinship organisation in Madagascar.* London.

Bloch, M. 1982. Death, women and power. Bloch, M. & Parry, J. (eds.). *Death and the regeneration of life,* pp 211-230. Cambridge University Press.

Bloch, M. & Parry, J. 1982. Introduction. Bloch, M. & Parry, J. (eds.). *Death and the regeneration of life,* pp 1-44. Cambridge University Press.

Bonney, D.J. 1966. Pagan Saxon burials and boundaries in Wiltshire. *Wiltshire Archaeological Magazine* 61, pp 25-30. London.

Bonney, D.J. 1976. Early boundaries and estates in Southern England. Sawyer, P. (ed.). *Medieval settlement: continuity and change,* pp 72-82. London.

Bonney, D.J. 1973. The pagan Saxon period. c. 500-700 AD. *Victoria County History: Wiltshire,* vol 1:2, pp 468-484. London.

Bowen, H.C. 1990. *The archaeology of Bokerley Dyke.* RCHME. London.

Bradley, R.J. 1987. Time regained: the creation of continuity. *Journal of the British Archaeological Association* 140, pp 1-17. London.

Bradley, R.J. 1997. *Rock art and the prehistory of Atlantic Europe.* London.

Bradley, R.J. 1998. *The significance of monuments.* London.

Carver, M. 1989. Kingship and material culture in early Anglo-Saxon East Anglia. Bassett, S. (ed.). *The origins of the Anglo-Saxon kingdoms,* pp 141-158. Leicester University Press.

Carver, M. 1995. Boat burial in Britain; ancient custom or political signal? Crumlin-Pedersen, O. & Tye, B. Munch (eds.). *The ship as symbol in prehistoric and medieval Scandinavia,* pp 111-124. PNM Publications from the National Museum 1. Copenhagen.

Carver, M. 1998. *Sutton Hoo – burial ground of kings?* British Museum. London.

Charles-Edwards, T. 1976. Boundaries in Irish Law. Sawyer, P. (ed.). *Medieval settlement: continuity and change.* London.

Charles-Edwards, T. 1989. Early medieval kingships in the British Isles. Bassett, S. (ed.). *The origins of the Anglo-Saxon kingdoms,* pp 28-39. Leicester University Press.

Collins, A.E.P. & Collins, F.J. 1959. Excavations on Blewburton Hill, 1953. *Berkshire Archaeological Journal* 57, pp 52-73. Reading.

Conder, E. 1895. Communicating the following account of the exploration of Lyneham Barrow, Oxon. *Proceedings of the Society of Antiquaries* 15, pp 404-410. London.

Dickinson, T.M. 1973. Excavations at Standlake Down in 1954: the Anglo-Saxon graves. *Oxoniensia* 38, pp 239-257. Oxford.

Dickinson, T.M. 1974. *Cuddesdon and Dorchester-upon-Thames.* BAR British Series 1. Oxford.

Dickinson, T.M. 1976. *The Anglo-Saxon burial sites of the Upper Thames Region and their bearing on the history of Wessex. c. AD 400-700.* Unpublished D.Phil thesis. Oxford.

Dickinson, T.M. & Speake, G. 1992. The Seventh-Century cremation burial in Asthall barrow, Oxfordshire: a reassessment. Carver, M. (ed.). *The age of Sutton Hoo,* pp 95-131. Woodbridge.

Doggett, N. 1986. The Anglo-Saxon see and cathedral at Dorchester-on-Thames: the evidence reconsidered. *Oxoniensia* 51, pp 49-62. Oxford.

Dumville, D. 1997. The terminology of overkingship in early Anglo-Saxon England. Hines, J. (ed.). *The Anglo-Saxons from the Migration Period to the Eighth Century: an ethnographic perspective,* pp 345-373. Woodbridge.

Eagles, B. 1994. The evidence for settlement in the fifth to seventh centuries AD. Aston, M. & Lewis, C. (eds.). *Medieval landscapes of Wessex,* pp 13-32. Oxford.

Eagles, B. In press. The age of assimilation and the Anglo-Saxon period.

Eagles, B. & Struth, P. In press. An Anglo-Saxon barrow cemetery in Greenwich Park.

Eliade, M. 1954. *The myth of eternal return.* Princeton University Press.

Ellis, H. 1943. *The road to Hel – a study of the conception of the dead in Old Norse literature.* Cambridge University Press.

Everson, P. 1993. Pre-Viking settlement in Lindsey. Vince, A. (ed.). *Pre-Viking Lindsey,* pp 91-100. City of Lincoln Archaeological Unit. Lincoln.

Farley, M. 1987. An Anglo-Saxon cemetery at Bourne End, Wooburn. *Records of Buckinghamshire* 29, pp 170-174. Aylesbury.

Foucault, M. 1988. Technologies of the self. Martin, L.H.; Gutman, H. & Hutton, P.H. (eds.). *Technologies of the self – a seminar with Michel Foucault,* pp 16-49. Massachusetts.

Fulford, M.J. & Rippon, S. 1994. Lowbury Hill, Oxon: a re-assessment of the probably Romano-Celtic temple and the Anglo-Saxon barrow. *Archaeological Journal* 151, pp 158-211. London.

Gaffney, V & Tingle, M. 1989. *The Maddle Farm project: an integrated survey of Prehistoric and Roman landscapes on the Berkshire Downs.* BAR British Series 200. Oxford.

Gates, T. 1975. *The Middle Thames Valley: an archaeological survey of the river gravels.* Berkshire Archaeological Committee Publication no.1. Oxford.

Geake, H. 1992. Burial practice in Seventh- and Eighth-Century England. Carver, M. (ed.). *The age of Sutton Hoo,* pp 83-94. Woodbridge.

Geake, H. 1997. *The use of grave-goods in Conversion-Period England c.600-850.* BAR British Series 261. Oxford.

Gelling, M. 1974. *The place-names of Berkshire part II.* English place-name society volume L. Cambridge.

Gelling, M. 1978. *Signposts to the Past.* London.

Gelling, M. 1979. *The early charters of the Thames Valley.* Leicester University Press.

Goodier, A. 1984. The formation of boundaries in Anglo-Saxon England: a statistical study. *Medieval Archaeology* 28, pp 1-21. Leeds.

Grinsell, L.V. 1936. An analysis and list of Berkshire barrows. Part II. *Berkshire Archaeological Journal* 40(1), pp 20-58. Reading.

Grinsell, L.V. 1957. Archaeological Gazetteer. Pugh, R.B. (ed.). *The Victoria history of the County of Wiltshire, volume I, part I,* pp 21-272. Oxford University Press.

Grundy, G. B. 1919. The Saxon land charters of Wiltshire (First Series). *Archaeological Journal* 76, pp 193-201. London.

Grundy, G.B. 1933. *Saxon Oxfordshire*. The Oxfordshire Record Society. Oxford.

Hamerow, H. 1992. Settlement on the gravels in the Anglo-Saxon period. Fulford, M. & Nichols, E. (eds.). *The developing landscapes of Lowland Britain: the archaeology of the British gravels: a review*, pp 39-48. Society of Antiquaries of London.

Hamerow, H. 1993. An Anglo-Saxon cemetery near West Hendred, Oxon. Filmer-Sankey, W. & Griffith, D. (eds.). *Anglo-Saxon studies in archaeology and history* 6, pp 113-123. Oxford Committee for Archaeology. Oxford.

Härke, H. 1994. A context for the Saxon barrow. Fulford, M.J. & Rippon, S. Lowbury Hill, Oxon: a re-assessment of the probably Romano-Celtic temple and the Anglo-Saxon barrow. *Archaeological Journal* 151, pp 158-211. London.

Härke, H. 1997. Material culture as myth: weapons in Anglo-Saxon graves. Jensen, C.K. & Nielsen, K.H. (eds) *Burial and society: the chronological and social analysis of archaeological burial data*, pp 119-127. Århus.

Härke, H. & Williams, H.M.R. 1997. Angelsächsische Bestattungsplätze und ältere Denkmäler: Bemerkungen zur zeitlichen entwicklung und Deutung des Phänomens. *Archäologische Informationen* 20/1, pp 25-27. Bonn.

Hassal, W.O. 1939. Cuddesdon. *Victoria County History: Oxford Volume 5*, pp 96-116. Oxford University Press.

Hawkes, S.C. 1986. The Early Saxon Period. In Briggs, G.; Cook, J. & Rowley, T. (eds.). *The archaeology of the Oxford region*, pp 65-108. Oxford.

Hertz, R. 1906. *Death and the right hand*. London.

Hooke, D. 1987. Anglo-Saxon estates in the Vale of the White Horse. *Oxoniensia* 52, pp 129-143. Oxford.

Hooke, D. 1988. Regional variation in southern and central England in the Anglo-Saxon Period and its relationship to land units and settlement. Hooke, D. (ed.). *Anglo-Saxon settlement*, pp 123-151. Oxford.

Hooke, D. 1995. The administrative and settlement framework of Early Medieval Wessex. Aston, M. & Lewis, C. (eds.). *Medieval landsapes of Wessex*, pp 83-95. Oxford.

Hooke, D. 1998. *The landscape of Anglo-Saxon England*. Leicester University Press.

Hunter, M. 1974. Germanic and Roman antiquity and the sense of the past in Anglo-Saxon England. *Anglo-Saxon England* 3, pp 29-50. Cambridge.

Huntingdon, R. & Metcalf, D. 1991. *Celebrations of death*. Cambridge University Press.

James, E. 1989. Burial and status in the Early Medieval west. *Royal Historical Society Transactions*. 5th ser. 39, pp 23-40. London.

Llobera, M. 1996. Exploring the topography of mind: GIS, social space and archaeology *Antiquity* 70/269, pp 612-622. Cambridge.

Johnston, R. 1998. The paradox of landscape. *European Journal of Archaeology* 1/3, pp 313-326. European Association of Archaeologists.

Kan, S. 1989. *Symbolic immortality: the Tlingit potlatch of the Nineteenth Century*. Smithsonian Institute Press. Washington.

Kelly, S. 1990. Anglo-Saxon lay society and the written word. McKitterick, R. (ed.). *The uses of literacy in Early Medieval Europe*, pp 36-62. Cambridge University Press.

Kennett, D.H. 1969. The Anglo-Saxon grave from Battle Edge, near Burford, Oxfordshire. *Oxoniensia* 34, pp 111-115. Oxford.

Leeds, E.T. 1939. Anglo-Saxon remains. Salzman, L.F. (ed.). *Victoria County History of Oxford*, volume 1 pp 346-372. Oxford University Press.

Lucy, S. 1998. *The Early Anglo-Saxon cemeteries of East Yorkshire*. BAR British Series 272. Oxford.

Malpas, F.J. 1987. Roman roads south and east of Dorchester-on-Thames. *Oxoniensia* 52, pp 23-34. Oxford.

Margary, I.D. 1955. *Roman roads in Britain, volume 1: south of the Foss Way – Bristol Channel*. London.

Meaney, A. 1964. *A gazetteer of Early Anglo-Saxon burial sites*. London.

Meyer, R.E. (ed.). 1993. *Ethnicity and the American cemetery*. Bowling Green State University Popular Press. Ohio.

Morris, R. 1993. Baptismal places 600-800. Wood, I. & Lund, N. (eds.). *People and places in northern Europe, 500-1600*, pp 15-24. Woodbridge.

Musty, J. 1969. The excavation of two barrows, one of Saxon date, at Ford, Laverstock, near Salisbury Wiltshire. *Antiquaries Journal* 49, pp 98-117. London.

Overing, G.R. & Osborn, M. 1994. *Landscapes of desire – partial stories of the medieval Scandinavian world*. Minnesota University Press. Minneapolis.

Peake, H. 1937. Excavations on the Berkshire Downs 24th November 1934. *Transactions of the Newbury District Field Club* 7/1. Newbury.

Parker Pearson, M. 1993. The powerful dead: archaeological relationships between the living and the dead. *Cambridge Archaeological Journal* 3, pp 203-229. Cambridge.

Reynolds, A. 1997. The definition and ideology of Anglo-Saxon execution sites and cemeteries. De Boe, G. & Verhaeghe, F. (eds.). *Death and burial in Medieval Europe: Papers of the Medieval Europe Brugge 1997 Conference*, volume 2, pp 33- 41. Brügge.

Richards, J. C. 1979. *The archaeology of the Berkshire Downs: an introductory survey*. Berkshire Archaeological Committee Publication Number 3. Reading.

Semple, S. 1998. A fear of the past: the place of the prehistoric burial mound in the ideology of middle and later Anglo-Saxon England. *World Archaeology* 30(1), pp 109-126. London.

Scull, C. 1992. Excavation and Survey at Watchfield, Oxfordshire, 1983-1992. *Archaeological Journal* 149, pp 124-281. London.

Scull, C. 1993. Archaeology, Early Anglo-Saxon society and the origins of Anglo-Saxon kingdoms *Anglo-Saxon Studies in Archaeology and History* 6, pp 65-82. Oxford University Committee for Archaeology.

Shephard, J. 1979. The social identity of the individual in isolated barrows and barrow cemeteries in Anglo-Saxon England. Burnham, B. & Kingsbury, J. (eds.).

Space, hierarchy and society: interdisciplinary studies in social area analysis. BAR British Series 59, pp 47-79. Oxford.

Smith, R. 1905. Anglo-Saxon remains. Page, W. (ed.). *The Victoria County History of the County of Buckingham,* volume 1, pp 195-206. Haymarket.

Speake, G. 1989. *A Saxon bed burial on Swallowcliffe Down.* English Heritage. London.

Stocker, D. & Went, D. 1995. The evidence for a pre-Viking church adjacent to the Anglo-Saxon barrow at Taplow, Bucks. *Archaeological Journal* 152, pp 441-450. London.

Tilley, C. 1994. *A phenomenology of landscape: places, paths and monuments.* Oxford.

Tilley, C. 1996. The powers of rocks: topography and monument construction on Bodmin Moor. *World Archaeology* 28(2), pp 161-177. London.

Tingle, M. 1991. *The Vale of the White Horse Survey – the study of a changing landscape in the clay lowlands of southern England from prehistory to the present.* BAR British Series 218. Oxford.

Van De Noort, R. 1993. The context of Early Medieval barrows in western Europe. *Antiquity* 67, pp 66-73. Cambridge.

Welch, M. 1992. *Anglo-Saxon England.* London.

Warren, C. 1993. Disrupted death ceremonies: popular culture and the ethnography of Bali. *Oceania* 64, pp 36-56. Sydney.

Williams, H.M.R. 1997a. Burnt Germans in the age of iron? Anglo-Saxon cremation practices in context. Paper presented at the TAG 97 conference, Bournemouth, UK.

Williams, H.M.R. 1997b. Ancient landscapes and the dead. *Medieval Archaeology* 41, pp 1-32. Leeds.

Williams, H.M.R. 1998. Monuments and the past in early Anglo-Saxon England. *World Archaeology* 30(1), pp 90-109. London.

Williams, H.M.R. 1999. Cremation: ritual, technology and the transformation of identities. Paper presented at the University of Reading, March 18th 1999.

Williams, H.M.R. In press. Identities and cemeteries in Roman and Early Medieval archaeology. Forcey, C. & Witcher, R. (eds.). *TRAC 98. Proceedings of the eighth annual Theoretical Roman Archaeology Conference, Leicester 1998.* Oxford.

Yorke, B. 1990. *Kings and kingdoms of Early Anglo-Saxon England.* London.

Yorke, B. 1994. *Wessex in the Early Middle Ages.* Leicester University Press.

Swords and brooches. Constructing social identity.

Siv Kristoffersen, Department of Archaeology, University of Bergen, Norway

This paper focuses on a sample of Germanic burials from the 5th and 6th centuries AD in south and west Norway, all containing gilded objects decorated in Nydam Style and Salin's Style I. The material has been chosen against a background of questions concerning the social context of these decoration styles. I will give a brief presentation of the archaeological material, theoretical framework and interpretations. The paper refers to a thesis in manuscript and a further developed and rewritten version which is to be published (Kristoffersen 1997, in prep; see also in press a).

South and west Norway is a primary area for the distribution of Migration Period animal art (fig. 48, table 4) and seems to be central in the development of Style I. The area is united by other cultural similarities as well.

Within this area, there are 93 finds with 137 gilded objects decorated in Nydam Style and Style I. The number of objects increases through the Migration Period and is by far the greatest in the last phase. There is also a change in the types of decorated objects (tab. 3). 83 finds are from burials. Most of them are found under mounds, usually large ones. The majority are inhumation burials in stone cists. They are richly furnished, many with gold and silver objects, and imported glass and bronze vessels. There is, however, variation, especially in the last phase. Skeletons are seldom preserved.

Against this general background of archaeological context, combinations of various types of objects have been studied. Two categories are distinguished: burials with weapons (14) and burials with relief brooches (43). Weapons and relief brooches are never combined. When these objects occur together in a grave, they seem to have belonged to different individuals. Relief brooches are often combined with smaller brooches and spindlewhorls. Keys and iron weaving battens occur in these assemblages (fig. 51-54), as well as gold bracteates. In seven of the weapon assemblages, decorated sword equipment occurs; usually pommels, scabbard mounts or buckles (fig. 50). Scales are also found in these graves (fig. 49). This small group consists of often exceptionally rich assemblages that include the well-known Evebø and Snartemo burials. The categories with weapons and brooches are through correlation with osteological sex-assessments related to different gender-related social identities.

In terms of theoretical framework, the graves are regarded as products of rituals, and I focus on social aspects of rituals as they are discussed by Turner (1967), Bloch & Parry (1982) and Bourdieu (1977, 1996). Rituals are emotionally charged, public situations in which social construction works very well – social categories and relationships become real, because they are presented as real.

Type of decorated object	D1	D2a	D2b	D	Total
Relief brooches	8	10	27		45
Relief brooches with a spatulate foot			19		19
Cruciform brooches	3	1			4
Clasp buttons	3	10	19	1	33
Clasps	3	1	1		5
Sword equipment	3	2	3		8
Buckles	4	1			5
Golden scabbard mounts			3		3
Mounts for glass vessels		5			5
Miscellaneous	5	1	4		10
Total	20	31	76	1	137

Table 3. Object-types with animal art from the three phases of the Migration Period.

Table 4. *List of finds referring to numbers on map in fig. 48.*
B = Inventory number for Bergen Museum.
C = Inventory number for Universitetets Oldsaksamling, Oslo.
S = Inventory number for Arkeologisk Museum, Stavanger.

All listed finds are published in the accession lists of the museums. A catalogue of published lists until 1950 is found in Gjessing & Fett 1950. A catalogue up to 1993 is found in Hines 1993:103-106.

F1. Langlo, Stokke pgd. og k. Vestfold. C5947-5962.

F2. Veierland, Stokke pgd. Nøtterøy k. Vestfold. C18714-15.

F3. Nordheim, Hedrum pgd. Larvik k. Vestfold. C19858.

F4. Ommundrød, Hedrum pgd. Larvik k. Vestfold. C29300.

F5. Roligheten, Hedrum pgd. Larvik k. Vestfold. C14338-50, 14534, 89-90, 711.

F6. Skåra, Tjølling pgd. Larvik k. Vestfold. C18892-904, 18917-18, 19095.

F7. Berg, Brunlanes pgd. Larvik k. Vestfold. C19227.

F8. Tveitane, Brunlanes pgd. Larvik k. Vestfold. C11220-36.

F9. Tveitane, Brunlanes pgd. Larvik k. Vestfold. C11237.

F10. Bratsberg, Gjerpen pgd. Skien k. Telemark. C26566.

F11. Falkum, Gjerpen pgd. Skien k. Telemark. C21856.

F12. Søtvet, Solum pgd. Skien k. Telemark. C9440-49, 9811.

F13. Stenstad, Holla pgd. Nome k. Telemark. Nat. Mus. Copenhagen 8031, 8306-08, 8411, 8420.

F14. Nordgården, Seljord pgd. og k. Telemark. C19269-19280, 19615-16.

F15. Vik, Fjære pgd. Grimstad k. Aust-Agder. C7072-7082.
F16. Trygsland, Bjelland pgd. Marnardal k. Vest-Agder K DCCXI-III, DCCXV, DCCXXII-IVb, DCCCXXXII-VII.

F17. Ågedal, Bjelland pgd. Audnedal k. Vest-Agder. B3410a-t, B4132.

F18. Snartemo II, Hægebostad pgd. og k. Vest-Agder. C28026, C8897.

F19. Snartemo V, Hægebostad pgd. og k. Vest-Agder. C26001.

F20. Hægebostad-Ødegården, N.-Audnedalen pgd. Lindesnes k. Vest-Agder. C13697.

F21. Løland, Nord-Audnedalen pgd. Lindesnes k. Vest-Agder. C18301-309.

F22. Gitlevåg, Sør-Audnedalen pgd. Lyngdal k. Vest-Agder. B5060.

F23. Bergsaker, Lyngdal pgd. og k. Vest-Agder. C25813.

F24. Høyland, Vanse pgd. Farsund k. Vest-Agder. B5037.

F25. Lunde, Vanse pgd. Farsund k. Vest-Agder. B3543.

F26. Sletten, Vanse pgd. Farsund k. Vest-Agder. B4234.

F27. Spanskslottet, Vanse pgd. Farsund k. Vest-Agder. B4286.

F28. Åmdal, Lista pgd. Farsund k. Vest-Agder. C25077.

F29. Gyland, Bakke pgd. Flekkefjord k. Vest-Agder. C7453-63, 7539-40, 7563.

F30. Ådland, Bakke pgd. Flekkefjord k. Vest-Agder. C8713-21.

F31. Abeland, Helleland pgd. Bjerkreim k. Rogaland. S306-311.

F32. Hovland, Helleland pgd. Egersund k. Rogaland. S2276.

F33. Kvassheim, Egersund pgd. Hå k. Rogaland. B5343.

F34. Kvassheim, Egersund pgd. Hå k. Rogaland. B5994.

F35. Kvassheim, Egersund pgd. Hå k. Rogaland. B5362.

F36. Anisdal, Hå pgd. og k. Rogaland. S2062-2066.

F37. Voll, Hå pgd. og k. Rogaland. S927-938.

F38. Jorenkjøl av Skretting, Hå pgd. og k. Rogaland. S6970.

F39. Skjerpe, Hå pgd. og k. Rogaland. S3741.

F40. Torland, Hå pgd. og k. Rogaland. S440.

F41. Rimestad, Hå pgd. og k. Rogaland. S4268.

F42. Fosse, Time pgd. og k. Rogaland. S6697.

F43. Garpestad, Time pgd. og k. Rogaland. B1781-1784, 1877.

F44. Vestly, Time pgd. og k. Rogaland. S8635.

F45. Eikeland, Time pgd. og k. Rogaland. S9181.

F46. Erga, Klepp pgd. og k. Rogaland. S7131.

F47. Hauge, Klepp pgd. og k. Rogaland. B2269-82, 88-92, 94-99.

F48. Hauge, Klepp pgd. og k. Rogaland. B4000.

F49. Tu, Klepp pgd. og k. Rogaland. C21407.

F50. Anda, Klepp pgd. og k. Rogaland. B2973-74.

F51. Nord-Braut, Klepp pgd. og k. Rogaland. S2451.

F52. Fristad, Klepp pgd. og k. Rogaland. S1961.

F53. Vatshus, Klepp pgd. og k. Rogaland. C3300-3313.

F54. Lunde, Høyland pgd. Sandnes k. Rogaland. C1638.

F55. Hogstad, Hetland pgd. Sandnes k. Rogaland. S1520-26.

F56. Syre, Skudesnes pgd. Karmøy k. Rogaland. S9269.

F57. Melberg, Strand pgd. og k. Rogaland. S7577, S7858.

F58. Rivjaland, Hjelmeland pgd. og k. Rogaland. S2547.

F59. Vatland, Jelse pgd. Suldal k. Rogaland. S2772.

F60. Nærheim, Suldal pgd. og k. Rogaland. S2848.

F61. Åm, Skjold pgd. Vindafjord k. Rogaland. S4116.

F62. Østbø, Vikedal pgd. Vindafjord k. Rogaland. S2695.

F63. Etne pgd. Hordaland. B2049.

F64. Grindheim, Etne pgd. og k. Hordaland. B10202 II (S2617).

F65. Sørheim Etne pgd. og k. Hordaland. B10205 (S2850).

F66. Sæbø, Fjellberg pgd. Kvinnherad k. Hordaland. B3358.

F67. Øvsthus, Fjellberg pgd. Kvinnherad k. Hordaland. B3731.

F68. Nordhus, Fjellberg pgd. Kvinnherad k. Hordaland. B4096.

F69. Indre Ålvik, Kvam pgd. og k. Hordaland. B6899.

F70. Løining under Øystese, Kvam pgd. og k. Hordaland. B6809.

F71. Hæve, Voss pgd. og k. Hordaland. B6474.

F72. Mittun, Voss pgd. og k. Hordaland. B7190.

F73. Gjermo, Voss pgd. og k. Hordaland. B7607.

F74. Døsen, Os pgd. og k. Hordaland. B6090 I.

F75. Haugland, Fana pgd. Bergen k. Hordaland. B5541.

F76. Hartveit, Haus pgd. Osterøy k. Hordaland. B4291, B5208.

F77. Indre Arna, Haus pgd. Bergen k. Hordaland. B564-569.

F78. Hodneland, Lindås pgd. og k. Hordaland. B4704, B4846.

F79. Hodneland, Lindås pgd. og k. Hordaland. B4950, B5705.

F80. Hove, Vik pgd. og k. Sogn og Fjordane. B319.

F81. Hove, Vik pgd. og k. Sogn og Fjordane. B6691.

F82. Skjervum, Vik pgd. og k. Sogn og Fjordane. B8830.

F83. Holum, Leikanger pgd. og k. Sogn og Fjordane. B8045.

F84. Nornes, Sogndal pgd. og k. Sogn og Fjordane. B9688.

F85. Kvåle, Sogndal pgd. og k. Sogn og Fjordane. B6516.

F86. Kvåle, Sogndal pgd. og k. Sogn og Fjordane. B13954.

F87. Ugulen, Hafslo pgd. Luster k. Sogn og Fjordane. B6071, B6092 I-II.

F88. Sørheim, Luster pgd. og k. Sogn og Fjordane. B3720.

F89. Bolstad, Luster pgd. og k. Sogn og Fjordane. B3724.

F90. Sandal, Jølster pgd. og k. Sogn og Fjordane. B6656.

F91. Gjemmestad, Gloppen pgd. og k. Sogn og Fjordane. B12549.

F92. Evebø, Gloppen pgd. og k. Sogn og Fjordane. B4590.

F93. Indre. Bø, Stryn pgd. og k. Sogn og Fjordane. B4842.

Fig. 48. *Distribution of finds with objects decorated in Nydam Style and Style I in southwest Norway. C.f. table 4.*

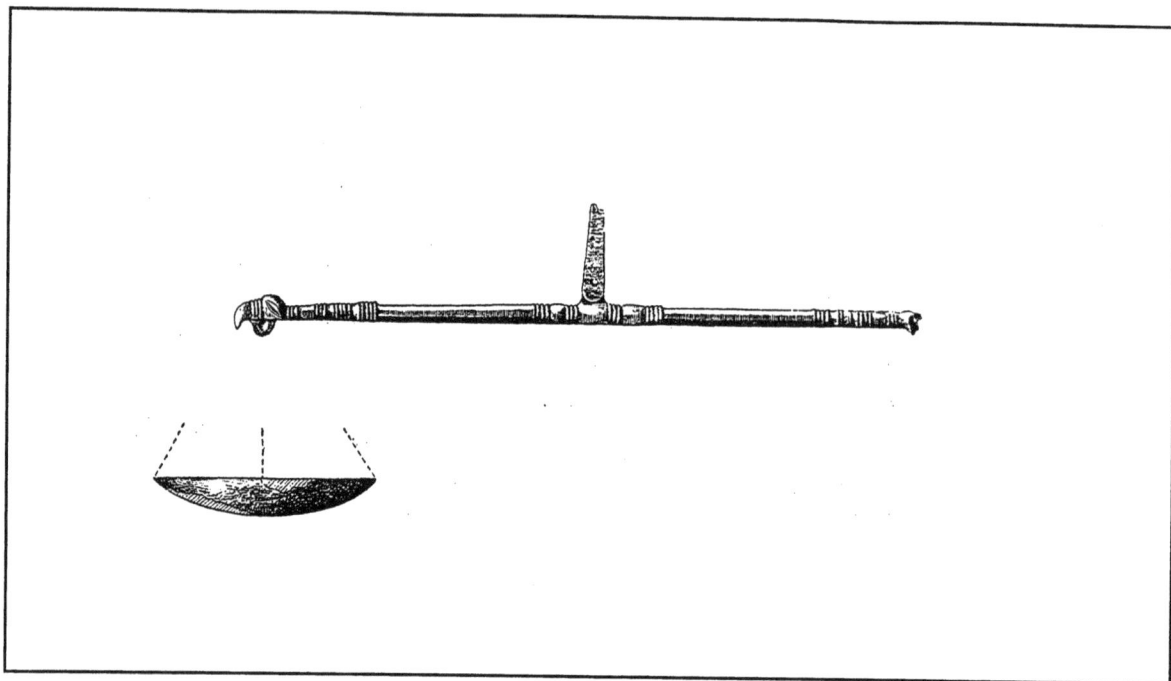

Fig. 49. Scales from Evebø, Sogn og Fjordane (B 4590). After Shetelig 1912, fig. 261. Scale 1:2.

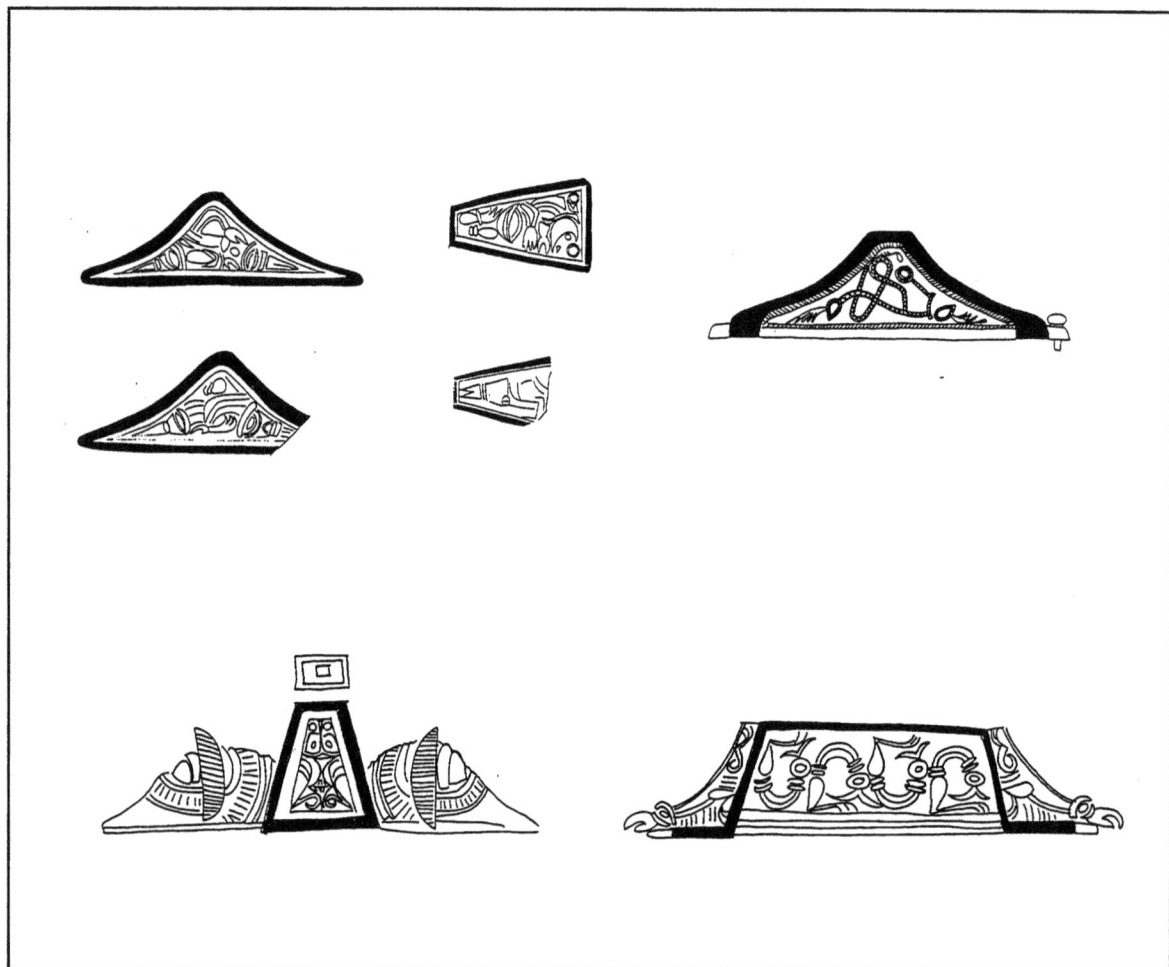

Fig. 50. Top: Sword pommels from Haugland, Hordaland (B 5541) (left) and Hodneland, Hordaland (B 4950) (right). Bottom: Sword pommel and grip mount from Snartemo II, Vest-Agder (C 28026). Drawings by S. Kristoffersen. Scale 71%.

Social order consists of relations manifested through different social identities. Inequality is fundamental to social structure and often draws on categories which can easily be presented as biologically determined – as gender and age (Moore 1994:24 f, 92 f; see also Bourdieu 1996). In defining social identity, the performed aspect is important – what people do – their roles or sets of roles (ibid.). Objects which are used in rituals often relate to what people do, although not necessarily directly, and are, as such, at work in defining these roles. Some of these objects are left for us: keys – iron weaving battens – scales – swords.

The gender categories expressed in the burials referred to above are then to be understood as symbolically and contextually situated – that is, if there is a need to express inequality, difference between the genders and polarity in the relationship are focused upon. If, on the other hand, there is a need to express equality or transformation, roles are mingled, or variations between the poles are emphasised (ibid.).

I see in the burials, thus, the construction of social identities. The burials are constructed images of social roles – images that existed in society, but not necessarily described the individual in the burial. And in this construction, objects, left for us in the graves, were important.

There is, however, no way to control the associations evoked by these objects. The objects are, through their use, coded with different levels of meaning and could be read in various ways. This implies that construction is open to negotiation.

Returning to the patterns in the archaeological material and interpreting them within this framework, the result might turn out as follows. The few burials with decorated sword equipment represent a small group of people, while the numerous group of burials with relief brooches represents a larger group, in which there are variations which seem to be of social significance. There are variations in the brooches as well as in the dress equipment they are part of. Within Germanic society, or a part of that society, the sword worked as a strong and definite symbol of power. Presented on the sword, animal art became charged with this strong expression of power, and was therefore probably of restricted use – reserved for the role of the political leader. The restriction, in turn, would have strengthened the expression of exclusiveness. The small, exclusive group of burials is, thus, regarded as a medium in which the role of the political leader is defined – the role as one would have expected it within the context of the Germanic warrior aristocracy or in groups which related themselves to this identity. Animal art would have been considered less threatening on brooches – or would have been presented as less dangerous. There would not, then, have been the same restrictions on the use of animal art in the brooches. They would have been allowed to be used in the burials of the larger group of wealthy families.

According to this, then, the relationship between the burials with decorated sword equipment and the burials with relief brooches expressed the definition of the relationship between political leaders and wealthy families. Symbolism related to gender constructed inequality in the social structure. The artefact combinations in the burials show that there was pure and precise presentation of the roles. The relationship of inequality was presented as biologically determined.

It is further argued that through the occurrence of relief brooches, sets of bronze keys and iron weaving battens, a group of burials can be related to the construction of the image and role of the *Lady of the house.* The interpretation of the keys is central to this understanding (Steuer 1982, Dübner-Manthey 1990). Due to their design, lack of use-wear and the way they were carried, their symbolic function is argued to have been of importance. In later written sources (*The Lay of Thrym* and *The Lay of Rígh* in the Poetic Edda, translation by Hollander 1962; legislation referred to in KLMN XII:384-386, IV:133-136) keys are related to wedding ceremonies where the *Lady of the house* is given responsibility for valuables which could be locked in chests and caskets. These ceremonies constitute a situation where the definition of the role would have been an essential concern.

It is of importance that the keys are mentioned in plural in the written sources – as sets. The development from single keys to the sets of bronze keys can be followed chronologically in the burials with relief brooches. The keys found in the graves were made as sets and would have been handed over to women as such, probably on a special occasion. In analogy with the written sources, I argue that these occasions were wedding ceremonies or other rites of transition. Through these the role of the *Lady of the house* would have been defined, a definition which was repeated in the burial ritual, in which we know that the keys played a part. The keys relate the role to the farmstead, and it is important to bear in mind that the farmsteads where these burials are found were the large, central ones which constituted the very core of society. The relation to the farmstead is underlined by the local tradition expressed in the ornamentation of the brooches, which is distinguished from the common Scandinavian tradition generally found in the sword equipment.

The role of the *Lady of the house,* however, has implications which extend beyond the local through the distribution of the valuables in her care and through marriage alliances. The textile equipment – spindlewhorls, hook-mounts for distaffs (in the Kvåle grave, fig. 52, there were nine) and iron weaving battens – adds the aspect of highly developed textile production to the role. This aspect is, on one hand, of economic relevance, and would have had implications on the political level as well, through the assumed role of the textiles in the exchange systems. The textile equipment, however, additionally carries cultic connotations, which can be deduced through the relation of such tools to metaphors of prophecy and scrying. Important to this discussion are later written sources and the occurrence of related presentations on contemporary gold bracteates (Bæksted 1988, Enright 1991, Hauck 1985,

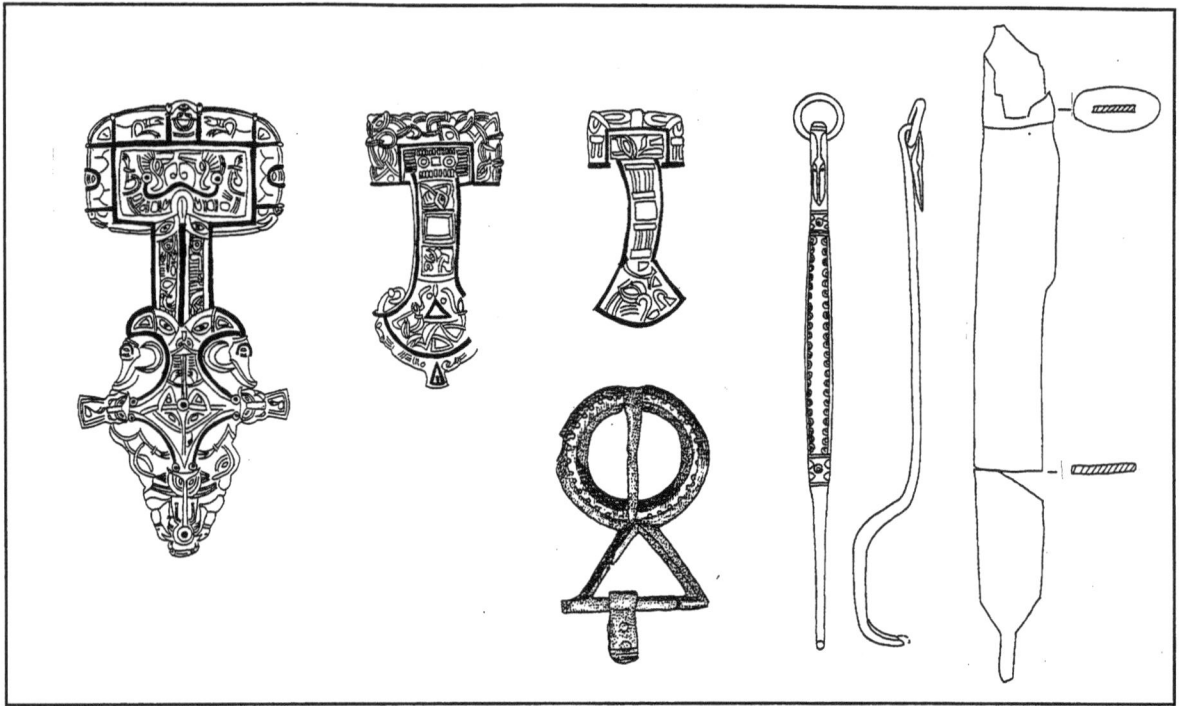

Fig. 51. *Relief brooches, bronze key with key ring and iron weaving batten from Ågedal, Vest-Agder (B 3410). Key and key ring drawn by E. Hoff, Bergen museum, otherwise by S. Kristoffersen. Scale 1:2, weaving batten 1:4.*

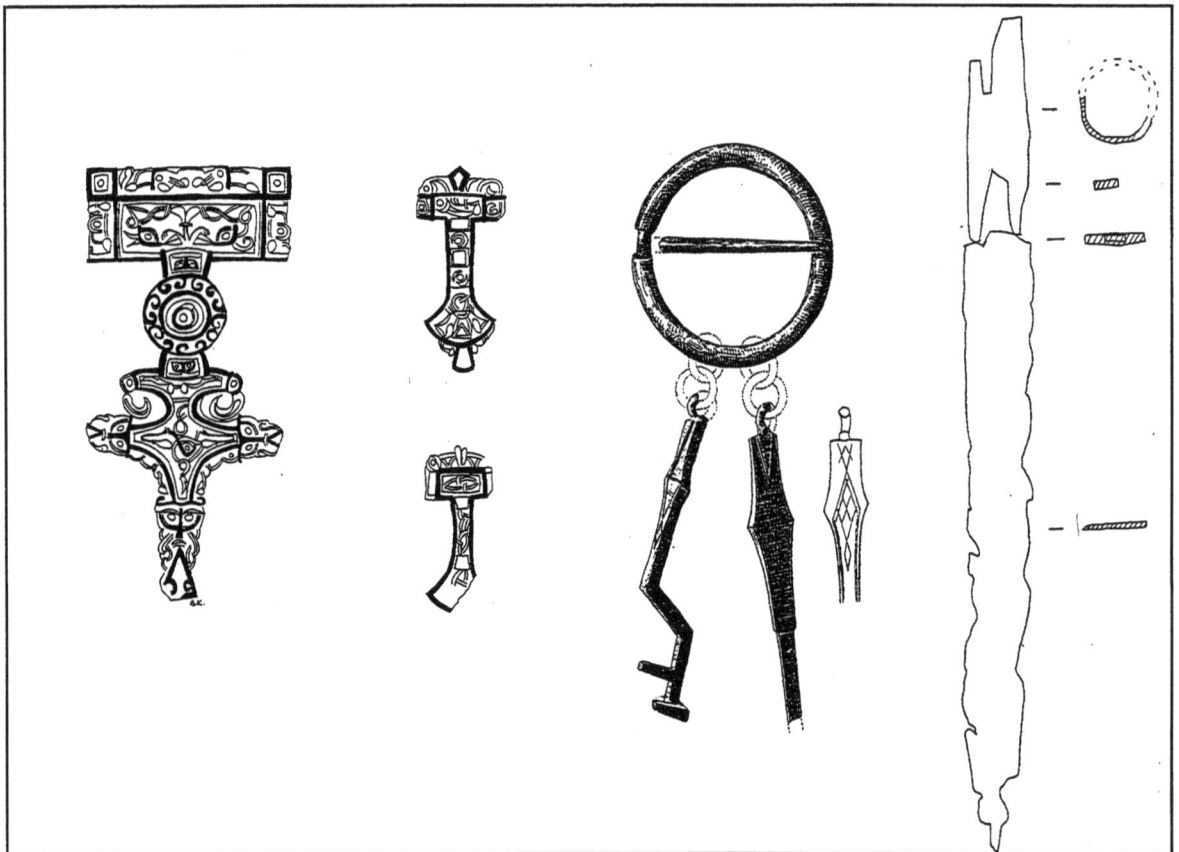

Fig. 52. *Relief brooches, set of bronze keys and iron weaving batten from Kvåle, Sogn og Fjordane (B 6516). Keys after Shetelig 1912, fig. 357, otherwise drawn by S. Kristoffersen. Scale 1:2, weaving batten 1:4.*

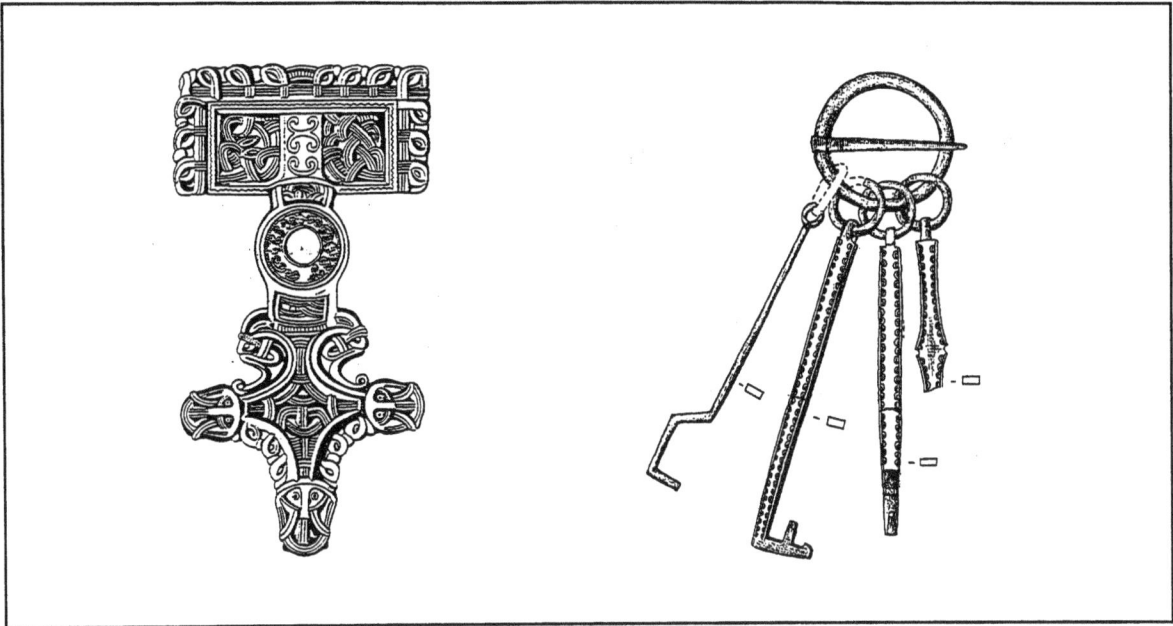

Fig. 53. Relief brooch and set of bronze keys from Indre Arna, Hordaland (B 564-569). Drawings by L. Tangedal (brooch) and E. Hoff (keys), Bergen museum. Scale 1:2.

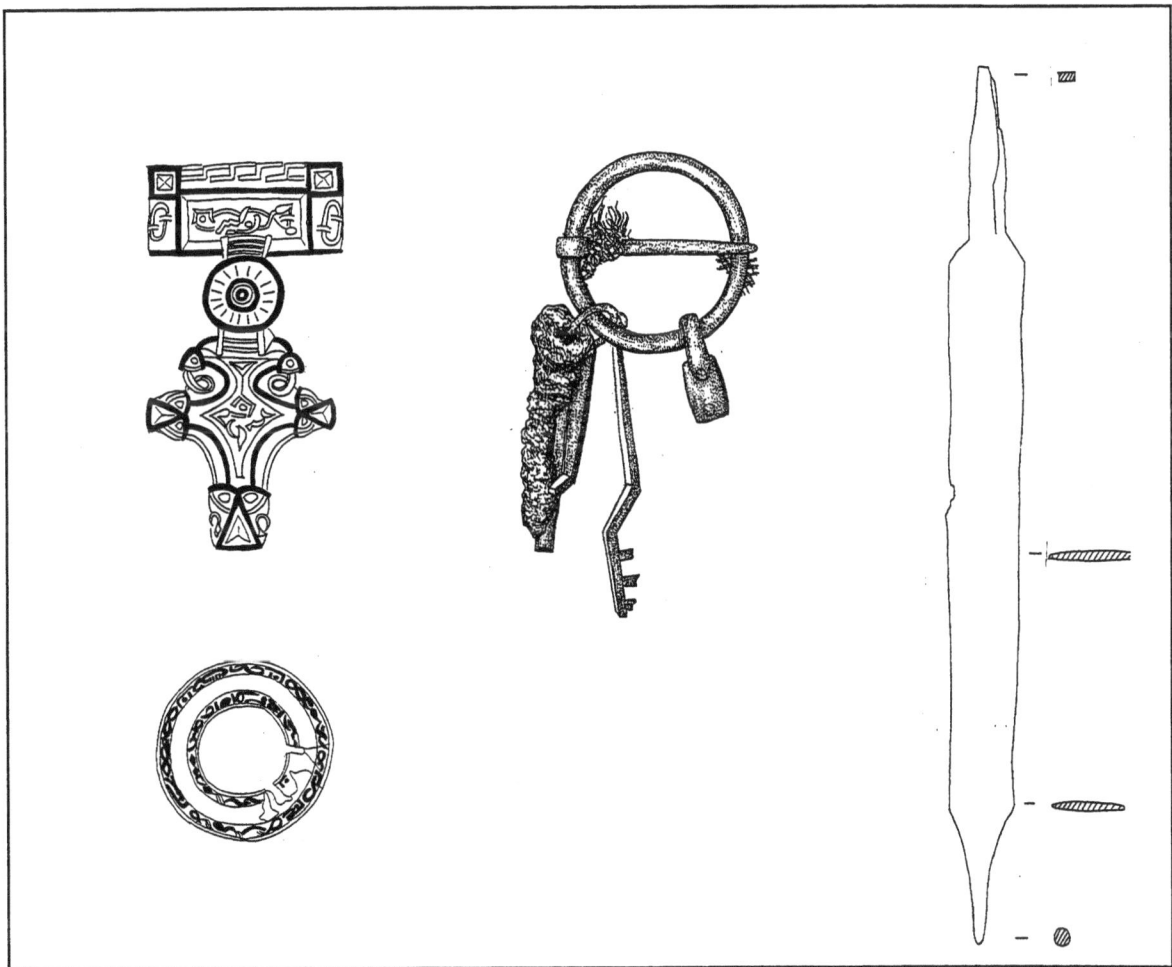

Fig. 54. Relief brooch, decorated silver sheet disc, set of bronze keys and iron weaving batten from Holum, Sogn og Fjordane (B 8045). Keys drawn by E. Hoff, Bergen museum, otherwise by S. Kristoffersen. Scale 1:2, weaving batten 1:4.

Strøm 1985, Wamers 1988; see also the discussion in Kristoffersen 1995). Furthermore, we know from later written sources that the *Lady of the house* performed rituals which took place at the farmsteads. This has been argued to have been of greater importance in an earlier cult of the Vanir (M. Olsen 1926, O. Olsen 1966, Steinsland 1985).

In the tools related to the textile production, there is embedded a plurality of potential meanings which constitute a basis for different interpretations and definitions of the role. The economic and cultic aspects would have had the ability to function in different contexts and would have been able to serve different interests. The economic aspect would function in relation to the political system and the social structure, that is, the preservation of the social order. By focusing on the economic and political associations one would also be in a position, through rituals, to transform the cultic aspect – and conversely.

These different aspects of meaning, then, constitute a foundation for negotiation and freedom from the imposed symbols in the social construction. This also refers to the social relationship between the role of the political leaders and the wealthy families, as interpreted in the symbolic representation of the gender-related burials. There is a possibility of the on-looker not being convinced by the social construction in the ritual, because the associations evoked may be different.

The social context which I have discussed presupposes controlled production and use of animal art. Further consequences concerning the character and spatial distribution of the art are implicit. If the art is connected to burials of the political elite and wealthy families, it should occur in concentrations in areas which stand out with respect to resources and strategic potential. It would also support my arguments if the decorated objects within an area could be associated through the ornaments

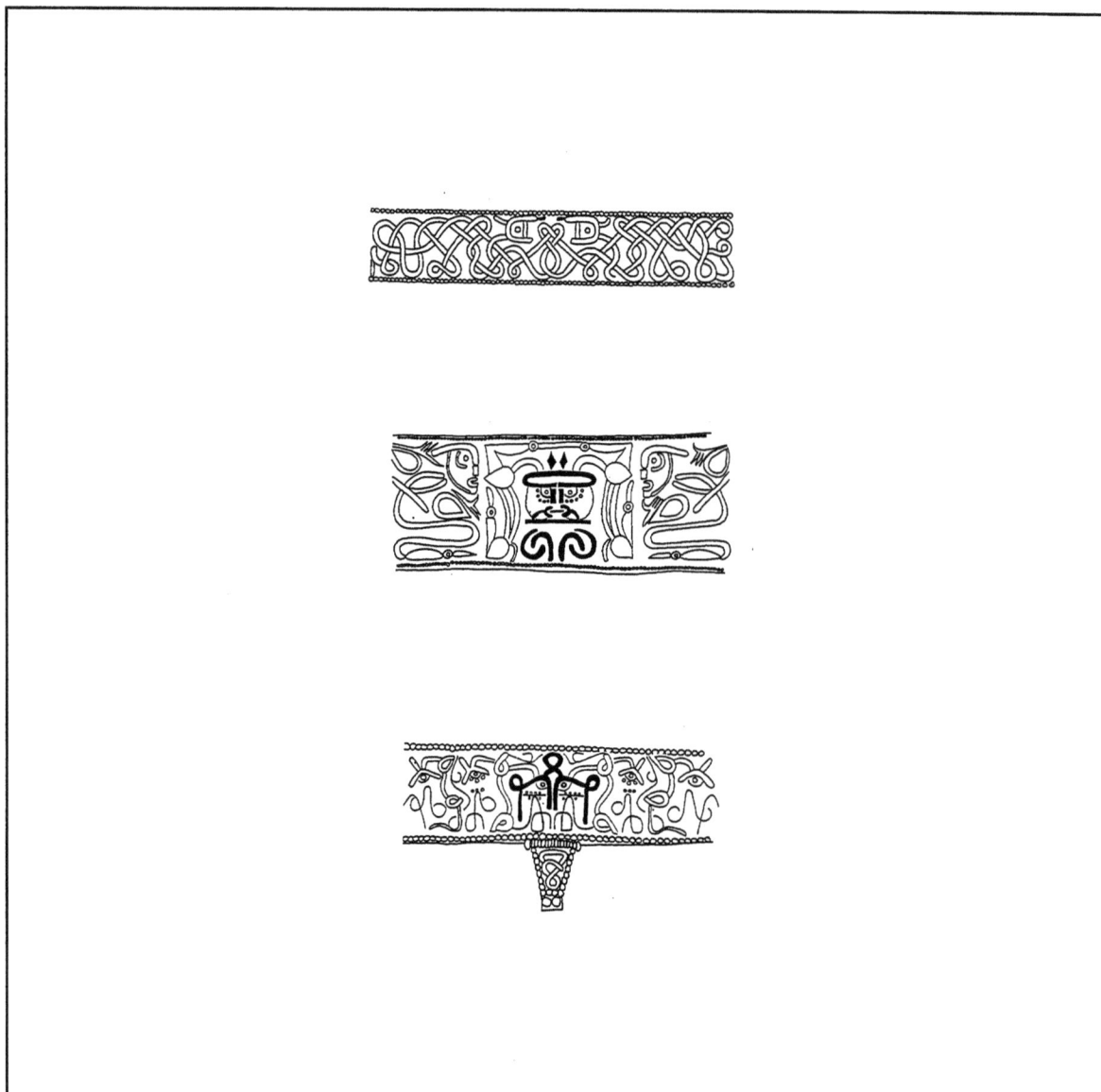

Fig. 55. Golden scabbard mounts. Top: Bergsaker, Vest-Agder (C 25813). Middle: Åmdal, Vest-Agder (C 25077). Bottom: Etne, Hordaland (B 2049). Drawings by S. Kristoffersen. Size 1:2.

themselves. Jæren in county Rogaland and parts of county Vest-Agder constitute areas with such potential where characteristic local traditions of animal art are found.

As the production and use of animal art would have been under political control, so would the dispersion of ornamented objects from the central areas. Large parts of Rogaland and Vest-Agder are interconnected through such shared traditions of animal art. The Jæren tradition is dispersed over large areas – a dispersion which, then, probably expresses political influence established through gift-giving and alliances.

Further north in western Norway there are small concentrations of burials with animal art, which taken by themselves do not make much sense. They do, however, correspond with distinct concentrations of weapon burials and high-quality meaningful objects such as gold scabbard mounts of different types (fig. 55) – objects which can be argued to indicate an association with the warrior aristocracy. These features occur together in Jæren and the abovementioned parts of Vest-Agder as well. There are, however, variations within this pattern, which indicate variations in the basis for power as well.

Animal art might, thus, be related to the political processes of its time (see also discussions in Hedeager 1992, 1993, 1996). Several aspects of the decorated objects contribute to their efficacy in such contexts, as well as the contexts discussed above. Apart from the potential of material culture in general in terms of the different levels of meaning, their aesthetic value appeals to the senses and evokes a positive emotional response which opens the viewer to the social code they may communicate (Kristoffersen in press b, with reference to Morphy 1996; Turner 1967). Their visual effect is powerful, especially when combined with the idea of magic embedded in their highly developed technology and artistry (for a discussion of enchanted technology, see Gell 1996). Magic can also be related to these objects through more distinct aspects of meanings (Kristoffersen 1995, in press b).

It is interesting that the dispersion of objects is first distinguishable in the Style I phase. As distinct from Nydam Style, Style I has, through the local traditions, the ability to signal nuanced relations of loyalty, and would as such function well in relation to alliances. An important aspect might, however, also be the fact that the meanings and significance of the objects with animal art developed through the use of the Nydam Style and became more charged with specific meanings in the later part of the Migration Period.

References

Bloch, M. & J. Parry 1982. Introduction: death and the regeneration of life. In Bloch, M. & Parry, J. (eds.). *Death & the regeneration of life*. Cambridge University Press. Cambridge.

Bourdieu, P. 1977. *Outline of a theory of practice*. Cambridge University Press. Cambridge.

Bourdieu, P. 1996. *Symbolsk makt*. Pax forlag. Oslo.

Bæksted, A. 1988. *Nordiska gudar och hjältar*. Oslo.

Dübner-Manthey, B. 1990. Zum Amulettbrauchtum im frühmittelalterlichen Frauen- und Kindergräbern. In Affeld, W. (ed.). *Frauen in Spätantike und Früh-mittelalter. Lebensbedingungen – Lebensnormen – Lebensformen*. Sigmaringen.

Enright, M. 1991. The Goddess who weaves. Some iconographic aspects of bracteates of the Fürstenberg type. *Frühmittelalterliche Studien* 24. University of Münster.

Gell, A. 1996. The technology of enchantment and the enchantment of technology. In Coote, J. & Shelton, A. (eds.). *Anthropology, art and aesthetics*. Oxford studies in the anthropology of cultural forms. Oxford.

Gjessing, H. & Fett, P. 1950. Register over trykte tilvekster av norske oldsaker. *Universitetets Old-saksamlings Årbok* 1949/50. Oslo.

Hauck, K. 1985. Motivanalyse eines Doppelbrakteaten. Die Träger der goldenen Götterbildamulette und die Traditionsinstanz der fünischen Brakteatenproduktion. *Frühmittelalterliche Studien* 19. University of Münster.

Hedeager, L. 1992. Kingdoms, ethnicity and material culture: Denmark in a European perspective. In Carver, M. O. H. (ed.). *The Age of Sutton Hoo. The seventh century in north-western Europe*. New York.

Hedeager, L. 1993. The creation of Germanic identity. A European origin-myth. *Frontières d'empire. Actes de la table ronde internationale de Nemours 1992*. Memoires du Musee de Prehistoire d'Ile-de-France 5. Nemours.

Hedeager, L. 1996. Myter og materiel kultur – den nordiske oprindelsesmyte i det tidlige kristne Europa. *Tor 28*. Department of Archaeology, University of Uppsala.

Hines, John. 1993. *Clasps, hektespenner, Agraffen. Anglo-Scandinavian clasps of classes A-C of the 3rd to 6th centuries A.D. Typology, diffusion and function*. KVHAA. Stockholm.

Hollander, L. M. 1962. *The poetic Edda*. University of Texas Press. Austin.

KLNM. *Kulturhistorisk Leksikon for nordisk middelalder fra vikingetid til reformasjonstid*, I-XXII. Rona, G. (ed.). Copenhagen 1956-1978.

Kristoffersen, S. 1995. Transformation in Migration Period animal art. *Norwegian Archaeological Review, Vol. 28, No. 1*. Oslo.

Kristoffersen, S. 1997. Dyreornamentikkens sosiale til-hørighet og politiske sammenheng. Nydamstil og Stil I i Sør- og Sørvestnorge. Unpublished doctoral thesis.

Kristoffersen, S. In press a. Migration Period chronology in Norway. In Hines, J.; Høilund-Nielsen, K. & Siegmund, F. (eds.). The Pace of Change: Studies in Early Medieval Chronology. Oxbow books. Oxford.

Kristoffersen, S. In press b. Expressive objects. In Olausson, D. & Vandkilde, H. (eds.). *Form – funksjon – kontekst*. Acta Archaeologica Lundensia. Department of Archaeology, University of Lund.

Kristoffersen, S. In prep. Sverd og spenne. Dyre-ornamentikk og sosial kontekst. A revised version of Kristoffersen 1997.

Moore, H. 1994. *A passion for difference. Essays in anthropology and gender.* Polity Press. Cambridge.

Morphy, H. 1996. From dull to brilliant. The aesthetics of spiritual power among the Yolungu. In Coote, J. & Shelton, A. (eds.). *Anthropology, art and aesthetics.* Oxford studies in the anthropology of cultural forms. Oxford.

Olsen, M. 1926. *Ættegærd og helligdom. Norske stedsnavn sosialt og religionshistorisk belyst.* Instituttet for sammenlignende kulturforskning. Oslo.

Olsen, O. 1966. *Hørg, hov og kirke. Historiske og arkæologiske vikingetidsstudier.* Copenhagen.

Steinsland, G. 1985. Kvinner og kult i vikingetid. In Andersen, R.; Dommasnes, L. H.; Stefansen, M. & Øye, I. (eds.). *Kvinnearbeid i Norden fra vikingetiden til reformasjonen. Foredrag fra et nordisk kvinne-historisk seminar i Bergen 3-7 august 1983.* Bergen.

Steuer, H. 1982. Schlüsselpaare in frühgeschichtlichen Gräbern. Zur Deutung einer Amulett-Beigabe. *Studien zur Sachsenforschung* 3. Hildesheim.

Ström, F. 1985. *Nordisk hedendom. Tro och sed i förkristen tid.* Arlöv.

Turner, V. 1967. *The forest of symbols. Aspects of Ndembu ritual.* Cornell University Press.

Wamers, E. 1988. Die Völkerwanderungszeit im Spiegel der Germanischen Heldensagen. In Menghin, W.; Springer, T. & Wamers, E. (eds.). *Germanen, Hunnen, Awaren. Schätze der Völkerwanderungszeit.* Aus-stellungskatalog des Germanischen Nationalmuseums Nürnberg.

Late Iron Age barrows at Lyckås, Skärstad parish, Småland, southern Sweden

Påvel Nicklasson, Halland County Museum, Sweden

Introduction

This paper briefly describes the excavation of two barrows at Lyckås in Skärstad parish, Småland, southern Sweden. The barrows are dated to the Late Iron Age, most probably the middle Vendel period, 7th century AD. The first one was excavated in 1985-86 by Björn Varenius, then of the Jönköping County Museum. The second was excavated by the author as a training excavation for students from the Department of Archaeology at the University of Lund, in collaboration with the Jönköping County Museum. The barrows yielded rich finds. Both graves were cremations. Especially the deposition of several animals in the graves is very interesting. In the first barrow a woman was most probably buried and in the second a man. They may be

seen as a chieftain couple and the graves can be interpreted as the founders' graves of a large, now completely plowed-over cemetery. In the second part of the paper I present a survey of historical sources. From the written records it is possible to conclude that there were originally most probably four cemeteries from the Late Iron Age in the Skärstad valley. Apart from the two barrows excavated, only one additional grave is known in any detail.

The Lyckås barrows

In 1993 and 1994 I directed the excavation of a barrow (Sw. *storhög*, "large mound") at Lyckås, Skärstad parish, in the north of the province of Småland, southern Sweden (fig. 56). The work was organised as a training excavation

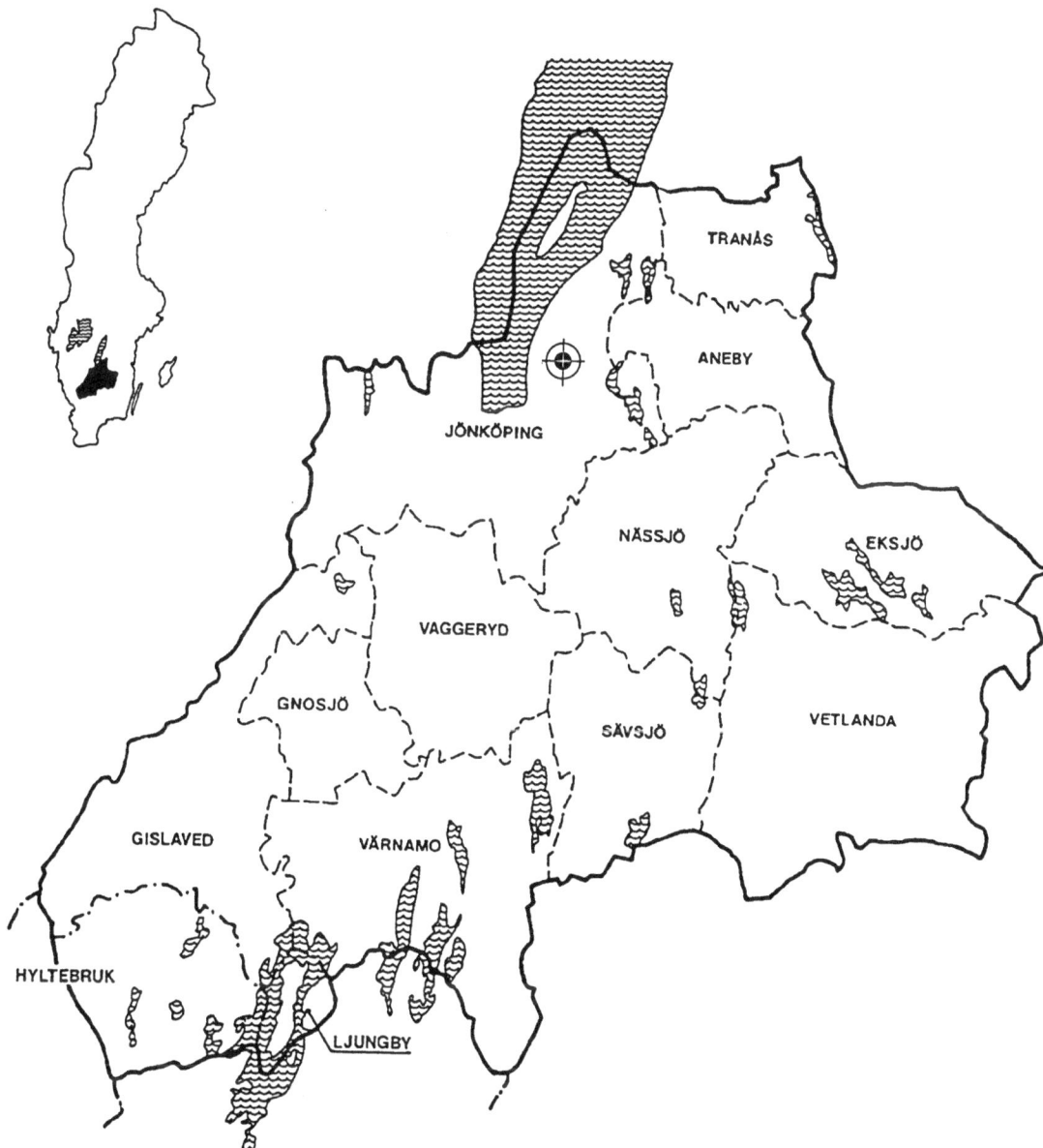

Fig. 56. Map of Jönköping County with Skärstad indicated by a crossed circle.

97

Fig. 57. A view from the valley floor toward the ridge with the second barrow under excavation. The first barrow excavated by Varenius was located immediately to the left of the visible trench.

for students from the Department of Archaeology at the University of Lund in collaboration with the Jönköping County Museum.

Skärstad is situated on the eastern shore of Sweden's second-largest lake, Lake Vättern. In Sweden, Småland is known as cold and inhospitable. The Skärstad valley is, however, part of the Vättern depression and the local climate is favourable. The Skärstad valley has more in common with western Östergötland than the Småland uplands. The soil is very fertile and Skärstad is famous for its orchards, especially the apples.

From an archaeological point of view, Skärstad is very rich. The best-known site is a very large pitted ware Middle Neolithic settlement at Gisebo, where large amounts of flint artefacts and pottery have been found. There is also a well known hoard find of the Bronze Age from Hillinge, containing a belt box, bronze arm rings and golden finger rings. There are many hilltop cemeteries. These should most probably be dated to the Late Bronze Age or the Early Iron Age, but none of them has been excavated. Two weapon graves dated to the Early Roman Iron Age are known from Sandvik near Lake Landsjön (Nicklasson 1997:234 f). They probably belong to a cemetery invisible above ground. Cemeteries of this kind are common in Västergötland and Östergötland.

In modern times there have been two barrows visible at

Lyckås. They were situated on a ridge overlooking the central parts of the fertile Skärstad valley (fig. 57). South of the barrows is the above-mentioned Lake Landsjön. There are good grounds to suspect that the barrows were once part of a considerably larger cemetery that has been completely plowed-over. I will discuss this in detail in the second part of the paper. Both barrows had been badly damaged through cultivation and only the central cairns remained intact. The first barrow was excavated in 1985 and 1986 by Björn Varenius, then of the Jönköping County Museum (Varenius 1996). Here a large cremation layer was found. Among the cremated bones were about 20 glass beads, mounts and rivets from a chest, mounts from a drinking bowl, spinning whorls and a pottery vessel. The grave was dated to the Late Iron Age. The cremation layer contained bones from a human, three dogs, a horse and a goshawk. Additionally there were small amounts of bones from hen, cow and pig. These were interpreted as remains of animal parts only, not whole carcasses placed on the pyre. Most probably edible cuts had been chosen as food for the dead. Altogether the grave yielded about 5.8 kg of cremated bones. Osteological analysis could not determine whether the grave contained a man or a woman. Swedish Iron Age barrows with several animals have hitherto only yielded male or male + female sex determinations. The grave goods from the first barrow at Lyckås, however, definitely indicate a female burial.

The grave excavated in 1993 and 1994 had a somewhat

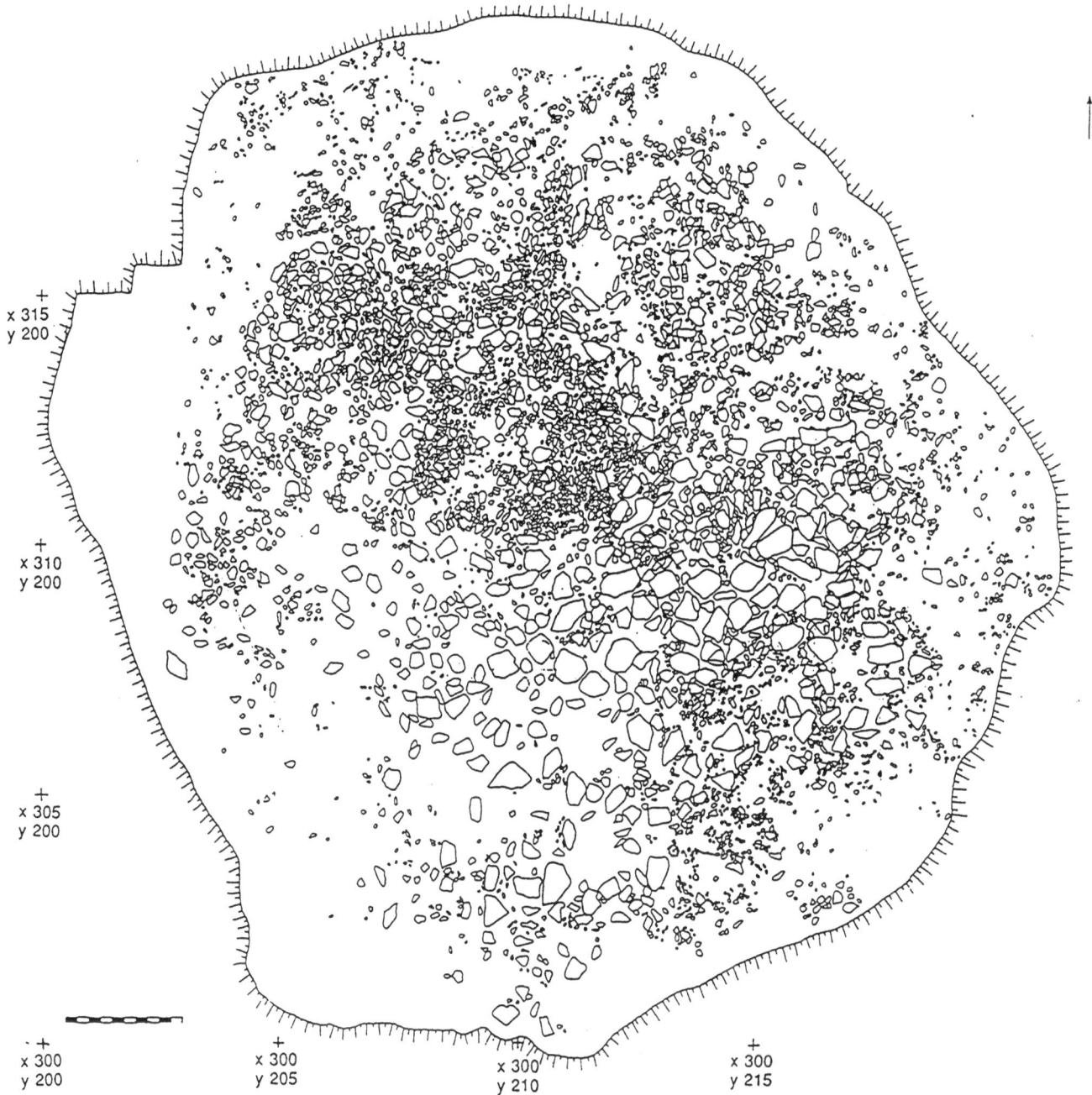

Fig. 58. The central cairn of the second Lyckås barrow.

more complicated construction. The central cairn was about 20 meters across (fig. 58, 60). In the centre an internal stone circle could be discerned. Inside this only small fragments of scattered cremated bones were found. This kind of grave is typical of the Early Iron Age. Most probably the barrow had been built on top of an older stone-setting. This is rather common for Late Iron Age barrows e.g. in the Lake Mälaren valley (Zachrisson 1994). Under the southwest part of the cairn a large cremation layer was found. It measured up to 8 meters across and was up to 20 cm thick. About 10 kg of cremated bones were found in the cremation layer.

The cremation layer was excavated in 25 by 25 cm squares. This method was chosen to enable us to study how different bodies and objects had been situated before they were burned. Of course, this method supposes that the barrow was erected directly on the cremation site. This

should be possible to determine from the position of different objects in the cremation layer. In a number of other Swedish barrows the cremation layers have been excavated in 1 meter squares and in one case in ½ meter squares. In some graves it has been possible to get a picture of how the bodies were arranged before the pyre was lit (Sjösvärd 1989). In the first barrow at Lyckås the cremation layer was excavated in 1 meter squares.

It was possible to make a reconstruction of the second Lyckås pyre before it was set on fire (fig. 59). This clearly indicates that the funeral pyre was lit on the spot of the subsequently erected barrow. The cremation layer contained nails and rivets spread over an area approximately 4 meters long, probably the remains of a small boat. The cremation layer contained few other artefacts, among which should be mentioned a knife and a pottery vessel. Bones from an old man; a horse; three dogs, produced a lot of bones, could not be placed better than in general terms on the grounds of which squares contained a lot of horse bones. The smaller animals were easier. The birds and the three dogs could be placed with great accuracy. Especially one of the dogs could be very exactly placed from the tip of the tail to the muzzle. The very thorough method of excavating the cremation layer in small squares clearly shows that it is possible to discuss the placement of objects and bodies in a cremation burial of this type.

The exact date of the grave is somewhat problematical. It is clearly datable to the Late Iron Age. However, it contained no objects that could be more precisely dated. Two charcoal samples were submitted to radiometric dating. The result showed that the grave most probably should be dated to the middle of the 7th century AD. In addition to the central stone-setting, probably dating from the Early Iron Age, and the Vendel period cremation burial, a small concentration of cremated bones was found on top of the cairn. This may indicate a secondary grave dug from the top of the barrow. This deposit was, however, almost totally destroyed through cultivation.

The two barrows at Lyckås contained the remains of a man and most probably a woman buried with several animals each. In fact the only difference in the animal contents is the presence of an eagle-owl in the second grave. In spite of the dating difficulties this could most tentatively be interpreted as the graves of a chieftain couple. Since their graves occupy the highest point of the hill the graves could be discussed in terms of founders' graves.

Birds of prey in Late Iron Age graves

Both of the Lyckås barrows contained cremated bones from birds of prey. This is a common feature of Swedish Iron Age barrows, as shown by Sabine Sten and Maria Vretemark who analysed the bones from a number of such sites (Vretemark 1983, Sten & Vretemark 1988). They interpreted the presence of birds of prey in connection with dogs and horses as indicating falconry. The horses and dogs in the barrows were of course also used by hunters: the horse for transportation, and the dogs in a number of ways. They could scare game out of hiding to enable the birds of prey to strike it. They could be used to mark the killing spot where the bird had succeeded in catching game, it being essential for the hunter to arrive at this spot quickly to keep the bird from feeding. A sated bird will not be interested in more hunting that day.

Birds of prey are used in different ways depending on the species of bird. The most spectacular hunting is performed by eagles and falcons. Especially falcons, such as the peregrine, are very skilled aviators and make big show before swooping down to strike. Goshawks hunt differently. They are very aggressive birds and may attack anyone close enough, including the falconer and his dogs. This also means that the goshawk may be trained to hunt down a broad spectrum of game. There are even examples of falconers training their birds to attack large animals

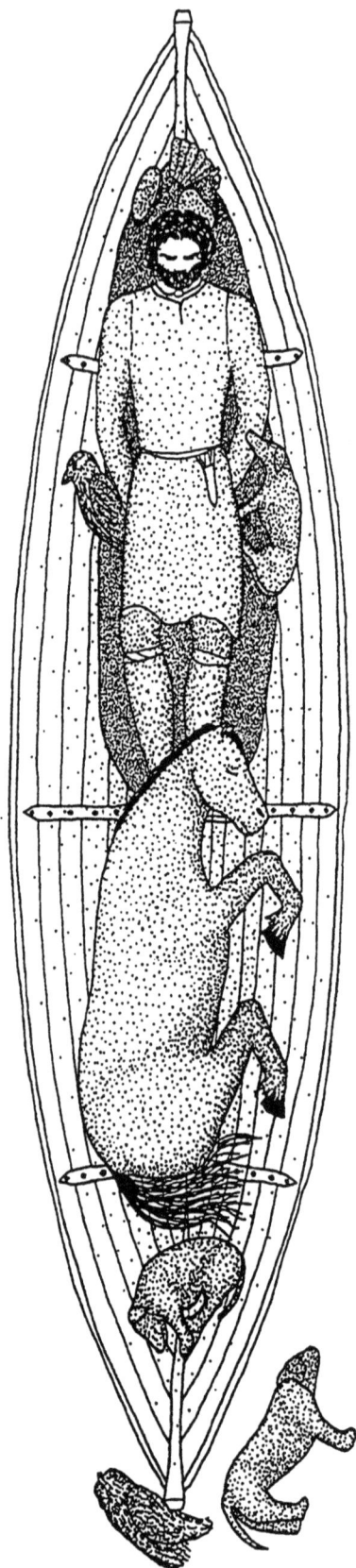

Fig. 59. A reconstruction of the pyre of the second Lyckås barrow before it was lit. Drawing by Anna Lihammer.

two big and one small; a goshawk and an eagle owl were found. There were also small parts of sheep. The reconstruction of the placement of the individual animal bodies varied somewhat in accuracy. The horse, which

Fig. 60. The large cremation layer during excavation under the supervision of the author.

such as deer. The goshawk takes on such big game through attacks to the head and tries to blind the deer until the hunter and the dogs deliver the final blow. The goshawk does not make a big flying show before the kill. It chases the game into thick woods and goes directly for the kill. It is a very efficient hunter, and a trained bird may hunt down as many as 20 targets a day. Because of this, the goshawk is sometimes referred to as the "cook's bird".

The eagle owl is not used for hunting in the way described above. Rather, it is used as a decoy. The falconer straps the owl to a pole in broad daylight. It is blinded by the light and totally defenceless. Its appearance is intensely disturbing to other birds, especially corvids, who attack the poor owl furiously. The eagle owl serves to attract other birds and soon the area is filled with enraged birds trying to scare off or maim the poor thing. In advance, the cunning falconer has prepared the area around the owl's pole with nets or glue-rods to catch and kill scavenger birds. The use of the eagle owl as a protector of crops was current into the 20th century.

Birds of prey have been found in most of the Iron Age barrows excavated in Sweden. The most common birds are the goshawk and the eagle owl. Since these are the bird species that make the most valuable contribution to the gathering of food and not the ones mostly used only for sport, falconry may have had a serious side as a complement to other food sources. One should bear in mind that birds of prey shed their feathers in the summer, and because of this the falconer does not use them for hunting during this season. Instead, the birds of prey are most efficient in the autumn, winter and spring seasons, when other resources may be scarce. Perhaps one side of being a local chieftain was the ability to obtain meat in the middle of winter. Of course one could argue that the presence of birds in the cremation layer might be interpreted not as hunting indicators. The birds may have been caught simply to accompany the dead on the pyre. Vretemark (1983) has however shown that hunting with birds of prey is mentioned in the Norse saga literature and that hunting motifs are present on Late Iron Age picture stones. Further proof of the birds being present in aristocratic environments in southern Scandinavia is that goshawk bones have been found at the aristocratic Late Iron Age settlement at Toftegård in Seeland (Tornbjerg 1998). In the same context bones from several other bird species were also found. These are some of the goshawk's game-birds, and such birds are also present in several of the Swedish barrows. Barrows of the Swedish type have hitherto not been found in Denmark. The evidence from Toftegård tells the same story though: falconry was practised across northern Europe.

The Lyckås barrows compared to other aristocratic graves from the Late Iron Age

Voluminous cremations including several animals under barrows are concentrated to the Lake Mälaren valley in middle Sweden. This is the area with the most surviving barrows and where most excavations of them have taken place. It may therefore be that rich graves with similar contents are also to be found in other parts of Sweden. There are examples of this kind of graves from Halland, Bohuslän, Västergötland and Östergötland (e.g. Lindqvist 1929, Arbman 1941, Wideen 1955, Augustsson 1976). In Småland, only one additional barrow has been excavated, at Gamleby in Gunnerstad parish outside Västervik (Friberg-Johansson 1978). This grave was very similar to the second grave in Skärstad. The Gamleby grave contained a boat, in which the dead had been placed. The animals in the cremation layer were identical to the ones from the Lyckås grave: a horse, three dogs, a goshawk and an eagle owl. The difference is that the Gunnerstad grave

101

contained parts of a helmet. Weapons are very scarce in Late Iron Age graves in Östergötland and the Lake Vättern area in Småland. Perhaps the local burial custom prohibited the deposition of weapons in graves. In the Lake Mälaren region, Peter Bratt has shown that the presence of weapons in barrows varies over time and is not to be seen as something generally linked with barrows (Bratt 1996).

How should one understand the barrows at Lyckås? Clearly, they do not feature regalia in the sense discussed by Birgit Arrhenius (1995). They should therefore not be seen as graves of the extreme upper class. Perhaps the barrows should be seen as the graves of a local aristocratic family. This might be problematical, since there are other barrows at nearby Berghem too which might mean that there were too many chieftains in the Skärstad valley during the Late Iron Age. More on these graves further on. But since the barrows did not contain exceptional grave goods except for the animals, they should not be seen as indicators of extreme prestige.

Looking at the neighbourhood one might perhaps discern some of the Late Iron Age and Medieval power-structure. I believe that this may give some hints about why the barrows were erected in Skärstad parish. The island of Visingsö was the site of the first royal castle in Sweden, at Näs, built perhaps as early as the 12th century. No earlier installations are known, but it is fully plausible to assume a Late Iron Age harbour, trading post or stronghold somewhere on the island. South of the city of Jönköping there are remains of Late Iron Age iron production. From the north of Småland, iron may have been transported to Visingsö or even further north to western Östergötland. Western Östergötland shows a strong royal presence during the Early Middle Ages (11th century onwards), and the iron trade may have been one of the prerequisites of this power. On the southern side of Lake Landsjön is a hillfort called Vista kulle. From here one could observe the southern part of lake Vättern and every boat crossing. The old Eriksgata road passed through Skärstad. This was the road used by the Medieval Swedish kings on their circuit through the domain. There are signs of a royal presence in Skärstad during the Middle Ages, for instance the toponym Bosgård near Lake Landsjön. There is also documentary evidence that a daughter of the farmstead of Hallisa married into the royal line in the 14th century. Hallisa is situated across the valley from the Lyckås barrows. The road passed along the eastern side of the valley, with the Lyckås barrows in plain and impressive view. Those buried in the barrows should perhaps be seen as the key-holders to the roads connecting northern Småland and Östergötland, and as the guardians of the stronghold of Vista kulle.

Late Iron Age burial sites in Skärstad parish

As mentioned above, the two barrows had been badly damaged through cultivation and may originally have been part of a much larger cemetery. The Late Iron Age is almost unknown in the archaeological record of northern Småland. The great exception is of course the island of Visingsö with over 800 visible graves from the period. On the mainland, there are only few stray finds indicating Late Iron Age graves. A Viking Period shield boss has been found on top of a stone-setting in Svarttorp parish and female jewellery has been found at Bogla in Rogberga parish. In addition to these, I have excavated a Vendel Period grave in Vireda parish (Nicklasson 1996). These are the only known graves from the Late Iron Age in the area and one easily gets the impression that it was sparsely populated in the Late Iron Age. In Skärstad parish, there is only one other indication of a Late Iron Age grave. This is yet another plowed-over barrow at the farmstead of Berghem about 2 km northeast of the Lyckås graves. It has not been excavated. This situation contrasts sharply to the Early Iron Age in the area. Several large cemeteries are known, although few graves have actually been excavated. Among these are the two aforementioned weapon graves found near Sandvik at Lake Landsjön. Thus, it is clear that the Skärstad valley must have been densely populated in the Early Iron Age. What happened then? Did the people move to Visingsö or did they simply dwindle during the Late Iron Age?

I have conducted some research in the archives and tried to reconstruct the Late Iron Age landscape from written sources. Some of the work builds upon a compilation from the 1930s put together by Claes Claesson and Bror Kugelberg (Jönköping County Museum archives). A non-archaeological but rather amusing aspect of this work are the variations in the Swedish language and the way people have expressed their thoughts about ancient monuments in different times. This aspect is unfortunately lost in my English translations. Since I have been working with primary manuscript material it has not been possible to date all sources exactly. Some of the statements about graves in the Skärstad valley are only known to me from secondary sources that do not mention dates for the original observations. It is quite a task to locate books from the 18th and 19th century, so this is the best I have managed!

I have also studied old maps depicting Skärstad. The oldest surviving maps are from the 1770s. Most maps from the 18th and 19th centuries were drawn to clarify property boundaries and to regulate land divisions. The cartographers seldom marked ancient monuments on the maps. I have not been able to discern any cemeteries on the old maps of Skärstad. I believe maps must be used in a more indirect way for this purpose. If a field is marked as disused and mention is made of stones or earthen mounds it may indicate a prehistoric cemetery. The names of fields may also give indications; e.g. "Stenåker" (stony field), "Stengärdet" (stony plot) and "Högåkern" (mound field). I believe that old maps may give valuable information about ruined ancient monuments, but they need to be thoroughly interpreted and they do perhaps not always divulge the locations of graves. Reading old maps is very difficult and time-consuming work and I have not yet completed my studies of Skärstad.

The Halland County Museum conducts a project to find ruined and plowed-over cemeteries from the Iron Age. In at least one case, a name on the old maps that seems to indicate ancient monuments actually marks the spot of a Stone Age settlement rather than the Iron Age graves nearby (Nicklasson in press, map studies by Eva Bengtsson, Halland County Museum).

The earliest source that discusses the ancient monuments of Skärstad is the *Rannsakningar efter antikviteter* of 1667. The *Rannsakningar* was a centrally administered questionnaire concerning ancient monuments and other notable sites circulated among the parish priests of Sweden. The source states:

"On the land of Lyckås Manor is an earthen mound, somewhat large, in a meadow and a beautiful oak-grove, close to the eastern shore of Lake Landsjön. Similarly, there is an earthen mound in a beautiful oak-grove in the meadow of the Skärstad Vicarage, which is situated not far from the north end of Lake Landsjön. However, no information or old tale here tells of the origins of these mounds."

"Finnes på Säterijetz Lyckås äghor vthi en Engh och wacker Eekelundh, en jordHögh, något stoor, belägen strax widh Landhsiö på Östre sijdhan. Och i lijka måtto en Jordhögh vthi en wacker Eekelundh i Skierstads Prästegårdz ängh, hwilcken ängh är belägen ett lijtet stycke ifrån den Nordaste änden på Landsiö. Men någon weetskap eller gammal sagha här om huru bemelte Jordehöghar äro tijkompne, weet ingen man till det ringaste at berätta." (Ståhle & Stahre 1992:69).

Another undated part of the Rannsakningar states:

"Large burial mounds are abundant here, both large and small ones [!]. Among them are some which the people reckon to have some value, but they do not seem to have any distinctive names."

"Stoora hoop burne Jordehögar och ättebackar finnas här een heel hoop, bådhe stoora och Små, iblandh dhem ähro nogra, som folket menar wara af werdhe men serdeles nampn der wedh hahr man icke än försport." (Ståhle & Stahre 1992, p.100)

The two sites with graves are identical to the Late Iron Age graves at Raä 5 Lyckås and Raä 51 Berghem (numbers in the State Ancient Monuments registry). The directions and distances from Lake Landsjön are not altogether correct, but the sites can be identified with certainty. The source only mentions one barrow at Lyckås. The statement about a great number of burial mounds should most probably be interpreted to mean that there were large cemeteries both at Lyckås and at Berghem. The mention of oak-groves is interesting. Oaks are very long-lived. The excavation of the barrows at Lyckås showed that they date from the 7th century AD. Perhaps the oaks were planted at the very same time as the cemetery was in use. Perhaps a cemetery should be understood not only as containing the mounds of earth and stone, but also the surrounding vegetation.

After this early source all is quiet about the ancient monuments of Skärstad until 1770 when Samuel Rogberg writes in his *Historisk Beskrifning om Småland*:

"On the lands of Lyckås Manor and Skärstad are a large number of small hillocks or mounds on the flat field, which are indubitably burial places."

"På detta Säteris (Lyckås) äfwen som på Skärstads egor finnes på slätta fältet en myckenhet små kullar eller högar, där ofelbart äro begrafningsplatser."

This time the source claims that there is a cemetery at Lyckås. Another cemetery is also mentioned on the lands of Skärstad. This might be the aforementioned grave at Berghem, but in that case it should have been mentioned as being placed on the land of Berghem or the vicarage. Rather, I think this is the earliest claim for the presence of a third cemetery, probably from the Late Iron Age judging from the "small hillocks or mounds", of which no trace remains today. Of course the exact site and dating cannot be determined from the source. Later sources claim, as we shall see, that there were graves on the lands of the Råby and Skärstad farmsteads. Råby is situated on the other side of the valley from Lyckås and the cemetery was perhaps located near the church. Perhaps, there may even have been two more cemeteries, one at the church of Skärstad and one on the lands of Råby.

After this time it seems that systematic destruction of the ancient monuments of Skärstad began. From 1824 we have the following statement from a certain von Köhler:

"When I cultivated a meadow at Lyckås, and I wanted to make it level, I had a rather large hillock upon which several different tall trees grew removed with much labour. Upon reaching the level of the surrounding ground, a stone-setting of dressed stones marking a burial place was found. Three of these stones were set on end at each side, one at each end and three were placed on top. When these last-mentioned stones were removed, nothing more was found than a small amount of loam or ash, and a piece of iron, probably a piece of a sword, so insignificant that no-one bothered to keep it. This mound was probably erected in the Mound Age. I have nothing further to say on the subject.

"Då jag vid Lyckås uppodlade en äng till åker, och jag wille göra den jemn lät jag med mycket arbete bortköra en där warande ganska hög kulle, bevext med flere sorters höga träd. När man kom ned till den kringliggande markens yta, fants en stensättning af jämnhuggna stenar, som wisade ett grafställe. Af dessa stenar woro tre stälde på hwarje långsida, 1 hwarje ända, och 3 lagde ofwanpå. När de sistnämne borttogos fanns inuti stenarna ej mer än ganska litet mulle eller aska, och en järnbit, säkert et stycke af et swärd, som war så obetydligt, att man ej aktade det wärdt den behålla Säkert hade denna hög blifwit i högålderstiden. Jag kan föröfrigt därom ej lämna underrättelse."

The same excavation is mentioned later in the 19th century in Tuneld's *Geografi* III:

> "In the Skärstad meadow at Lyckås are distinct traces of several burial mounds, of which not one has been left unharmed. In a meadow further south, a mound with high trees and a stone cist was removed during cultivation in the second half of the last century."

> "På Skärstadsängen vid Lyckås äro tydliga lemningar efter flera grifthögar, af hvilka dock ingen enda blifvit fredad för åverkan. Längre i söder på en äng har man i sednare hälften af sistförflutna århundradet, vid odling, borttagit en med höga träd bevext kulle, i hvilken man funnit en stenkista."

That it is the same grave as the one von Köhler removed should be beyond doubt. Both sources mention the high trees and the stone cist. The relation may however not be about the graves at Raä 5. Possibly some other grave on the lands of Lyckås was removed. The somewhat uncertain geographical placement by Tuneld should however place it close to Raä 5. The mention of loam or ashes and iron points to an Iron Age cremation burial and rules out a Bronze Age barrow or some kind of megalithic structure under a mound.

A short statement from the early 19th century by a certain Wallman states:

> "A pagan burial ground on the lands of Lyckås ... pagan burial ground also at the vicarage"

> "På Lyckås egor hednisk grafplats ... hednisk grafplats, äfven vid prestgården."

This, of course, indicates the graves at Lyckås and Berghem. This is the earliest source to claim explicitly that there was an entire cemetery also at Berghem.

The last writer to give a more or less accurate description of Late Iron Age cemeteries in Skärstad was J. Allwin, who wrote *Beskrifning öfver Wista härad* (Allwin 1859).

> "On the great plain making up the lands of Lyckås, Skärstad, Råby and Berghem, many ancient remains have probably once been located, at least grave mounds; but the soil is too good for the plowman to hesitate to remove them."

> "På den stora slätten, som utgör Lyckås, Skärstads, Råby och Berghems egor, hafva troligen många lemningar från fornåldern funnits, åtminstone ättekullar; men jordmånen är af för mycket god natur, att odlaren deraf skulle draga i betänkande att bortaga dem."

It seems that vast destruction of ancient monuments had taken place between 1770 and 1859. Allvin seems to have recorded what the locals had told him. Therefore the massive destruction must have taken place in the last 20 or so years before Allvin visited Skärstad. The

abovementioned undertaking by von Köhler is only one example of this. Allvin mentions four places with mounds: Lyckås, Skärstad, Råby and Berghem. Perhaps the suggested third now unknown cemetery was instead two separate cemeteries? He gives this interesting piece of information about Berghem:

> "On the lands of the Berghem vicarage, however, three burial mounds still remain: two of them are situated not far apart in the lower or western part of the property, in a plot that was a meadow before the Laga Skifte land amalgamation reform, but is now mostly tilled. The mounds are low, 26 feet across and are constructed of earth and stone."

> "På Berghems prestgårds egor äro dock 3 ättekullar qvarblifna: två af dessa ligga ej långt från hvarandra på nedra eller vestra egorna, uti en derstädes före laga skiftet varande, men nu till det mesta odlad äng; dessa äro helt låga, 26 fot i tvärlinie samt bestå af jord och sten."

This is the only source that states an exact number of graves at Berghem. Of course there must have been more than the three graves before the meadow was tilled. The measurements of two of the mounds should perhaps not be taken literally, but instead denote two unusually large mounds. This may mean that the cemetery at Berghem once had the same structure as the one at Lyckås with two barrows placed together and several small mounds around these. Today, only one barrow is visible at Berghem. Allvin goes on:

> "On the lands of nearby Råby there used to be several burial mounds, but they have been removed through cultivation ... Because of the great number of burial mounds that are and have been on the great plain at Skärstad and the beautiful hill on which the church is placed ... In the corner of the crofter's holding Svängen are signs of one or more burial mounds, which must have been of some size, but they are altered. A number of oaks in the vicinity give the impression of being the remains of a holy grove also destroyed through cultivation."

> "På närbelägna Råby egor funnos fordom flera ättekullar, men hafva vid odlingar blifvit borttagna ... I anledning av den mängd ättekullar som finnas och bevisligen funnits på den stora slätten vid Skärstad och den vackra höjd på hvilken kyrkan ligger ... I hörnet av torpet Svängen märkas tecken efter en eller par ättekullar, som synas hafva varit af större höjd och vidd, men äro förändrade. Några deromkring befintliga ekar gifva anledning till den förmodan, att dessa äro qvarlefvor af en här befintlig helig lund, som äfven genom odling tillintetgjorts."

Allvin places cemeteries at Råby and at the church, sites that are now totally devoid of visible ancient monuments. In his more detailed description Allvin never mentions the graves at Lyckås. Instead he introduces the name of the crofter's holding Svängen as the place for a cemetery. This crofter's holding Svängen is not mentioned in any other written source. The crofter's holding may have been located a couple of hundred meters east of Raä 5. Is this another unknown cemetery? I cannot tell. The fact that Allvin does not mention the otherwise well-known cemetery at Lyckås and describes at least some of the graves at Svängen as of "some size" awakens the suspicion that in fact he is talking about Raä 5. He also mentions oaks that should be compared to the information on an oak-grove in the oldest source, *Rannsakningar*. Even today there are several oaks in the wood behind Raä 5. A source-critical observation may hold the key to why Allvin does not mention Lyckås. The manor-house of the Lyckås estate burned down in 1822 and a new one was not constructed until 1863 (Börjesson 1990:154). When Allvin wrote in 1859 there was, in a way, no Lyckås to refer to. Instead he may have referred to the closest standing building, i.e. the crofter's holding Svängen. The information that some graves had been "altered" should probably be read as they had been plowed-over. But since the crofter's place Svängen is somewhat too far from Raä 5, it is still possible to suspect that Allvin was in fact describing another cemetery.

A somewhat macabre piece of information originates from the clerical authorities in Skärstad. The foreman at Lyckås, Johan Larsson Kraft, confessed to the priest on his deathbed in the 1890s that:

"In the field near [Raä 5] there used to be stone cairns, which contained several large flat stones. They were removed in the 1880s."

"I åkern i närheten av [fornlämning 5] funnos förr stenrösen, som innehöllo flera stycken stora flata stenar. De borttogos på 1880-talet."

Perhaps Mr Kraft was haunted by ghosts from the mounds and wanted to meet his maker with a clean conscience. This source only mentions stone cairns. This may be an indication that the cemetery was already heavily plowed-over and the mounds badly damaged, with only the stones of the central cairns remaining for the ploughman to curse. Today, not one stone is to be seen in the field around Raä 5. Perhaps this is the result of Mr Kraft's efforts to remove the last traces of the Late Iron Age at Lyckås.

This is the last source stating the presence of cemeteries around the barrows in Skärstad. Even into the 20th century the destruction continued. In the 1930s the two barrows were noticed by local people interested in ancient monuments. There is correspondence between the museum in Jönköping and the National Board of Antiquities about an excavation of the two damaged monuments, but the discussions led to nothing. When Skärstad parish was surveyed for ancient monuments by the National Board of Antiquities in 1954 the barrows were registered only as "possible graves", not as the barrows that are found in the written sources. When Skärstad parish was re-surveyed for ancient monuments in 1985 the two barrows were badly damaged by ploughing and cremated bones were found in the topsoil. This led to the funding of Varenius' excavation of the first barrow by the National Board of Antiquities, and later to the excavation of the second barrow by myself and the students. The last visible trace of the cemetery has finally been removed.

The following table summarises the different locations where graves probably from the Late Iron Age have been present.

Date	Lyckås Raä 5	Berghem Raä 51	Skärstad village	Others
1667	barrow	barrow		
1770	cemetery		cemetery	
18xx (Wallman)	cemetery	cemetery		
1824	mound?			
1859	cemetery?	3 mounds	cemetery	Svängen, Råby
1890	cemetery			

The frequent mentions of the cemetery at Lyckås give the impression that this cemetery was the most impressive one and perhaps featured the largest graves. The cemetery is mentioned in all the sources. The site at Berghem also featured one or more barrows, but is not mentioned as frequently and may therefore have been somewhat less impressive. Both at Lyckås and Berghem there have without doubt been extensive cemeteries that are now totally plowed-over, and the only remaining visible grave is the barrow at Berghem, which is still plowed-over each year. With some certainty we may also conclude that there have been cemeteries somewhere near the church and also on the lands of the farm Råby. The exact locations and dates of these sites are unknown. They are described in the same way as the cemeteries at Lyckås and Berghem with

grave mounds. Because of this they should probably be dated to the same period. No source mentions any barrows or other impressive grave structures on these spots. Perhaps one might therefore conclude that they were more ordinary cemeteries.

Altogether there may have been up to four cemeteries in the central parts of Skärstad parish. This means that the grave density should be compared to Visingsö and other Swedish sites with extreme numbers of Late Iron Age graves. Conclusive proof of an overwhelming number of graves once to be found in Skärstad might of course be had through trial excavations at Berghem and Lyckås around the known graves, and at other locations with cemeteries mentioned in the written sources.

It seems that we are standing at a peephole, seeing the Skärstad valley as it once was, with a visibly present past. The ancient monuments and their associated mythical lore are now irrevocably lost. Instead we have the scientific discipline of archaeology with its mythical lore to lean upon. The first scientifically acceptable excavations of Iron Age barrows in Sweden were the excavations of the royal barrows at Old Uppsala in 1846-47 and 1874 (Lindqvist 1936). At the very same time barrows and cemeteries were being levelled in Skärstad. Perhaps archaeology is a substitute for a past that is no longer present.

References

Allwin, J. 1859 [1993]. *Beskrifning öfver Wista härad uti Jönköpings län.* Stiftelsen Grännamuseernas skriftserie 4. Gränna.

Arrhenius, B. 1995. Regalia in Svealand in Early Medieval times. *TOR* 27. Department of Archaeology, University of Uppsala.

Augustsson, K. 1976. Gävehögen i Ås socken. *Halland. Årsbok för kulturhistoria och hembygdsvård i Hallands län* 59. Halland County Museum. Halmstad.

Bratt, P. 1996. Storhögar och maktstruktur i Mälaren under järnåldern. Renck, A.M. & Stensköld, E. (eds.). *Aktuell Arkeologi V.* Stockholm Archaeological Reports 30. Department of Archaeology, University of Stockholm.

Börjesson, K. (ed.) 1990. *Regionalt kulturminnesvårdsprogram för Jönköpings län, del 2: kulturmiljöer.* Småländska kulturbilder. Meddelanden från Jönköpings läns hembygdsförbund och Stiftelsen Jönköpings läns museum 61. Jönköping County Museum. Jönköping.

Friberg-Johansson, B. 1978. Om en utgrävning i Gamleby sn för 20 år sedan. *Tjustbygden.* Tjustbygdens kulturhistoriska förening. Västervik.

Lindqvist, S. 1936. *Uppsala högar och Ottarshögen.* KVHAA Monografier 23. Stockholm.

Nicklasson, P. 1996. Vendeltid i Vireda. *Bulletin för arkeologisk forskning i Sydsverige* 4. Department of Archaeology, University of Lund.

Nicklasson, P. 1997. *Svärdet ljuger inte – vapenfynd från äldre järnålder på Sveriges fastland.* Acta Archaeologica Lundensia, series in quarto no 22. Department of Archaeology, University of Lund.

Nicklasson, P. In press. *Ett sönderplöjt gravfält vid Menlösa i Voxtorps socken.* Halland County Museum. Halmstad.

Sjösvärd, L. 1989. *HaukR – en rinker från Vallentuna. Arkeologisk undersökning av fornlämning 27, Rickeby, Vallentuna sn, Uppland.* Raä UV rapport 1989:2. Board of National Antiquitites. Stockholm.

Ståhle, C.-I. & Stahre, N.-G. (eds.) 1992. *Rannsakningar efter antikviteter. Band III.* KVHAA. Stockholm.

Tornbjerg, S.Å. 1998. Toftegård – en fundrig gård fra sen jernalder og vikingetid. Larsson, L. & Hårdh, B. (eds.). *Centrala platser, centrala frågor – en vänbok till Berta Stjernquist.* Uppåkrastudier 1. Department of Archaeology, University of Lund.

Varenius, B. 1996. *Arkeologisk undersökning, vikingatida grav. Raä 5, Skärstad sn, Jönköpings kn.* Jönköping County Museum. Jönköping.

Vretemark, M. 1983. *Jakt med dresserad rovfågel i Sverige under yngre järnålder.* Unpublished seminar paper. Department of Archaeology, University of Stockholm.

Zachrisson, T. 1994. The odal and its manifestation in the landscape. *Current Swedish Archaeology* 2. Swedish Archaeological Society. Stockholm.

Communities in southeast Scandinavia in the Viking Period. An introduction to research in progress.

Fredrik Svanberg, Department of Archaeology, University of Lund, Sweden

Classifications of the "peoples" of Scandinavia c. AD 800-1000

Some aspects of culture and society were similar over large parts of Scandinavia during the Viking Period. There existed great similarities in ideas concerning a world of metaphors. For example, common myths seem to be expressed in Gotlandic picture stones, skaldic poetry and some burial rituals represented in many areas (Andrén 1993). The social elite of different areas shared certain cultural traits. Characteristic artefacts, such as the oval brooches, were widely spread. On the other hand, there were great differences in terms of cultural traditions, social structure, economic strategies, centre-periphery relations and participation in networks of trade and exchange.

How important were such differences and how should they be characterised? What terminology should be used? In the latest generation of syntheses on Viking Period Scandinavia, there are three basic ways of classifying the "peoples" of the area:

1. They are all discussed as *Norsemen* or *Vikings*.
2. They are separated into *Danes*, *Swedes* and *Norwegians*, the Swedes sometimes being further separated into *Götar* and *Svear*.
3. They are seen as separated into many small areas or groups of people with certain characteristics. These, however, are always areas *of the same kind*, for example "Settlement districts" or "Regions". Differences are termed "regionality", which primarily denotes *similarity* with other (greater) structures.

The frame of the historical developments is the *political* history, the history of power and kings, and, most importantly, the "unification" of the three Scandinavian kingdoms.

I will argue that the common picture of "peoples" in Scandinavia at the time concerned is highly over-simplified, and that political conditions are not a suitable frame for the general historical developments of the Viking Period. The rest of this paper is mainly concerned with the first of these arguments, while I will argue briefly for the second here.

First of all, we must start with an understanding of the character of Viking Period Scandinavian "politics". Although there seems to have existed phenomena that contemporary written sources sometimes discuss as "kings" ruling "kingdoms", it must be made clear that these were not unified territorial bodies with powerful administrations. Rather, they appear to have been weak and ever-changing organisations. Power over anything beyond small regions should perhaps best be described as temporary "overlordships". Power in this time was a power

over *people*, not over *territories*, and the territorialisation of power mainly belongs to later periods.

This should, in my view, lead us to concentrate on how to characterise the *peoples*, or rather, "communities" of this period, and primarily in a cultural sense; not on "kingdoms" or other such loose and temporary organisations.

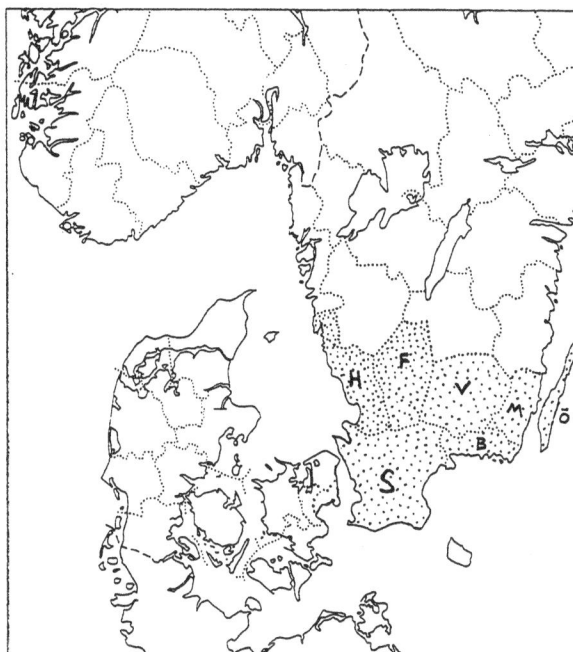

Fig. 61. *The parts of present-day southern Sweden treated in research by the author. H=Halland, F=Finnveden, V=Värend, M=Möre, Ö=Öland, S=Scania, B=Blekinge.*

Classifications of communities in present-day southern Sweden

Previous research has demonstrated that people in present-day southern Sweden (fig. 61), in the Late Iron Age, were living in many small "settlement areas" separated by zones with no or extremely sparse settlement. It should be emphasised that it is possible to gain a very good general picture of the demography of this period in the area in question. The most detailed work on the demography has been published by Johan Callmer (fig. 62). It has also been demonstrated that obvious differences in the archaeological record can be observed between different settlement areas. This has led quite a few scholars to discuss the characteristics of different areas or groups of people. The discussion has revolved around a number of concepts, the most important of which are presented in table 5.

Author and work	Conceptualisation (translated by the author)
Burström 1991	"Societies" – politically relevant social networks with a spatial dimension
Callmer 1991	"Social aggregates" – territorial units
Callmer 1992	"Ethnic groups" – specific cultural traits
Fabech 1993	"Regions" or "Petty kingdoms"
Callmer 1994	"Special cultural areas" – regions with special features, ethnicity?
Hyenstrand 1996	"Archaeological regions" – can be seen as tribal areas / chiefdoms / "large estates". Can be a "chessboard" for the unification of the Swedish kingdom

Table 5. Recent conceptualisations of different groups of people, or differences between areas, in present-day southern Sweden

As shown by this table, previous research has been slightly confused about how to characterise different groups of people. Research by the present author is directed to a discussion of a better terminology, as well as to an understanding of *what different groups of people were*, through a study of the available archaeological material.

The written sources

Different groups of people and different "lands" in present-day southern Sweden are mentioned in several written sources from the Late Iron Age and the earliest Middle Ages. The earliest source with obvious interpretational possibilities is the list of peoples in the history of Jordanes from the mid-6th century AD. Among his many "peoples", Jordanes mentions *Hallin* and *Finnaithae* (Jordanes 1997), who were possibly "peoples" living in areas partly corresponding to the Medieval provinces of Halland and Finnveden. Around AD 900, the traveller Wulfstan gives a slightly more detailed picture of different "peoples" and "lands". He mentions *Sconeg* (Scania), *Burgenda land* (Bornholm), *Blekingaeg* (Blekinge), *Meore* (Möre) and *Eowland* (Öland). He also claims that some of these "lands" belonged to *Denemearcan* or *Sweon* (Lund 1983; cf. fig. 61), which has been interpreted as meaning that they belonged to a "Danish" or "Swedish" kingdom at this time. However, the interpretation of these last two concepts remains complicated. It is by no means clear what Wulfstan meant, and nothing suggests a political interpretation of the type that has hitherto been the most common.

The information from Jordanes and Wulfstan demonstrates that different collectives of people existed, and that these were denoted by certain names and connected to certain geographical areas. The picture we can gain from these sources is, however, incomplete and difficult to interpret, even though it can be compared to the rather detailed demographic picture demonstrated above. There are also a few other relevant written sources, but I will not discuss these further in the present context. In order to approach a more detailed picture of different groups of people, and of how they can be characterised, we must turn to the archaeological record.

Cultural traditions and cultural contacts: the evidence of graves and imports

As has been demonstrated by the author in another context, different groups of people in the area in question had very specific cultural traditions and very differing contacts with other groups during the Viking Period (Svanberg 1998). Especially the burial customs can be grouped in several quite obvious "traditions" – customs which were reproduced over several generations and were specific to certain regions. This is still work in progress, but I will briefly outline some of the specific differences (fig. 63).

In southwest Scania, the known burials of the Viking Period are almost exclusively inhumations. In southeast Scania, the burial customs are heavily dominated by cremations, but a small number of inhumations occur. In northeast Scania, the burials are exclusively inhumations. In Blekinge, the burials are almost exclusively cremations and placed in cemeteries with a variety of superstructure types not found anywhere else. These brief characterisations of burial customs could, of course, be made more detailed. I have only mentioned a few areas here, since my work has as yet not fully grasped the traditions of the whole area in question.

As I have previously demonstrated (ibid), these differences in burial customs correspond to other differences in the available material. The most important are differences in what jewellery was put in the women's graves and what types and combinations of weapons were used in different

Fig. 62. Densely populated parts of present-day southern Sweden in the Late Iron Age. After Callmer 1991, p. 270, fig. 6.

areas. It is obvious that different groups of people had very differing cultural traditions and preferred different artefacts. Different groups of people also had differing contacts with other groups, as can be demonstrated by the spread of imported artefacts (ibid; Callmer 1992).

To a certain extent, these cultural differences can be correlated with the information about peoples or lands from Jordanes and Wulfstan, or to the earliest known Medieval administrative territories. But a full correspondence is not to be expected, since:

1. Jordanes and Wulfstan can not be supposed to have had complete knowledge about the area in question.

2. We know neither what Jordanes' nor Wulfstan's "peoples" or "lands" were. They need not have corresponded completely to the *cultural geography* which is the focus of the differences discussed above.

A revised view of the communities of Scandinavia c. 800-1000

My main argument is that when writing the history of the Viking Period, we should be more interested in the culture of different groups of people which can be grasped through the archaeological record, rather than in a very vague political history built on the scanty written sources. The old picture of Scandinavia with three large kingdoms or a small number of "peoples" during the Viking Period simply cannot be held as valid anymore. It is also noteworthy that different groups of people met very differing historical developments in relation to classical problems of historical research, such as "Christianisation", participation in Viking raids to the Continent and Britain, or, indeed, the formation of large-scale power-structures in the late Viking Period.

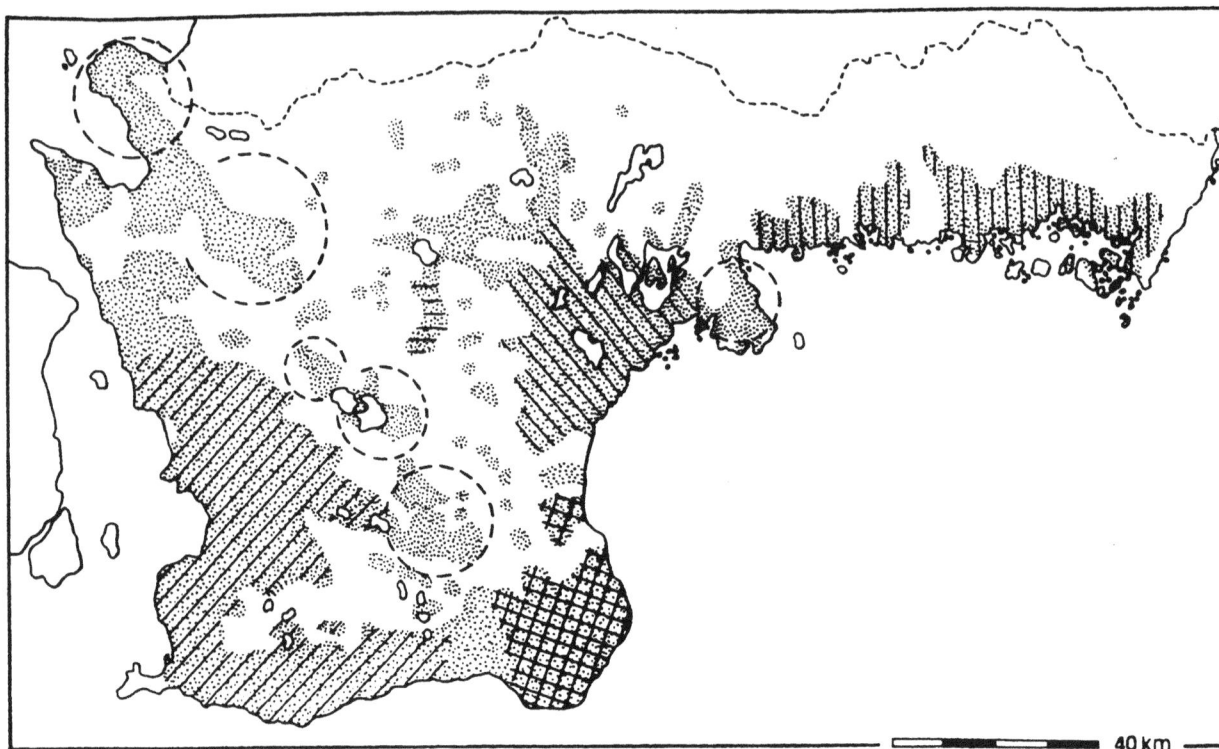

Fig. 63. *Culturally distinct communities in present-day Scania and Blekinge c. AD 800-1000 (Svanberg 1998). Hatching represents the distribution of distinctive burial customs etc. The dashed circles delimit settlement areas with more nebulous cultural characteristics.*

References

Andrén, A. 1993. Doors to other worlds – Scandinavian death rituals in Gotlandic perspectives. *Journal of European Archaeology* 1. European Association of Archaeologists. Aldershot.

Burström, M. 1991. *Arkeologisk samhällsavgränsning. En studie av vikingatida samhällsterritorier i Smålands inland.* Stockholm Studies in Archaeology 9. Department of Archaeology, University of Stockholm.

Callmer, J. 1991. Territory and dominion in the Late Iron Age in southern Scandinavia. Jennbert, K.; Larsson, L.; Petré, R. & Wyszomirska-Werbart, B. (eds.). *Regions and reflections – in honour of Märta Strömberg.* Acta Archaeologica Lundensia. Series in octo no. 20. Department of Archaeology, University of Lund.

Callmer, J. 1992. Interaction between ethnical groups in the Baltic region in the Late Iron Age. Hårdh, B. & Wyszomirska-Werbart, B. (eds.). *Contacts across the Baltic Sea – during the Late Iron Age (5th-12th centuries).* Report Series no. 43. Department of Archaeology, University of Lund.

Callmer, J. 1994. Interaktion mellan etniska grupper i östersjöområdet i yngre järnålder. Edlund, L-E. (ed.). *Kulturgränser – myt eller verklighet.* Diabas – skrifter från den dialektgeografiska databasen inom institutionen för nordiska språk vid Umeå universitet 4. Department of North Germanic languages, University of Umeå.

Fabech, C. 1993. Skåne – et kulturelt og geografisk grænseland i yngre jernalder og i nutiden. *TOR* 25. Department of Archaeology, University of Uppsala.

Hyenstrand, Å. 1996. *Lejonet, draken och korset. Sverige 500-1000.* Lund.

Jordanes. 1997. *Getica. Om goternas ursprung och bedrifter.* Översättning Andreas Nordin. Stockholm.

Lund, N. 1983. Af den oldengelske Orosius. Madsen, J.S. (ed.). *Ottar og Wulfstan. To rejsebeskrivelser fra vikingetiden.* Roskilde.

Svanberg, F. 1998. Cultural diversity in present Scania and Blekinge ca AD 800-1000. *Lund Archaeological Review* 1997. Department of Archaeology, University of Lund.